CIPS Study Matters

Level 4

Foundation Diploma in Purchasing and Supply

Developing Contracts in Purchasing and Supply

Bernadette King
Open University
(Study sessions 1–13, 15–17, 20)

and

Patricia Elliot
Thetes Group
(Study sessions 14, 18, 19 and revision questions)

THE
CHARTERED INSTITUTE OF
PURCHASING & SUPPLY

Published by

The Chartered Institute of Purchasing and Supply
Easton House, Easton on the Hill, Stamford, Lincolnshire PE9 3NZ
Tel: +44 (0) 1780 756 777
Fax: +44 (0) 1780 751 610
Email: info@cips.org
Website: http://www.cips.org

© The Chartered Institute of Purchasing and Supply 2006

First published September 2006

The right of Bernadette King and Patricia Elliot to be identified as authors
of this work has been asserted by them in accordance with the Copyright,
Design and Patents Act, 1988 in force or as amended from time to time.

Technical reviewers: Patricia Elliot, Thetes Group (study sessions 1–13,
15–17, 20) and Margaret Griffiths, University of Glamorgan (study
sessions 14, 18, 19 and revision questions).

Instructional design and publishing project management by Wordhouse
Ltd, Reading, UK

Content management system, instructional editing and pre-press by
Echelon Learning Ltd, London, UK

Index prepared by Indexing Specialists (UK) Ltd, Hove, UK

ISBN 1-86124-153-4
ISBN 978-186124-153-5

Contents

Introduction

This course book has been designed to assist you in studying for the CIPS Developing Contracts in Purchasing and Supply unit in the level 4 Foundation Diploma in Purchasing and Supply. The book covers all topics in the official CIPS unit content document, as illustrated in the table beginning on page xi.

As a professional purchaser you may become involved in a 'purchasing' contract at any of the different stages in its development or you may be involved in most of the process. Whatever your role, it is important to have an overview of how and why contracts are developed and the pivotal position that the purchasing department has in that process. This course book will take you through the various stages in the development of contracts, but remember you can also supplement your course book studies by reading other appropriate texts and by examining how the principles and practices dealt with in this course book are applied in the development of your organisation's contracts.

In the first three sessions (1-3) the course book looks at the early stages where the purchasing professional needs to be aware of how the purchasing professional's role changes according to the category of procurement, identifying purchasing objectives and achieving them by using specifications, measuring performance and using contractual terms to enforce compliance with the contract. In the next four sessions (4-7) the formation of contracts is studied including the problems arising when the 'battle of the forms' arises with the use of standard terms and conditions. Session 7 considers what is important to ensure that contracts are effective before examining in the next six sessions (8-14) the various types of terms in contracts. In session 8 the classification of terms is explained, then implied terms are examined before going on to consider various different types of express contract terms. Session 14 then explains the use of standard model form contracts. Sessions 15 and 16 consider international contracts for the sale of goods and services. Sessions 17 to 19 consider the tendering process, EU Procurement Directives and e-tendering. Finally session 20 considers the whole process of contract management review and improvement.

How to use this book

The course book will take you step by step through the unit content in a series of carefully planned 'study sessions' and provides you with learning activities, self-assessment questions and revision questions to help you master the subject matter. The guide should help you organise and carry out your studies in a methodical, logical and effective way, but if you have your own study preferences you will find it a flexible resource too.

Before you begin using course this book, make sure you are familiar with any advice provided by CIPS on such things as study skills, revision techniques or support and how to handle formal assessments.

If you are on a taught course, it will be up to your tutor to explain how to use the book – when to read the study sessions, when to tackle the activities and questions, and so on.

If you are on a self-study course, or studying independently, you can use the course book in the following way:

Scan the whole book to get a feel for the nature and content of the subject matter.

Plan your overall study schedule so that you allow enough time to complete all 20 study sessions well before your examinations – in other words, leaving plenty of time for revision.

For each session, set aside enough time for reading the text, tackling all the learning activities and self-assessment questions, and the revision question at the end of the session, and for the suggested further reading. Guidance on roughly how long you should set aside for studying each session is given at the beginning of the session.

Now let's take a look at the structure and content of the individual study sessions.

Overview of the study sessions

The course book breaks the content down into 20 sessions, which vary from three to six or seven hours' duration each. However, we are not advising you to study for this sort of time without a break! The sessions are simply a convenient way of breaking the syllabus into manageable chunks. Most people would try to study one or two sessions a week, taking one or two breaks within each session. You will quickly find out what suits you best.

Each session begins with a brief **introduction** which sets out the areas of the syllabus being covered and explains, if necessary, how the session fits in with the topics that come before and after.

After the introduction there is a statement of the **session learning objectives**. The objectives are designed to help you understand exactly what you should be able to do after you've studied the session. You might find it helpful to tick them off as you progress through the session. You will also find them useful during revision. There is one session learning objective for each numbered subsection of the session.

After this, there is a brief section reproducing the learning objectives and indicative content from the official **unit content document**. This will help you to understand exactly which part of the syllabus you are studying in the current session.

Following this, there are **prior knowledge** and **resources** sections if necessary. These will let you know if there are any topics you need to be familiar with before tackling each particular session, or any special resources you might need, such as a calculator or graph paper.

Then the main part of the study session begins, with the first of the numbered main subsections. At regular intervals in each study session, we have provided you with **learning activities**, which are designed to get you actively involved in the learning process. You should always try to complete the activities – usually on a separate sheet of your own paper – before reading on. You will learn much more effectively if you are actively involved in doing something as you study, rather than just passively reading the text in front of you. The feedback or answers to the activities are provided at the end of the session. Do not be tempted to skip the activity.

We also provide a number of **self-assessment questions** in each study session. These are to help you to decide for yourself whether or not you have achieved the learning objectives set out at the beginning of the session. As with the activities, you should always tackle them – usually on a separate sheet of paper. Don't be tempted to skip them. The feedback or answers are again at the end of the session. If you still do not understand a topic having attempted the self-assessment question, always try to re-read the relevant passages in the textbook readings or session, or follow the advice on further reading at the end of the session. If this still doesn't work, you should contact the CIPS Membership and Qualification Advice team.

For most of the learning activities and self assessment questions you will need to use separate sheets of paper for your answers or responses. Some of the activities or questions require you to complete a table or form, in which case you could write your response in the study guide itself, or photocopy the page.

At the end of the session are three final sections.

The first is the **summary**. Use it to remind yourself or check off what you have just studied, or later on during revision.

Then follows the **suggested further reading** section. This section, if it appears, contains recommendations for further reading which you can follow up if you would like to read alternative treatments of the topics. If for any reason you are having difficulty understanding the course book on a particular topic, try one of the alternative treatments recommended. If you are keen to read around and beyond the syllabus, to help you pick up extra points in the examination for example, you may like to try some of the additional readings recommended. If this section does not appear at the end of a session, it usually means that further reading for the session topics is not necessary.

At the end of the session we direct you to a **revision question**, which you will find in a separate section at the end of the course book. Feedback on the questions is also given.

Reading lists

CIPS produces an official reading list, which recommends essential and desirable texts for augmenting your studies. This reading list is available on the CIPS website or from the CIPS Bookshop. This course book is one of the essential texts for this unit. In this section we describe the main characteristics of the other essential text for this unit, which you are strongly urged to buy and use throughout your course.

The other essential text is *Law for Purchasing and Supply*, 3rd edition by Ivor and Margaret Griffiths, published by Pearson in 2002. It deals with the various topics covered in sessions 4-6 and 8-19. The areas of the course covered in sessions 1-3, 7 and 20 are not covered in that text but you could read the relevant chapters in Lysons and Farrington (2006) and Carter and Kirby (2006) as well as the relevant documentation on the CIPS website as mentioned at the end of the relevant study session.

Unit content coverage

In this section we reproduce the whole of the official CIPS unit content document for this unit. The overall unit characteristics and learning outcomes for the unit are given first. Then, in the table that follows, the learning objectives and indicative content are given in the left hand column. In the right hand column are the study sessions, or subsections, in which you will find coverage of the various topics.

Unit Characteristics

This unit is designed to help students to gain an appreciation of the complexities of both the legalities and commercial issues of contractual arrangements entered into with external organisations. The unit provides an underpinning knowledge of the legalities of the formation of contracts as well as the key ingredients of any commercial arrangement - a specification, the contractual terms and key performance indicators.

Students will be able to apply a variety of terms to contracts in given situations, and will be aware of the significance of a range of different contractual terms that are typically applied to a range of procurements affecting both direct and indirect expenditures. The unit also analyses the processes used for tendering or for requests for proposals from external suppliers through to contract award.

Learning Outcomes

On completion of this unit, students will be able to:

- Recognise the use of specifications, performance measures and contract terms for procurements of products and services from suppliers
- Identify a range of legal aspects in relation to the contracting process
- Describe and apply the legalities linked to the formation of contracts
- Explain the impact of both implied and express terms in contracts
- Recognise the remedies for breaches of contracts and draft terms to cover such risks
- Appreciate and discuss the legal and relationship issues arising through the use of tendering procedures, including e-tendering, and the application of EU procurement directives
- Outline the practices that can be adopted for contract review and award

Learning objectives and indicative content

1.0 Develop commercial agreements (Weighting 20%)

1.1 Identify the various categories of procurements that organisations typically undertake.

Study session 1

- The types of products and services that are typically purchased by organisations, such as purchases for re-sale, capital equipment, sub-contracted work, facilities, ICT and MRO items
- Categories of expenditures on goods and services
- The procurement function's role in setting up agreements for purchased goods and services

1.2 Formulate objectives for the procurement of both goods and services.

Study session 2

- The five rights of purchasing
- Achieving a balance between objective: time versus cost
- The use of specifications, performance measures and contractual terms in supply agreements

1.3 Recognise the impact of specifications on achieving value for money.

Study session 3

- The functions of a specification
- The types of specification
- Choosing the most appropriate type of specification for the purchase decision

1.4 Discuss the use and application of key performance indicators in agreements with suppliers.

Study session 3

- The development of performance measures that can be applied to commercial agreements
- Examples of performance measures
- Developing targets for supplier performance

1.5 Recognise the use and the content of contractual terms for purchased goods or services.

Study session 3

- Purchasers' and suppliers' standard contracts
- The differences between purchasers' and suppliers' terms

2.0 The formation of contracts (Weighting 25%)

2.1 Identify and apply the legal aspects relating to the formation of contracts.

Study session 4
Study session 5

- Offer
- Acceptance
- Consideration
- Intention to create legal relations
- Capacity
- The contractual promise
- The distinction between framework and call off contracts

2.2 Discuss the legalities and commercial considerations linked to   Study session 6
the battle of the forms.
   • The exchange of suppliers' and purchasers' terms in the
      contract formation process
   • Counter-offers and acceptance
   • Precedent set by case law on contract formation
   • The creation of e-contracts
2.3 Identify and discuss the legal aspects relating to the formation of   Study session 15
contracts in international trade.
   • International law
   • The Vienna Convention, Uniform Law for International
      Sale of Goods (1980)
2.4 Discuss standard model form contracts and their uses and   Study session 14
applications.
   • The use of model form contracts
   • Examples of model form contracts such as CIPS, the New
      Engineering Contract, Joint Contracts Tribunal

3.0 Contractual terms (Weighting 30%)
3.1 Analyse and discuss the effectiveness of a supply agreement.   Study session 7
   • Contractual obligations
   • Contract termination
3.2 Recognise different contract terms and their impact on any   Study session 8
breach of contract.
   • Conditions
   • Warranties
   • Innominate terms
3.3 Discuss and apply implied terms.   Study session 5
   • Key legislation relating to contracts   Study session 9
      – Sale of Goods Act (as amended)   Study session 12
      – Supply of Goods and Services Act
      – Unfair Contract Terms Act
      – Contracts (Rights of Third Parties) Act
3.4 Discuss standard contracts terms for indemnities.   Study session 11
   • Intellectual property rights
   • Insurances
   • Accidents and damage
   • Third parties
3.5 Recognise and discuss the use of express contractual terms.   Study session 10
   • Liquidated damages   Study session 12
   • Guarantees
   • Passing of property
   • Sub-contracting and assignment
   • Payment
   • Transfer of undertakings and protection of employment
      regulations
   • Confidentiality
   • Other terms

3.6 Identify the provision in contracts for amendments, change, review and renewal.
- Contract duration
- Dispute resolution
- Default and termination clauses
- Variation and change control
- Contract renewal

3.7 Appreciate and discuss international considerations in contract terms
- The choice of legal system
- Arbitration
- The use of incoterms

4.0 Letting contracts (Weighting 20%)

4.1 Discuss the stages of the procurement process underlining the tendering process.
- The stages of the procurement process
- The principles of tendering
- The use of pre-qualification and evaluation criteria
- Post-tender negotiation
- Contract award
- Contract transition arrangements

4.2 Outline and discuss the EU procurement directives.
- The objectives of the EU procurement directives
- Supplies, services, works and compliance
- Coverage of the directives - the thresholds
- The consolidated procurement directive
- Open, restricted, negotiated and competitive dialogue
- Award criteria
- Debriefing

4.3 Discuss the use of e-tendering and outline the legal issues.
- Supplier databases
- Electronic tender systems
- Electronic notice systems

4.4 Recognise the importance of reviewing the outcomes of contracts and identify problems that require immediate action.
- Contract management
- Contract review
- Improving the contracting process

Study session 1
Categories of procurements

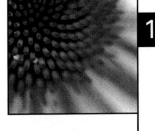

'What usually comes first is the contract.'
(I Gershwin (1896–1983), American lyricist and songwriter)

Introduction

During this course you will be studying the development of contracts – but in this session the contract will not come first! You will begin by identifying the different categories of procurements purchased by organisations, then you will go on to consider the types of expenditure used to obtain them before examining the role played by the purchasing professional in the acquisition process.

Session learning objectives

After completing this session you should be able to:

1.1 Identify, using examples, the types of products and services typically purchased by organisations.
1.2 Identify the categories of expenditure on goods and services.
1.3 Explain the role of the procurement function in setting up agreements for purchased goods and services.

Unit content coverage

This study session covers the following topic from the official CIPS unit content document.

Learning objective

1.1 Identify the various categories of procurements that organisations typically undertake.
  • The types of products and services that are typically purchased by organisations such as purchases for resale, capital equipment, sub-contracted work, facilities, ICT and MRO items.
  • Categories of expenditure on goods and services.
  • The procurement function's role in setting up agreements for purchased goods and services.

Timing

You should set aside about 5 hours to read and complete this session, including learning activities, self-assessment questions, the suggested further reading (if any) and the revision question.

1

1.1 Types of products and services purchased by organisations

Learning activity 1.1

List the goods and services typically purchased by your organisation.

Feedback on page 11

This section introduces you to the wide range of external resources purchased by organisations. The categories of purchased inputs that are required by organisations depend on many factors, including which of the primary, secondary or tertiary sectors the organisation is in as this will govern, to a large extent, the type of activity carried on. However, there are some categories of procurements that can be purchased by organisations in any of the sectors.

The categories of procurements can include capital equipment; production materials such as raw materials, components and semi-finished items used in manufacturing; consumables and maintenance, repair and operating (MRO) supplies; resale goods; and services.

Capital equipment

Capital equipment is sometimes referred to as capital goods or capital assets. Capital equipment provides utility or benefit to the organisation over a long period. Lysons and Farrington (2006) identify three important characteristics of capital equipment:

- it can be physically touched or handled
- it is used to produce further goods or services
- it has a lifetime of more than one year.

Marrian (1965: 10–23), distinguished six types of industrial equipment:

- Buildings: permanent constructions on a site to house or enclose equipment and personnel employed in industrial, institutional or commercial activities.
- Installation equipment: essential plant, machinery or other major equipment used directly to produce the organisation's goods and services, for example aircraft purchased by an airline.
- Accessory equipment: durable major equipment used to facilitate the production of goods and services or to enhance the operations of organisations, for example aircraft purchased by a manufacturing organisation to facilitate the movement of executive personnel.
- Operating equipment: semi-durable minor equipment which is moveable and used in, but not generally essential to, the production of goods and services – for example, special footwear, goggles, brooms.
- Tools and instruments: semi-durable or durable portable minor equipment and instruments, required for producing, measuring or calculating associated with the production of goods or services, for example, ICT equipment, all tools, surgical instruments, timing devices, cash registers.
- Furnishings and fittings: all goods and materials employed to fit buildings for their organisational purposes, but not equipment used

specifically in production, for example carpets, floor coverings, draperies, furniture, shelving, counters, benches.

Production materials used in manufacturing

The production inputs required in the manufacturing processes are usually raw materials, parts, components, sub-assemblies or assemblies. Risley (1972: 24–25) classified materials and parts used in manufacturing under three headings:

- Raw materials: primarily from agriculture and the various extractive industries: minerals, ores, timber, petroleum and scrap as well as dairy products, fruits and vegetables sold to a processor. Many of these raw materials are internationally traded commodities. Generally they are in an unprocessed state although they can enter into trade in a processed form rather than having just been mined or harvested, for example ores are extracted from rock and coffee and tea will be dried and processed before they reach a market.
- Semi-finished goods and processed materials: materials to which some work has been applied or some value added. Such items are finished only in part or may have been formed into shapes and specifications to make them readily usable by the buyer. These products lose their identity when incorporated into other products. Examples include: metal sections, rods, sheets, tubing, wires, castings, chemicals, cloth, leather, sugar and paper.
- Component parts and assemblies: completely finished products of one manufacturer, which can be used as part of a more complex product by another manufacturer. These do not lose their original identity when incorporated into other products. Examples include bearings, controls, gauges, gears, wheels, transistors, car engines and windscreens. In recent years there has been a trend in manufacturing to buy in more assemblies and fewer components. Assemblies are groups of components that have been assembled prior to purchase, such as car steering assemblies or gearboxes. In the past, many car manufacturers bought all the component parts for these items and actually put them together in the factory. Of course this meant many more suppliers and low-value orders. Nowadays, most car manufacturers buy in larger assemblies from suppliers who, effectively, make whole sections of the car. Most large car manufacturers make less than 50% of the items that are actually in the final automobile product that the consumer buys from a dealer. Indeed, the fact that most car factories are now called "assembly plants" is evidence of this trend.

Consumables and MRO supplies

A wide range of items is required in order to keep the infrastructure (buildings, administration and production facilities) of the organisation running. These are divided into consumable supplies and MRO items.

- **Consumable supplies** are defined as 'consumable items used in the operation of the business enterprise', such as stationery and office supplies, machine oil, fasteners, uniforms, safety apparel, insecticides, fuels, small tools, packaging and wrapping materials.

- **Maintenance, repair and operating supplies** are defined as 'items which are needed repeatedly or recurrently to maintain the operational efficiency of the business', such as fire and safety equipment, electrical supplies, caretaking requirements, and a wide variety of repair parts or spares for plant and equipment.

Resale goods

Unlike manufacturing organisations which transform purchased inputs into finished products, some merchandising organisations (wholesalers or retailers) buy completed products for resale. Wholesalers usually sell to other wholesalers, retailers or to individuals but not usually to the ultimate consumer, whereas retailers provide products and services to the ultimate consumers.

Services

Services involve supply where the main element is a task rather than the provision of tangible goods or materials. The provision of services is becoming more important with the increase in outsourcing. In recent years there has been a large increase in the range of services available to organisations such as catering, payroll, recruitment, training, building management, security, warehousing, transportation, maintenance, IT services, design, printing and management consultancy. Sometimes the service provider's staff will provide the service at the purchasing organisation's premises (a 'provider present' service) such as catering, cleaning or security. In other situations the service will be provided away from the purchasing organisation's premises ('provider not present' service) such as banking or insurance. Services such as transport will involve the service provider being present at the purchasing organisation's premises for only a short time.

You should be aware that sometimes, goods or services are provided by subcontractors and that in some procurement situations, such as with organisations in the construction industry, this is common.

Self-assessment question 1.1

Consider the items listed in learning activity 1.1 above and, in the light of what you have learned in this section, identify the procurement category to which each item belongs and give a definition for each of the categories you identify.

Feedback on page 11

1.2 Categories of expenditure on procurements

Learning activity 1.2

Reflect on your own professional experience. How would you categorise the expenditure on procurements made by your organisation?

Feedback on page 12

Capital expenditure is defined by the Inland Revenue as an expenditure on acquisition of tangible productive assets which yield continuous service beyond the accounting period in which they are purchased.

Various factors distinguish the purchase of capital goods from non-capital goods.

Total costs approach

The basic purchase price of a capital asset is only one of the elements of its total cost to the organisation as there are various costs associated with the purchase and other costs, which can arise during the life of a capital asset. In order to assess the true cost of a capital asset to the organisation, life-cycle costing was developed. **Life-cycle costing** has been defined by the Chartered Institute of Management Accountants as 'the practice of obtaining, over their life time, the best use of the physical assets at the lowest cost to the entity'.

The life-cycle costs of a capital item can be considered under three headings:

- Acquisition costs: these can include the initial costs of transportation, the costs of installation and commissioning, the cost of initial spares and the cost of training the operator/supervisor.
- Operation costs: these include the costs of supervisors, operators and employment costs, fuel and power expenditure, the cost of dealing with emissions or effluent, insurance, the costs of maintenance and downtime, and the cost of spares.
- Disposal costs: these include the costs of depreciation, the estimated value on disposal (if any) and the costs of disposal including the environmental costs.

High cost price

As the capital equipment may be of a high value there are various matters to be considered.

Should the item be purchased new or used? A used item may have a lower price than if it is bought new and be available more quickly. The buyer can perhaps see the machinery in operation and there may be incentives from the manufacturer.

As the purchase of capital equipment can be viewed as an investment, there are financial appraisal methods which can be used to compare the different options available as alternatives to not purchasing the capital asset and simply putting the money in the bank:

- **payback**, which is the time required for the cash returns to equal the initial cash expenditure
- **average rate of return**, which aims to assess the average net profit after depreciation and other cash outlays as a percentage of original cost
- **discounting**, which shows the extent to which a sum of money invested will grow over a period of time at a given rate of compound interest
- **net present value**, which determines the minimum required return on the capital investment.

1

Organisations will usually decide to purchase capital equipment as, after the running costs, maintenance and depreciation are considered, they expect to gain some benefit, which is often financial. This financial benefit from either reducing their overall costs (by doing the work themselves with the new equipment instead of sending out to another organisation to do it for them), or by gaining some additional earnings (by perhaps increasing their production capacity) is the *net cash flow* and it is this figure which is used to decide whether to purchase one particular capital item instead of another.

In addition, a decision needs to be made whether it would be better to lease, rent or hire the equipment instead of purchasing it outright.

Lack of purchasing experience

There is usually a lack of experience with capital items as they are non-recurring, unlike non-capital items which can be bought periodically or on a regular basis.

A team approach

This is usually needed for capital items, with other departments contributing expertise and the team being managed by the procurement specialist.

Negotiations

They will usually be more extended and complex with capital purchases due to the nature of the equipment being purchased.

Specifications

They are often more difficult to draft for capital purchases, which can often be technically complex.

Self-assessment question 1.2

Identify which of the following answers (a)–(c) are correct.

1   Life cycle costing:
    (a) is the practice of obtaining, over their lifetime, the best use of the physical assets at the lowest cost to the entity
    (b) can be considered under the headings of acquisition costs, depreciation costs and disposal costs
    (c) is used due to the low price of capital equipment.
2   Payback:
    (a) aims to assess the average net profit after depreciation and other cash outlays as a percentage of original cost
    (b) is the time required for the cash returns to equal the initial cash expenditure
    (c) shows the extent to which a sum of money invested will grow over a period of time at a given rate of compound interest.
3   With non-capital expenditure:
    (a) negotiations are usually more complex than with capital expenditure

(continued on next page)

Feedback on page 12

Self-assessment question 1.2 *(continued)*

(b) specifications are often more technically complex to draft than with capital expenditure

(c) there is usually a lot of experience with them as they are bought regularly.

1.3   The role of the purchasing professional

Learning activity 1.3

Roxanne is a procurement officer for Super Soggy Sandwiches, a national chain of sandwich sellers. Roxanne is responsible for purchasing and packaging of the sandwiches each week. There are only three types of packaging and the amount ordered each week is based on the remaining stock from the previous week and anticipated demand for the following week.

Rachel is the procurement officer for Exotic Engineering, a hi-tech engineering firm that specialises in developing prototype engine systems for racing cars. The goods Rachel is responsible for procuring tend to be highly specialised and need to be delivered to exacting standards. Rachel's job requires a lot of research into potential suppliers and ensuring the supplier understands the exacting and detailed requirements.

What are the similarities and differences in Roxanne's and Rachel's roles?

Feedback on page 12

In this section you will examine the role of the purchasing professional when purchasing different goods and services.

There are basic issues to be considered in purchasing whatever the category of procurement, such as what does the organisation need, who will supply it and how does the purchasing department get the best deal. As a result, some aspects of the purchasing professional's role can apply whatever the category of procurement. On closer examination however, the role does vary according to the type of goods/services being purchased, and different techniques are associated with buying in each of the procurement categories.

Capital equipment

In some organisations, the purchasing department has to persuade senior management and customers of the value-added contribution it can make in the purchase of capital equipment. In other organisations the procurement department buys centrally, often with participation by other specialists. The 'user', for example the production manager in cases where the equipment being purchased is manufacturing machinery, will often have a major role, and the more technical the equipment, the greater the technical department's role will be in the purchase. Purchasing capital equipment tends to be non-repetitive and so it can be challenging for the purchasing professional who will usually need to develop skills in management accountancy, project management, and teamwork and communication skills. Generally the purchasing role emphasises commercial, negotiating and contractual expertise, but purchasers could find that their role requires them to address issues such as:

- Questioning the need and deciding whether instead of purchasing the capital equipment to make a particular component the organisation should just buy the components instead.
- The financial impact of different options including not purchasing the equipment. Investment appraisal should be used (see section 1.2 above).
- Considering whether it would be better to lease, rent, hire or purchase the equipment.
- If it is to be purchased, should new or used equipment be acquired?
- If it is to be purchased and a decision is being made between different models, the total cost of acquisition should be considered by using life-cycle costing so the purchaser knows the true cost of the equipment over its lifetime.
- Preparatory steps of researching the possible suppliers, requesting quotes and evaluating bids on their merits. With the latter, matters such as price, lead time, operating characteristics, performance criteria, operating costs, spares, maintenance schedules and payment terms could be considered.
- Selecting the supplier. Sometimes the purchasing professional will need to combat prejudice in favour of one supplier who may not offer equipment that is as innovative or competitive as other makes on the market.
- Organising discussions and negotiations with the suppliers and agreeing and finalising terms and conditions.
- Once the contract is awarded the supplier's compliance will need to be checked, for example that they have submitted drawings and met deadlines. Performance should also be monitored during and after installation.

Production materials used in manufacturing

Manufacturing organisations have constant requirements for production materials, consequently purchasing and supply techniques and strategies are, generally speaking, most developed in this sector. The production inputs required in the manufacturing processes are usually raw materials, parts, components, sub-assemblies or assemblies. Without continuity of supply of these materials the production line can grind to a halt with consequential losses. This is another example of the key responsibility of purchasing to contribute to the profitability and quality standards of a business.

With raw materials, prices can fluctuate a great deal so it is important for purchasers to buy at the right time. Commodity purchasing is particularly challenging as prices tend to fluctuate on a daily basis due to uncontrollable variables such as political instability, natural disasters, crop failures and unfavourable weather conditions. In order to be able to purchase supplies at the most competitive price the commodity purchaser must be aware of the various political and economic factors which can influence market conditions. It is therefore the task of the purchasing function to evaluate the information available from various sources including the government (the Department of Trade and Industry (DTI)), publications and economic analysts, and to recommend purchasing policies to fit the circumstances. (*Supply Management*, the CIPS members' journal, publishes in each edition the latest market prices for a number of commodities and also gives the prices over the last 12 months so trends can be seen.) In situations when prices are falling, **hand-to-mouth buying** is appropriate, that is, purchasing according to need rather than in large quantities to obtain discounts. In situations when prices are increasing, **forward buying** can take place (organisations will buy more than they require in order to meet normal production needs). This bulk buying and stockpiling can be done during price increase periods provided the saving as a result of avoiding the future price increase is greater than any additional costs of storage and other such expenses. It can also avoid stoppages due to strikes or shortages. Commodities which can be stored without deterioration for a reasonable time, for example copper, can be sold for delivery at some time in the future. These 'futures' are a specific type of forward buying.

Purchasing component parts and assemblies also requires special attention from the professional purchaser. The following issues may need to be considered and appropriate steps taken:

- Should the organisation make or buy the components? If the decision is made to make them, then considerations such as purchasing capital equipment are relevant.
- Should the components be combined into sub-assemblies and then merely assembled by the organisation in the way that car manufacturers now tend to operate? Most car manufacturers now buy in larger assemblies and often manufacture less than 50% of the vehicle. Car plants tend to assemble rather than manufacture.
- Purchasers may need to liaise with designers over materials, costs, suppliers and possible alternatives to the product.
- Purchasers may enter into detailed negotiations, for example, on tooling costs.
- Where the product is being jointly developed the purchasing department will have an important role in negotiating and liaising with the supplier.

Consumables and MRO supplies

As some consumables and MRO supplies are critical to the organisation it is important that the MRO purchaser has an extremely disciplined approach. Potential disruption to production by a shortage in MRO items could be disastrous. The purchaser's role includes:

- Negotiating the purchase.
- Liaising with maintenance staff to ensure that information on cost, availability and delivery times is available to avoid having a build up of unnecessary levels of stock.
- Establishing a standardisation policy to avoid holding a variety of spares.
- Suggesting alternatives to purchasing such as outsourcing cleaning and catering which, for example, will avoid the need to hold cleaning and catering items.

1

- Minimising administration and storage costs by using small order procedures and direct purchasing by users using call-off contracts. (You will study call-off contracts in study session 4.)
- Analysing proposed maintenance contracts and advising whether they should be accepted. This affects MRO purchases because if total maintenance cover is provided, the organisation will not need to purchase spares as the maintenance contractor will provide them.
- Considering whether emergency or critical spares could be shared.

Resale goods

The term 'trade enterprises' can be used to refer to all types of wholesale and retail organisations involved in the resale of goods. Although the purchaser's role in buying resale goods is similar to buying for industrial organisations, there are some differences:

- Resale buyers often select the purchases and build ranges, unlike industrial purchasers who are told what to buy and in what quantities.
- Resale purchasers negotiate to a cost price which gives them an acceptable selling price/profit margin, whereas industrial purchasers analyse the supplier's material/labour costs and negotiate an acceptable contribution to the supplier's fixed costs/profit.
- Purchasers in trade enterprises purchase on a consignment stock basis so the supplier is paid when the goods are sold.
- With the development of bar-coding and EPOS (electronic point of sale) stocks can be reduced, service levels improved and warehouse/branch inventory policy can be improved. Due to automatic reordering systems with items in demand being reordered automatically without the need for purchaser intervention, purchasers can spend more time on value-added activities.
- With resale goods, purchasing and selling are closely integrated. In trade enterprises, purchasing professionals often have a higher profile.

Services

Services are purchased similarly to the way products are purchased. The purchaser will be involved at the specification stage and will often be involved in negotiating/drafting service level agreements. To ensure that the correct amount of service provision is made whilst avoiding waste and reducing costs, purchasers should work closely with users, as, unlike with products, there is usually a cost involved in making a service available even if it is not used, for example an airport cleaning team will still need to be paid even if there is a strike by aircrew. The purchaser's role can include negotiating with suppliers, using tendering, call-off contracts or spot buying arrangements.

Self-assessment question 1.3

Outline the role of the purchasing professional in the acquisition of capital equipment.

Feedback on page 13

Revision question

Now try the revision question for this session on page 237.

Summary

In this session you have examined the various categories of procurements that organisations will typically acquire. You should be able to:

- Identify and give examples of the different types of products and services that are purchased by organisations, for example capital equipment, production materials used in manufacturing such as raw materials, components and assemblies, consumables and MRO supplies, resale goods and various types of services.
- Identify the categories of expenditure, namely capital and non-capital, used to acquire products and services, and be able to explain the main considerations with these categories of expenditure such as life-cycle costing, new/used purchases and financial appraisal.
- Identify and explain the role of the purchasing professional in acquiring the various different types of products and services involving capital and non-capital expenditure for the benefit of the organisation.

Suggested further reading

Lysons and Farrington (2006). You should read the chapter on contrasting approaches to supply.

Feedback on learning activities and self-assessment questions

Feedback on learning activity 1.1

You should have listed all the goods and services which your organisation uses to extract raw materials or create agricultural produce if you are in the primary sector, to manufacture goods if for example you are in the secondary sector, and to resell finished goods or provide services if you are in the tertiary sector. Your list should include not only the items purchased, for example, for an organisation to manufacture goods or to provide a service, but also the goods purchased for the staff canteen or alternatively the outsourced catering services provided for the organisation's workers.

Feedback on self-assessment question 1.1

You should be able to identify the procurement category for each item by using the information above. Your definitions of procurement categories could be as follows:

- Capital equipment is a tangible asset which provides benefit to the organisation over a long period.
- Raw materials are the products from agriculture and the various extractive industries, many of which are internationally traded commodities.

- Semi-finished goods and processed materials are materials to which some work has been applied or some value added, but which lose their identity when incorporated into other products.
- Component parts and assemblies are completely finished products of one manufacturer which can be used as part of a more complex product by another manufacturer. They do not lose their original identity when incorporated into other products.
- In order to keep the organisation running, consumable supplies and MRO items are required. Consumable supplies are items used in the operation of the organisation. Maintenance, repair and operating supplies are needed repeatedly or recurrently to maintain the operational efficiency of the organisation.
- Resale goods are completed products that are purchased by merchandising organisations (wholesalers or retailers) for resale.
- Services involve supply where the main element is a task rather than the provision of tangible goods or materials.

Feedback on learning activity 1.2

There are many ways in which you could have categorised your organisation's expenditure. You may have used the value of the contract, the method of purchase or the department/procurement officer involved, or you may have classified it according to the procurement categories you studied in section 1.1. There are many ways that expenditure can be classified depending on what use you want to make of the classification, but in this session you will consider capital and non-capital expenditure.

Feedback on self-assessment question 1.2

The correct responses are indicated below, with an explanation of why the other responses are wrong.

1   Life cycle costing:
    (a) correct
    (b) the headings are acquisition, operation and disposal costs
    (c) the cost of capital equipment is usually high
2   Payback:
    (a) this is the average rate of return
    (b) correct
    (c) this is discounting
3   With non-capital expenditure:
    (a) negotiations are usually less complex
    (b) specifications are often less technically complex to draft
    (c) correct.

Feedback on learning activity 1.3

In Roxanne's role, once suppliers have been established, the role can become relatively routine. Roxanne is involved with repetitive purchases where her role appears to remain the same as she purchases the same type of goods. Unless there are requirements for continuous improvements, Roxanne's role will remain essentially the same.

Rachel's role is very different. It is non-routine and will often involve close liaison with other departments in sorting out the specification, finding the right suppliers, then liaising with them to ensure they understand exactly what the requirement is.

Feedback on self-assessment question 1.3

Your answer should include reference to the following.

Often the procurement department buys capital equipment centrally with participation by other specialists; the more technical the equipment, the greater the technical department's role will be. As it is non-repetitive it can be challenging for the purchasing professional who requires skills in management accountancy, project management, and teamwork and communication skills. The purchasing role emphasises commercial, negotiating and contractual expertise, with the purchaser addressing issues such as:

- whether to buy the product instead of manufacturing it
- the financial impact of different options using investment appraisal
- whether the equipment should be leased, rented or hired instead
- whether to buy new or used equipment
- total cost of acquisition using life-cycle costing
- researching the possible suppliers
- requesting quotes and evaluating bids
- selecting the supplier
- negotiating and agreeing the terms and conditions, and
- checking the supplier's compliance once the contract is awarded.

1

Procurement objectives

Introduction

In study session 1 you considered categories of procurements and expenditure and the role of the purchasing professional. In this session you will be examining the overall task of procurement professionals, then you will focus on the objectives that a purchasing department may develop to enable it to realise the overall strategy of the department or the organisation as a whole. Finally you will consider how specifications, performance measures and contractual terms can be used to achieve those objectives.

Purchasing is 'buying the right quality in the right quantity at the right price from the right source'.

(Attributed to HG Selfridge (1858–1947), American businessman and founder of Selfridges – Britain's first department store)

Session learning objectives

After completing this session you should be able to:

2.1 Define the overall purchasing task.
2.2 Formulate objectives that enable purchasing departments to realise overall strategy.
2.3 Explain why specifications, performance measures and contractual terms are used in supply agreements.

Unit content coverage

This study session covers the following topic from the official CIPS unit content document.

Learning outcome

Recognise the use of specifications, performance measures and contract terms for procurements of products and services from suppliers.

Learning objective

1.2 Formulate objectives for the procurement of both goods and services
 • The five rights of purchasing.
 • Achieving a balance between objectives: time versus cost.
 • The use of specifications, performance measures and contractual terms in supply agreements.

Prior knowledge

Study session 1

2

Resources

Appendix 5, Advice on answering examination questions.

Timing

You should set aside about 5 hours to read and complete this session, including learning activities, self-assessment questions, the suggested further reading (if any) and the revision question.

2.1 The purchasing task

Learning activity 2.1

What do you consider is the overall task of your department?

Feedback on page 21

Many quotations relating to purchasing have been attributed to Harry Gordon Selfridge, including the one above, which indicates what the founder of Selfridges apparently considered the purchasing task to be, that is, purchasing 'the right quality in the right quantity at the right price from the right source'.

However, in order to know what is right, first the purchasing professional must identify what the specific needs of the organisation are. It is only then that the 'right' purchases can be recognised.

One of the basic principles in purchasing is that of the 'five rights', which have strong echoes emanating from the quotation above. The five rights of purchasing are:

- the right quality
- the right quantity
- the right place
- the right time
- the right price.

If the rights are satisfied then the purchased inputs are of the right quality and the right quantity is delivered to the right place at the right time for the right price. In situations where the 'rights' are not achieved, however, there will be repercussions for the organisations and for the purchasing department. Inputs may be acquired which are of the wrong quality and which do not therefore satisfy the need. If the quantity supplied is less than expected your organisation may face severe problems especially if the items in question are vital components for production or they are critical maintenance, repair and operating (MRO) items. If the goods are delivered to the wrong location or are delivered late, problems can also occur. Finally, if the inputs are not acquired at the right price there will be financial implications for the organisation. As far as the purchasing department is concerned, if the inputs acquired for internal customers do not meet requirements this could cause other departments in the organisation to be dissatisfied with the performance of the purchasing department and if the purchasing department gives poor customer service to internal clients other departments may overlook it and purchase directly, or in some circumstances the purchasing department may even face being outsourced.

In *Purchasing and Supply Chain Management* (2006), Lysons and Farrington examine the purchasing department's function and consider the classic definition of the purchasing task, which is:

'To obtain materials of the right quality in the right quantity from the right source delivering to the right place at the right time at the right price.'

This classic definition extends the five rights of purchasing to six, with the addition of the 'right' source. It therefore recognises the importance of choosing the right supplier for the organisation's inputs.

Before finishing this section, you should consider the terminology used. The use of the word purchasing would suggest that only the actual purchase of goods and services is being considered when establishing what the task of the department is. However, you may well find that in your department not only are you involved with outright purchases but the department may also be involved in other methods of acquisition of goods such as leasing or by hire purchase. Referring to the 'purchasing' task therefore does not really reflect the department's true role. The 'procurement' task is wider in its scope and is more accurate for many organisations. Often, however, 'purchasing department' is the name used to cover the department which deals with all types of procurement.

You should always remember that whatever an organisation's 'rights' are, they should be in keeping with its goals and objectives. In section 2.2 below you will consider the operational objectives of purchasing.

Self-assessment question 2.1

Identify the 'rights' of purchasing.

Feedback on page 22

2.2 Purchasing and supply objectives

In order to formulate a corporate strategy, an organisation will scan the environment to discover opportunities and threats outside the organisation and to discover strengths and weaknesses within the organisation. It will then formulate its strategic vision stating what kind of organisation the management is trying to create. From this a mission statement can be written to set out how the organisation is managed and what its overall aim is. The organisation's corporate objectives will then explain how the aims will be achieved. As far as the purchasing department is concerned, its objectives are derived from the corporate objectives. If, for example, an organisation's corporate objectives included a plan to develop specific new products or a plan to introduce a cost reduction plan, the purchasing department could have corresponding departmental objectives of a plan to develop appropriate suppliers and a plan to introduce supplies standardisation and supplier reduction programmes.

Learning activity 2.2

Find out what your organisation's strategic vision, mission statement and corporate objectives are, and make a note of them. Find out what the objectives of your organisation's purchasing department are and make a note of them. If you discover that your department does not have its own specific objectives, use the organisation's corporate objectives to help you write appropriate ones for your department.

Feedback on page 22

Corporate objectives tend to be strategic, long term and general. The objectives of a purchasing department are functional and they are therefore tactical, short term and specific.

The five rights of purchasing and also the very similar classic definition of purchasing which you saw in section 2.1 above define purchasing from the point of view of objectives. Difficulties can arise with simplistic definitions of the 'rights' of purchasing just as they can arise with objectives due to the following reasons.

'Right' is usually defined differently by each organisation. What is perceived to be right for one organisation will not necessarily be right for another. In the same way the objectives which are relevant for one purchasing department will be different from those of a different organisation's purchasing department.

Rights and objectives do not remain constant for an organisation or a purchasing department. Change may occur in the overall purchasing environment just as it may occur within an organisation. Consequently the rights of purchasing for that organisation are likely to be affected. What is right for a particular organisation is likely to change within different purchasing contexts over a period of time. It is likely, however, that change will come sooner to the objectives of the purchasing department than to those of the organisation as the former's objectives are short term whereas the latter's are long term.

Further problems can arise because objectives may sometimes be irreconcilable, that is, it may be impossible to achieve all of the objectives just as it can be impossible to achieve all 'rights'.

If, for example, you required goods to be supplied at a very competitive price (the 'right' price), but you also required them to be delivered very quickly, for example, within 24 hours (the 'right time'), you may have two 'rights' and also objectives based upon them that could not be reconciled.

It is possible that you will be expected to pay more than what you consider to be the 'right' price for goods in order to achieve the 'right' quality, in other words the high quality that you require. If this is the case, those two 'rights' (price and quality) are irreconcilable, and so too are any objectives based upon them.

It is also possible that goods of the right quality are only available from a specialised high-quality manufacturer who is very busy. As a result, you may not be able to obtain them at the right time in order to achieve your objective but instead you may have to wait for delivery. Again these two 'rights', or rather the objectives based upon them, are seen to be irreconcilable in these circumstances.

The problem highlighted above, that objectives are irreconcilable, means that sometimes the purchasing professional must weigh up the importance of one objective against the other and achieve a balance between them, for example between time and cost. If inputs cannot be sourced at the 'right' cost and within the 'right' delivery time, the procurement department must balance the importance of cost against that of time and decide which of the two is preferable. If it is time then the higher price will be paid. If it is cost then the goods will be delivered at a later time. As a procurement professional, you may need to re-evaluate objectives or what is considered to be 'right' in situations where it is impossible to achieve all objectives as they are irreconcilable.

Self-assessment question 2.2

Formulate three typical objectives for a procurement department and explain, using examples, how they may be irreconcilable in connection with purchases of certain inputs.

You should answer this question by way of a short essay of approximately 300 words.

As this is the first essay that you have been asked to write in this course you may find it helpful to read the information in appendix 5, Advice on answering examination questions about the best approach to take when writing essays as success in the exam depends not only on you knowing and understanding the content of this course but also being able to demonstrate that knowledge and understanding in your examination.

Feedback on page 22

2.3 Requirements – specifying them, measuring compliance to them and enforcing them

Learning activity 2.3

How can purchasing professionals set standards to show what is required in a particular input?

Feedback on page 23

In order to achieve the purchasing objectives and acquire goods and services which satisfy the five rights, the purchasing function needs to address key issues to ensure that the purchasing professional is able to acquire inputs of the right quality, quantity and price which are delivered to the right place at the right time and from the right source to meet objectives.

It is important that the procurement professional takes steps to try to ensure that the inputs an organisation acquires meet its requirements. Often in contracts the important issues that must be monitored are quality and time of delivery. Therefore, it is vital that these and any other relevant issues for the contract are clearly defined and agreed at the outset so that both parties know what is required, that they are carefully monitored to establish whether standards are being maintained according to the agreed standards and that a mechanism is in place to make sure that steps can be taken to ensure compliance or make other provision where standards are not met. The way that the procurement function does this is by the use of specifications, performance measures and contract terms.

Specifications

It has been suggested that the procurement department's primary purpose is to obtain the best-quality products or services, bearing in mind fitness for use, at the lowest possible price. That is how it contributes to the profitability of an organisation.

'Fitness for purpose or use' was Juran's (1988) definition of quality, and one aspect of this is whether the product or service conforms to its specification. Therefore, the specification itself is an important part of the quality aspect of a product. If the specification is wrong then quality may be wrong and this can cause unnecessary cost to the organisation. The specification should give a clear picture to the supplier of what is needed by the organisation. You will be considering specifications in more detail in study session 3.

Performance measurement

Performance measurement in this sense measures how well a supplier is performing in supplying the required inputs. Performance measurement is important because if performance cannot be measured it is not possible to assess whether appropriate performance levels are being provided and it cannot be effectively managed, so improvement cannot be achieved. Often the procurement function needs to measure the quality aspects of the products and services provided by their suppliers as well as supplier performance with delivery time. You will be considering this further in study session 3.

Contractual terms

Once agreement has been reached between the organisation and its supplier, that agreement should be set out formally in a contract. The contract should be clear as to the requirements of the organisation in terms of the product or service that is to be provided by the supplier, and it should also make provision for what will happen in the event of difficulties arising. Once they enter into the contract both parties should carry out their obligations by supplying the specified goods in the right quantity to the right place at the right time and by making the appropriate payment in the right way at the right time. However, if the organisation finds that its supplier has not complied with its obligations under the terms of the contract, the organisation will be able to rely on provisions of the contract which may enable it to seek compliance by the supplier or payment of money to compensate for losses and in some circumstances to terminate the contract. Likewise the organisation could face similar measures if it fails to comply with its obligations under the contract. You will be examining contract terms in more detail in later sessions of this course book.

Self-assessment question 2.3

In the light of what you have covered in this section, explain in simple terms the purpose of specifications, performance measures and contractual terms.

Feedback on page 23

Revision question

Now try the revision question for this session on page 237.

Summary

In this session you have:

- Examined the overall task of procurement professionals by reference to the 'rights' of purchasing.
- Formulated objectives to enable the purchasing function to realise overall strategy.
- Considered how those objectives can be achieved to satisfy the rights of purchasing by the use of:
  - specifications
  - performance measures
  - contract terms.

Suggested further reading

Carter and Kirby (2006). You should read the chapter on fundamentals of procurement.

Lysons and Farrington (2006). You should read about the rights of purchasing, purchasing objectives and specifications.

Feedback on learning activities and self-assessment questions

Feedback on learning activity 2.1

You may consider that the task is to procure goods and/or services which give best value to your organisation, are delivered promptly, are of consistently high quality, meet your specifications and so on. You may have given a simple definition of the task or you may have gone into more detail, but however you approached the question, it is likely that you considered some or all of the aspects mentioned and you may well have thought of others too.

Feedback on self-assessment question 2.1

The 'rights' should be described as the original 'five' rights of purchasing:

- the right quality
- the right quantity
- the right place
- the right time
- the right price.

You could then have mentioned the additional 'right' of the right source.

Feedback on learning activity 2.2

The objectives that you draft should be SMART: **S**pecific, **M**easurable, **A**chievable, **R**ealistic, **T**imed.

Feedback on self-assessment question 2.2

You should have read the question carefully and realised that there were two main tasks:

- formulate three typical objectives for a procurement department, and
- explain, using examples, why purchases of certain inputs may be irreconcilable.

For the first point, you could indicate what the objectives are and state the three typical examples you have drafted.

To answer the second point you could find some information in the text above which deals with circumstances where objectives or 'rights' are irreconcilable. If you consider the rights of time and price, for example, you may be negotiating to purchase goods at a particular price but you may then wish the supplier to provide them very quickly. This may cause difficulties for the supplier who might require a higher price if the goods are to be supplied as a matter of urgency. Similarly difficulties may arise with goods being supplied at a particular price at a particular place. Your organisation may want them at a good price but may want them supplied to various sites when the supplier is prepared to supply them at a price which is right for you but will only supply to one central point for that price. Your answer should also include some examples from your own experience of situations where it has been difficult to obtain all the 'rights' of purchasing in a particular contract, or situations where you could envisage this happening. In such situations usually if the deal is struck there has to be some compromise where you do not achieve all the 'rights' exactly as you originally thought and you may find that this has happened in your organisation.

Remember, your answer should be around 300 words long.

Feedback on learning activity 2.3

You should have considered how procurement professionals could:

- use specifications to state what is required for a particular product or service that is being sourced
- use performance measures to set targets for suppliers and then measure whether suppliers perform at target levels or not
- use terms in contracts to be able to control the situation by the use of sanctions for failure to comply with what has been agreed.

Feedback on self-assessment question 2.3

Your answer should include reference to:

- specifications giving a clear picture to the supplier of what is needed by the organisation
- performance measurement being used to measure how well or not a supplier is providing the input, and
- contractual terms ensuring that the agreement between the parties states clearly the requirements of the organisation in terms of the product or service that is to be provided by the supplier and the consequences of certain difficulties arising.

2

Study session 3

Achieving procurement objectives

'First, have a definite, clear practical ideal, a goal, an objective. Second, have the necessary means to achieve your ends: wisdom, money, materials and methods. Third, adjust all your means to that end.'
(Aristotle (384–322 BC))

Introduction

In this session you will consider the importance of specifications in achieving value for money, examine why performance measures and targets are used in agreements with suppliers, and summarise the differences between purchasers' and suppliers' contractual terms.

Session learning objectives

After completing this session you should be able to:

3.1 Explain the importance of specifications in achieving value for money.
3.2 Explain, using examples, why performance measures and targets are used in agreements with suppliers.
3.3 Summarise the differences between purchasers' and suppliers' contractual terms.

Unit content coverage

This study session covers the following topic from the official CIPS unit content document.

Learning outcome

Recognise the use of specifications, performance measures and contract terms for procurements of products and services from suppliers.

Learning objectives

1.3 Recognise the impact of specifications on achieving value for money.
 • The functions of a specification.
 • The types of specification.
 • Choosing the most appropriate type of specification for the purchase decision.
1.4 Discuss the use and application of key performance indicators in agreements with suppliers.
 • The development of performance measures that can be applied to commercial agreements.
 • Examples of performance measures.
 • Developing targets for supplier performance.
1.5 Recognise the use and the content of contractual terms for purchased goods or services.
 • Purchasers' and suppliers' standard contracts.
 • The differences between purchasers' and suppliers' terms.

3

Prior knowledge

Study sessions 1 and 2.

Timing

You should set aside about 5 hours to read and complete this session, including learning activities, self-assessment questions, the suggested further reading (if any) and the revision question.

3.1 Specifications

Learning activity 3.1

Consider your own organisation. Is the procurement function involved in the specification process? If so, note down how, and with what product categories it becomes involved.

If the purchasing function does not get involved then note down the reasons why you think this is the case.

Feedback on page 34

It is fair to assume that an organisation will only purchase the items that it needs for its operations, as it would be a waste to purchase items that are not required. An organisation may need to purchase goods for use in production, for example a car manufacturer will need to buy components and assemblies in order to make cars, just as a hospital will need to purchase drugs and equipment to treat patients. This is known as **direct purchasing**. When the need arises on the non-production side of the operations, for example when a car manufacturer needs to purchase office supplies or cleaning services for its premises, this is known as **indirect purchasing**.

In order to source the right product to meet the need, whether it is in direct or indirect purchasing, the need itself must be described. This is what a specification should do. A **specification** is a statement of the attributes of a product, process or service. A well-written specification should describe the need accurately. Some specifications can describe the need in a few words where simple products are involved, whereas others describing the need for a specialised piece of equipment could run to several pages and include designs, drawings and detailed instructions for the manufacturer.

Functions of specifications

Specifications have two basic functions: communication and comparison.

- Communication: clear unambiguous specifications facilitate communication between the purchasing organisation and the supply market and also facilitate communication internally with users.

3

- Comparison: clear and unambiguous specifications facilitate a fair and more accurate comparison of suppliers' bids for contracts, as all bids are being compared on the same basis.

If the specification enables clear communication to take place between the parties at the beginning of the contract then there is less chance of disputes later on. So if in a specification for outsourced cleaning services an organisation wanted their office building to be 'clean', the specification should define what it means by the term 'clean' to ensure the cleaning contractors are aware of what the need is. Also, if the purchasing organisation clearly specifies what its needs are in respect of cleaning, if the contract is put out to tender for example, the organisation will be able to compare the bids as they will be made on the same basis and this will avoid the competing suppliers having different interpretations of what is meant by 'clean' and consequently basing their bids on different assumptions.

Types of specification

Specifications can be divided into two categories: conformance and performance.

Conformance specifications are strict, technical specifications which usually describe the requirement, that is, the specific product or service. A conformance specification uses a description of the physical attributes of the product and perhaps its manufacturing process. If the specification is for a service, it will usually state what the service providers are expected to do in sufficient detail so that they will be able to provide that service. The description in a conformance specification emphasises inputs and limits a supplier's freedom.

Performance specifications state what the requirement is expected to do. They should include what the typical performance is expected to be as well as the minimum and maximum performance expectations. The performance specification for a service will define the results that are required from successful performance of the service. Performance specifications emphasise outputs and encourage a supplier's freedom.

Methods of specification

Procurement professionals use various methods to specify requirements in a wide range of environments. Some of the common methods are described below. When reading through the list, consider how many of them are used in specifications in your department.

- Standards – for example A4 paper. Lysons and Farrington (2006) regard these as specifications intended for recurrent use. They are existing specifications which are national or international standards or manufacturer's standards as the specification has general, widespread acceptance within a product category, organisation, industry, profession or geographical trading area.
- Brand or trade names – for example a Peugeot car or Levi jeans. Using brand names can lead to higher costs as branded items are often more expensive, and if a brand is specified then alternatives cannot be used.

3

However, using brand names can be an advantage if there is a need to duplicate an existing product.

- Samples – for example the dress given by the designer to a manufacturer to use as the specification. You will consider the implications of sale by sample when you study the terms implied into sales contracts by the Sale of Goods Act 1979 (as amended) (in study session 9).
- Drawings/blueprints – for example in a construction project.
- Market grade – for example first-pressed olive oil, high-tensile steel.
- Method of manufacture – for example halal and kosher meat.
- Physical or chemical properties – for example animal feed, paints, concrete.

Choosing the most appropriate specification

As specifications are important in achieving value for money, choosing the appropriate specification for the particular requirement, whether it is for products or services, can be vital.

A decision has to be made whether a conformance or performance specification is more appropriate, or even whether the specification will have some elements that are conformance and other elements that are performance.

There are circumstances where conformance specifications are necessary and desirable. This may be because the purchaser has detailed technical knowledge and specifies precisely what is required by way of description of what will satisfy the need. The specification may include plans, physical properties or a brand name. As you read above, there is little or no supplier innovation in conformance specifications.

Sometimes, however, there are advantages in using performance specifications:

- They are easier to draft and so are appropriate to use when the purchaser has little knowledge of the product.
- They place the burden upon the supplier because if the product does not perform, the purchaser is entitled to seek redress from the supplier. This is due to section 14(3) Sale of Goods Act 1979 (as amended) under which a term can be implied into contracts for sale that goods are of satisfactory quality. You will examine this further when you study implied terms in study session 9.
- They widen the potential supplier base because if suppliers are expected to supply a product which will perform a particular function, a wide range of possible solutions could be provided by the expertise of different suppliers.

The method of specification must also be considered. As different methods are appropriate in different situations, the procurement professional must decide whether the appropriate method is being used to specify the input. Any specifications which are tight and restrictive should be reviewed and sometimes questioned as they limit both purchaser and supplier freedom.

The procurement function can play an important part in adding value at the specification stage and avoiding waste through unnecessary costs. The greatest opportunity for reducing costs is at the design/specification stage. The procurement professional can ensure that things are not over-specified. Additional requirements cost money and if they are not really necessary they can be dispensed with early and unnecessary costs can therefore be avoided. As branded items are usually more expensive they could be avoided in the specification, allowing suppliers to provide suitable cheaper alternatives. Packaging should be considered with a view to cost avoidance. Minimum packaging should be specified to avoid the cost of disposing of it, or alternatively returnable or recyclable packaging could be specified.

Self-assessment question 3.1

You are presently writing the specification for the catering service for your organisation's canteen. Identify three conformance specifications and three performance specifications that you might include in your overall specification.

Feedback on page 34

3.2 Key performance indicators (KPI)

Learning activity 3.2

Consider the various procurement items that are purchased by your organisation and the services that are provided to it. How do you know whether the supplier has supplied the items or provided the service in accordance with your requirements?

Feedback on page 35

Whether things or services are being provided, in order to decide whether the supplier or the service provider has satisfied the requirement, there are certain things that the procurement professional must know.

You must know what was expected of the supplier/provider. This is where the specification is relevant, as it communicates your requirement to the supplier. If the specification is for items, you can measure whether the supplier has performed the contract if the item meets the specification. As you saw in section 3.1 above, a conformance specification may include measurements, chemical properties, plans, named brands, samples and standards. Performance specifications will state what the item is expected to do. As far as measurements are concerned, if the item is measured against what is stated in the specification, if it conforms to the specification and perhaps if it is delivered by the time designated in the contract, then the supplier will have fulfilled his obligations under the contract. Likewise with a performance specification for an item, once the item has been delivered in accordance with any agreed delivery schedule, it will be put to use and

3

if it performs the function which was specified (for example a printer can produce a specified number of copies per minute to a specified quality level and is expected to function for a life of a specified number of pages), then that supplier too will have successfully fulfilled his obligations under the contract.

However, with providers of services, what is being supplied is not always so tangible, but nevertheless it will still have to be measured otherwise it will be impossible to tell whether the service provider has performed the service contract as agreed. First of all, therefore, it is important that the requirement for the service is clearly understood and communicated and that a range of features of the service is identified as being the 'measuring stick' of successful performance of the service contract. As with the supply of 'things', the provision of services should be clearly specified at the outset. Specifications for services state the minimum levels of service that are acceptable to the customer. They are usually the basis of agreements between the customer and service provider commonly referred to as service level agreements (SLAs). Service level agreements allow purchasers to state their minimum service level needs clearly and unambiguously and consequently they enable providers to focus their resources on providing services at the required level.

However, it is important that the service being provided can be measured. In SLAs a range of key performance indicators (KPIs) are used to measure the quality of performance. Obviously your KPIs must be measurable. They are important in providing qualitative or quantitative information that indicates whether current performance is reasonable and cost effective. The KPIs used will vary according to the nature of the service contract, but some quantitative examples of KPIs are workload and output-to-cost ratios, transaction ratios, error rates, consumption rates, inventory fill rates and timeliness measures (for example delivery times or waiting times). Qualitative service KPIs that could be used are responsiveness rates and user satisfaction rates.

As you have seen, it is important that KPIs are measurable and they must also be measured to assess whether the specified minimum service level is being achieved. They can also be used to set targets above the minimum expected service level. These targets give the supplier something to aim at to improve the quality of their performance, and when such targets are linked to supplier incentives, this can be a useful mechanism by which the purchaser can encourage and reward increased quality levels in the supplier's performance of the contract. For example, with a courier company, the incentive could be a bonus payment when delivery targets are met. The KPIs are also useful in identifying when suppliers fail to achieve minimum service levels, and when this happens the SLA may include penalties for the supplier for failure to achieve minimum service levels. This may entail a lower payment or no payment being forthcoming from the purchaser in cases, for example, of couriers failing to deliver parcels within the minimum required time. However, recognition of the failure to achieve can also allow remedial steps to be considered. This may involve changes to the agreement between the parties perhaps to increase the capacity for provision of the service, which may involve higher costs for the purchaser. Alternatively it could involve a decrease in the minimum level of service in the SLA where the supplier's expectations of the service level were initially too high.

3

Self-assessment question 3.2

Using a service level agreement, identify the parties, state what the agreement is for, identify three relevant KPIs and targets and say how you would measure them.

You can either use an SLA from your organisation or you can think up your own example.

Feedback on page 35

3.3 Differences between purchasers' and suppliers' contractual terms

Learning activity 3.3

How does having a written contract benefit purchasers and suppliers?

Feedback on page 35

Imagine that you are a supplier and make a mental list of what you would hope to have in a contract to give your organisation the advantage in relation to the supply of a particular service or an item. Now imagine yourself as the purchaser of that item or service and make a mental list of what you would hope to have in a contract to give your organisation the advantage in relation to the purchase of that item or service.

There is a wide range of matters that you could have thought of to include in your mental lists, depending on whether you were dealing with an item or a service and what those items and services were. The point of doing this, however, is to examine the differences in your lists. Although there are some matters that both the purchaser and the supplier would want to include in the contract in similar or identical ways, there are also many things that you might want to include as a purchaser but you would want to avoid them if you were a supplier, and vice versa.

Consider the range of items and services that your organisation procures, and the different types of commercial relationships that you may have with various suppliers. Some commercial relationships are partnerships where purchasers and suppliers have shared goals and work together to achieve them. Other relationships may be far removed from this situation and purchasers and suppliers can be adversaries. The nature of the relationship can be reflected in the terms of the contract between them, but even in the most cordial of relationships where both organisations appear to work well together, each organisation may want to ensure that the contract which is made between them will give it the stronger position in the relationship. It is important therefore to be aware of the general position regarding contract terms that may be preferable to purchasers or to suppliers.

During negotiations for the purchase of particular items from a supplier, there will come a point when either you or the supplier's negotiator will produce a first draft of the contract, which will set out the agreement reached thus far. At this stage, the advantage in negotiations lies with the party drafting the contract. Although the draft sets out matters agreed in the negotiations, those drafting it will naturally do so using their own language and preferred terms and will structure the sequence of the document whichever way seems most appropriate to them. The other party must then consider the first draft, familiarise themselves with the language, terms and structure, and then try to follow the drafter's logic through the document in order to decide if the reasons the drafters gave for writing it in a particular way are valid. They must also consider whether there are any hidden risks lurking in the document. Tactically drafting the contract can assist you.

One of the old principles of English contract law is that the parties have 'freedom to contract' and this, to an appreciable extent, still holds true today. This means that the terms can vary from one contract to another, as it is the parties' choice as to what they agree to include as express terms of their contract.

There are various matters which the parties may consider. Some will be important issues for the purchaser and some for the supplier, and other issues will be important to both of them.

Table 3.2

Matters to consider	Purchaser preference	Supplier preference	Possible contract terms to consider
Delivery times	Strictly as per P's delivery dates and in default of this a reduction in price	Would prefer some leeway and does not want sanctions for late delivery	'Time is of the essence'
What if production costs increase during the contract?	Purchaser wants to pay lower price applicable at date of contract even if they do not want delivery for some time	Supplier wants to charge increased price at time of subsequent delivery to take account of increased costs	Price variation clause
When does ownership of the goods pass to purchaser?	As soon as possible	Not until payment in full has been received for the goods	Retention of title clause
Is delivery short?	Expects missing goods to be delivered in 24 hours	Would like to avoid responsibility unless faults reported within 48 hours/will resupply within the week	Exclusion clause

Table 3.2 sets out some matters which may exercise the parties' minds and which can be dealt with by way of contract clauses. There are many other issues which may be relevant in contract negotiation, the list

is endless, but they could include situations where the goods do not match the specification, where they are defective, where the parties want different arrangements for payment terms, what financial sanctions for non-performance of the contract can be included and how disputes are to be resolved.

In study sessions 11 – 16 you will examine various express contract terms relied upon by both purchasers and suppliers, as well as terms that are implied into contracts.

Self-assessment question 3.3

Identify which, if any, of the following answers is wrong.

1 How does having a written contract benefit purchasers and suppliers?
   (a) They have an accurate record of the agreement and so can avoid misunderstandings
   (b) It clarifies what the buyer's obligations are to the supplier and what the supplier's obligations are to the seller
   (c) It clarifies what the purchaser's rights are against the supplier and what the supplier's rights are against the purchaser.
2 Suppliers would usually prefer clauses which:
   (a) Ensure that ownership of the goods does not pass to the purchaser until payment in full has been received
   (b) In a market where prices are increasing, state that the purchaser pays the lower price which applies at the date of the order even if delivery is not required for some time
   (c) Do not have strict delivery dates nor sanctions for late delivery.
3 The party drafting the contract has the advantage because:
   (a) They will use their own language and preferred terms and will structure the sequence of the document in whichever way seems most appropriate to them
   (b) The other party cannot influence what goes in the contract
   (c) The other party must also consider whether there are any hidden risks lurking in the document.

Feedback on page 36

Revision question

Now try the revision question for this session on page 237.

Summary

You have now completed your studies into the early stages in the development of contracts. In this section you have:

- Considered the importance of specifications in achieving value for money.

3

- Studied the functions of specifications, the various types of specifications, the methods of specifying requirements and choosing the most appropriate specification.
- Examined why performance measures and targets are used in agreements with suppliers.
- Identified differences between purchasers' and suppliers' contractual terms.

In study sessions 1 – 3 you have examined the categories of procurements, the objectives of procurement and how to achieve those objectives. In the following sessions you will begin to consider some of the legal aspects of developing contracts.

Suggested further reading

Carter and Kirby (2006). You should read the chapters on specification and performance measures.

Lysons and Farrington (2006). You could read about specifications.

Wyborn (2000). You could read the sections on 'Taking instructions', 'Who shall be draftsman?' and 'A simple synopsis'.

Feedback on learning activities and self-assessment questions

Feedback on learning activity 3.1

Depending on the type of procurements that are usually purchased by your department, it may have a major or minor role in the specification process. Within technical and production orientated environments, it is likely that there will be a high level of involvement by the users. Even so, purchasing should still have a role in avoiding waste, poor supplier performance and increased costs, although this will depend on the attitude to the purchasing function within the organisation. With less technical inputs the purchasing role could be greater as the user would usually have a lesser role in the specification process. In this situation too, however, some organisations do not value purchasing involvement in the specification process other than to receive specifications from end users and source the product or service, and so the purchasing function could still have only a minor role in the process.

Feedback on self-assessment question 3.1

Below are examples of conformance and performance specifications that could be used.

Conformance specifications:

1   A vegetarian choice must be offered.
2   The canteen must open at 7 am daily.
3   Must sterilise all work surfaces three times daily.

Performance specifications:

1 Food is tasty (measured by a customer survey).
2 No more than ten minutes waiting at peak times.
3 All complaints dealt with within 48 hours.

Feedback on learning activity 3.2

You might not realise that the service has not been provided until there is a complaint about it from the direct end users, or the component supplied is the wrong size and will not fit into the assembly on your production line, or the new laptops purchased for the production managers do not perform as expected. As a procurement professional you will then need to find out where the true problem lies and discover whether the supplier has failed to supply what was specified.

Feedback on self-assessment question 3.2

Below is a typical example for you to consider.

Service level agreement between Fun 4 U and Speedy Service Couriers

F4U is a book, DVD and games internet business which uses SSC, a courier service, to deliver goods to its customers. In table 3.1 there are examples of the KPIs and for each of them the 'measurements' are shown for the minimum service level (what the contract expects the courier service to perform), the target for the courier service to aim for in order to improve quality and perhaps gain any relevant bonus, and also the method of measurement.

Table 3.1

KPIs	Acceptable (minimum) level of service	Target level	How measured
Delivery time to UK address	90% next working day	100% next working day	Monthly customer survey
Response to pick-up time	85% collect within one hour	90% collect within one hour	Reception Signature
Damaged parcels	4%	0%	Monthly customer survey
Missing parcels	0%	0%	Contractor data

Feedback on learning activity 3.3

You could have listed several benefits including the following:

- To have an accurate record of what has been agreed in negotiation so as to avoid misunderstanding.

- To state what the purchaser's obligations are to the supplier and what the supplier's obligations are to the purchaser.
- To clarify what the purchaser's rights are against the supplier and what the supplier's rights are against the purchaser.
- So that at a later date the purchaser and supplier will have a written record of what was agreed in the event of problems arising.
- So that parties have guidance on what issues are important and can give themselves some protection against potential risks by introducing contractual sanctions for the other party if they do not comply with the agreement.

Feedback on self-assessment question 3.3

1   All true.
2   (b). This would be preferred by a purchaser. A supplier would want a clause in these circumstances which would allow the higher price applicable at the time of delivery to be the contract price charged for the item.
3   (b). The other party can influence what goes in the contract. The parties have to agree the terms of the contract for them to be included.

Contract formation – the agreement

'Men keep agreements when it is to the advantage of neither to break them.'
(Solon (630–560 BC), Athenian statesman and poet)

4

Introduction

Study sessions 1 – 3 consider different categories of procurements and procurement objectives and then go on to examine the achievement of those objectives. In this session you will begin studying contracts, which are the 'arrangements' by which the procurements are acquired and procurement objectives are attained.

Session learning objectives

After completing this session you should be able to:

4.1 Define the term contract.
4.2 Explain what an offer is and distinguish it from an invitation to treat.
4.3 Identify and describe the ways in which an offer can terminate.
4.4 Define acceptance and distinguish it from a counter offer.
4.5 Explain the rules on communication of acceptance.
4.6 Explain the distinction between framework and call-off contracts.

Unit content coverage

This study session covers the following topic from the official CIPS unit content document.

Learning outcome

Describe and apply the legalities linked to the formation of contracts.

Learning objective

2.1 Identify and apply the legal aspects relating to the formation of contracts.
 • Offer
 • Acceptance
 • The distinction between framework and call-off contracts

Resources

Appendix 1, The English legal system, appendix 2, Case law, appendix 3, Legislation.

Timing

You should set aside about 6 hours to read and complete this session, including learning activities, self-assessment questions, the suggested further reading (if any) and the revision question.

4

4.1 Introduction to contract law

Much of contract law was established many years ago and is based on 19th century cases. To be able to properly apply it therefore you will need to understand the legal principles established by judges in relevant cases and followed according to the rules of **judicial precedent**. Judicial precedent is the doctrine by which the lower courts follow the decisions of the higher courts in the court hierarchy. Judicial precedent and the hierarchy of the courts are explained in more detail in appendix 1, The English legal system. Appendix 2, Case law contains details of the cases referred to in this course book. In more recent years significant changes have been made in contract law by parliamentary intervention with the creation of primary legislation, namely Acts of Parliament (also referred to as statutes). In some areas of contract law therefore, such as with the terms implied into contracts for the sale of goods under the Sale of Goods Act 1979 (as amended)(see study session 9), you will also need to know and be able to apply relevant sections of the appropriate statutes. Secondary legislation (also referred to as delegated legislation) in the form of Statutory Instruments is also relevant in some areas of contract law, for example the Unfair Terms in Consumer Contracts Regulations 1999 (see study session 12). Finally, since the UK's entry into the EEC (now known as the EU) in 1970, we are subject to the law of the EU and this is relevant in this course in the area of the EU Procurement Directives (see study session 18). Appendix 3, Legislation contains excerpts from relevant legislation referred to in this course book.

When problems arise and one party sues the other, the court must first establish whether a *valid* contract exists between the parties before it can consider any terms of the contract which may have been breached and decide what, if any, remedies it will grant to the claimant.

Learning activity 4.1

Consider the various agreements that you have made during the last week. Do not just think about the workplace. Which of them do you consider to be contracts? Explain why. If you consider any of them were not contracts, explain why not.

Feedback on page 49

As contract law has a vital role to play in purchasing, it is important for procurement professionals to understand what creates a legally binding contract, which is **enforceable** under English law. Enforceable means that either party can sue the other on the basis of the contract to force the other party to comply with their obligations under the contract.

A contract is an agreement, enforceable by law, between two or more persons, to do or to abstain from doing some act or acts.

In order to decide if there is a contract the courts examine the situation objectively to see if the essential elements of a contract exist. For a simple contract to arise there must be an intention by the parties to form a legally binding agreement and some consideration must have passed from one party to the other.

At the heart of every contract lies an **agreement**. This has been referred to as the 'meeting of the minds' or the '*consensus ad idem*'. Unlike a contract, an agreement alone is not legally enforceable under English law. If someone decides not to abide by a simple agreement they have entered into they cannot be forced to comply as they cannot be sued in court.

To decide if there is an agreement, English law developed the objective approach to try to identify the elements of an agreement, namely offer and acceptance. Offer and acceptance are dealt with in more detail later in this session. In addition, for there to be a valid contract, English law requires that two further essential elements be present, namely consideration and intention to create a legal relationship. These are both dealt with in more detail in study session 5. The essential elements of any contract are therefore offer and acceptance, which together form the agreement, consideration and an intention to enter into legal relations. Further, the law also takes account of the capacity of the parties to enter into the contract and this is also dealt with in study session 5.

Normally, no formalities are required to make contracts; generally contracts do not have to be in writing to be valid. Contracts may be made orally, by conduct or in writing. In large commercial contracts however, it is desirable to have a written record of the terms and conditions agreed by the parties, although this is not a legal requirement unless the contract is of a particular type. Statute specifies several types of contract that must be in writing or evidenced in writing, for example consumer credit agreements, contracts for the sale of land and contracts of guarantee. You are not required to know about the exceptions to the general rule for the purposes of this course.

Even after you have entered into a seemingly valid procurement contract, having ensured that it has the essential elements of agreement (offer and acceptance), consideration and intention to enter into a legal relationship, and assuming that there are no difficulties presented by the capacity of the parties or the form of the contract, there may be vitiating factors which may affect your contract. The vitiating factors are misrepresentation, mistake, duress, undue influence and illegality, and after your contract has been made problems caused by these factors may come to light.

A **misrepresentation** is an untrue statement of fact made by one party to the contract to the other, before the contract is made, and which induces the other party to enter into the contract. If a misrepresentation is proven the court will decide if it is fraudulent, negligent or innocent. In such circumstances the contract is voidable and the claimant can have it rescinded and may be awarded damages.

If a mistake is made by one or both parties this may affect the validity of the contract and render the transaction void. Not all mistakes will affect a contract in this way but the two types of mistake which may do so are common mistake, where both parties make the same mistake, for example a mistake as to the subject matter of the contract, and mutual mistake where the parties are at cross-purposes either because each one makes a different

4

mistake or one party makes a mistake which the other is presumed to know about.

If a party to a contract has been compelled to enter into a contract then there is no true agreement and the contract will be voidable for duress. Originally the law recognised physical violence or threats of the same as duress, but now economic duress is also recognised. If an individual in a position of influence over another (such as in a solicitor/client relationship) exerts undue influence over the weaker person and influences that person to enter into a contract against their best interests, such a contract would be voidable as again there is no true voluntary agreement.

The courts will not enforce any contract that has an illegal purpose, for example contracts in restraint of trade which are void unless it can be shown that they are in the public interest and that they are reasonable, and contracts to oust the jurisdiction of the court which are also void except when the jurisdiction is ousted in a contractual term providing for disputes between the parties to be dealt with by arbitration or some other form of alternate dispute resolution. The latter will be examined further in study session 13.

Self-assessment question 4.1

Explain what a contract is.

Feedback on page 49

4.2 Offer

As you know, an offer is one of the elements forming an agreement. The offeror (the person making the offer) will give the details of the offer to the offeree (the person receiving the offer) so that it can be considered. In making an offer the offeror is indicating their willingness to enter into an agreement, which could be a legally binding contract, should the offeree accept the offer.

However, there are some situations where you might think that an offer has been made but in fact there is no offer at all, such as when there is a mere supply of information or when there is an invitation to treat. Therefore, it is important to be able to distinguish between these because whereas an offer is capable of being accepted and can have a binding legal effect, a statement of information or an invitation to treat have no legally binding effect as they are incapable of being accepted. Invitations to treat are a way of obtaining information or inviting offers from prospective offerors. They are an 'offer to negotiate' and occur in the stages prior to an offer being made. In the tendering process invitations to tender are invitations to treat. Tendering will be examined in more detail in study session 17.

Requests for information

A request for information is clearly not an offer, but what about the supply of that information? The answer to this question is not straightforward. If organisation A requests a quotation from organisation B, this is simply a request for information, which cannot constitute an offer. But what about the possible responses?

If, in reply, organisation B provides a detailed response with all the specifications, prices, dates and terms and conditions of supply, then this may be sufficient to amount to an offer.

If, however, the reply is a terse supply of prices and confirmation that the supplier has such goods in stock, then this will not be an offer.

As a general rule of thumb you could ask yourself whether in response to the supply of information the purchaser could simply say yes and the parties would reasonably consider themselves bound to supply and pay for the goods, in which case it was probably enough to form an offer in the first place. Applying this to the examples above, in example 1 organisation B has probably made an offer whereas in example 2, clearly it has only supplied information.

The courts have distinguished offers from requests and supply of information. You should use appendix 2, Case law to research the cases referred to in this session. In *Harvey* v *Facey* [1893] there was an exchange of telegrams between the parties about the possible sale of land. The court held that the respondent's reply was merely a statement of the minimum price he would accept if he decided to sell, not an offer.

Catalogues and price lists

In *Grainger and Son* v *Gough* [1896] a price list that had been circulated by a wine merchant was held to be an invitation to treat and not an offer.

Advertisements

Usually advertisements are attempts to induce offers but they are not offers themselves. In *Partridge* v *Crittenden* [1968] an advertisement in a newspaper for the sale of 'bramble finches, cocks and hens, 25 shillings each' was held to be an invitation to treat. Whether the advertisement appears in a newspaper or on an internet website the legal principle is the same: the advertisement is regarded as an invitation to treat and when you respond to the advertisement you are making the offer to purchase either to the person who placed the newspaper advertisement or to the organisation whose website you are using. These matters were considered in a relatively recent case involving Argos whose website had advertised £300 televisions for £3. Here, the advertisement on the website was an invitation to treat, but it is possible that, depending on the information on the website, it could be regarded as a unilateral offer (see later).

Display of goods in a shop window

In *Fisher* v *Bell* [1961] a shopkeeper displayed a flick knife for sale in his shop window. The court had to decide if this amounted to an offer to sell it or something else. The court held that it was an invitation to treat.

Display of goods self-service

The above rule (about display of goods in a shop window) has also been extended to self-service goods. In *Pharmaceutical Society of Great Britain*

4

v *Boots Cash Chemists (Southern) Ltd* [1953] the court held that goods displayed on a shelf are an invitation to treat. The purchaser makes the offer when the goods are taken to a checkout.

Auctions

In the case of *British Car Auctions Ltd* v *Wright* [1972], which involved the sale of an unroadworthy second-hand car, the court had to decide if an auctioneer actually offers the auction goods for sale. Technically under the law of contract the auctioneer does not. The court held that at auctions the auctioneer invites the people present to make offers. The bidders make the offers (the bids) and acceptance is usually signified by the fall of the gavel.

Learning activity 4.2

The following are situations where the courts have held that offers have not been made. For each one, state what has been made and identify a relevant case, briefly summarising the relevant facts of the case and explaining the legal principle involved.

1   A website advertising goods for sale.
2   A supplier circulating a price list.
3   Goods for sale in a shop window.
4   Display of goods in a self-service shop.
5   A request for a quotation and a simple quotation of price supplied.

When answering this question use the information provided in appendix 5, Advice on answering examination questions about using legal principles from decided cases. Also remember to use appendix 2, Case law, the case appendix.

Feedback on page 49

An offer can be made to a specific individual or company, in which case it is a bilateral offer. If an offer is made to the world at large, it is a unilateral offer and it can be accepted by anyone who knows about it and complies with its terms. You will be familiar with bilateral offers, but what form do you think a unilateral offer can take?

The courts considered unilateral offers in *Carlill* v *Carbolic Smoke Ball Co.* [1893]. This case involved an advertisement and although the general rule is that advertisements are usually invitations to treat, in Carlill it was not just any advert. The defendants argued that no offer had been made to Mrs Carlill by the advert and it was impossible to contract with the world. The court of appeal held that it was possible to make an offer to the world, and the defendants had done so in the detailed advertisement and Mrs Carlill had accepted that offer by her conduct.

Unilateral offers are also made when advertisements advertise a free item if you buy a particular product. Once you accept by buying the product the seller is legally obliged to give you your free item. This was held in the case of *Esso Petroleum Ltd* v *Commissioners of Custom and Excise* [1976].

Before we leave offers, remember it is important that if an offer is made it is communicated to the offeree. If the offeree does not know about the offer, it is incapable of being accepted.

Self-assessment question 4.2

Answer the questions below and insert your answers in the rows in figure 4.1. When you have answered all the questions correctly you should be able to identify the mystery word in the column marked with a star.

1   What is required to make an offer into an agreement?
2   What was the invitation to treat in *Fisher* v *Bell* [1961]?
3   Sometimes this can be an offer.
4   Who is the person making an offer?
5   What type of offer was made by the Carbolic Smoke Ball Company?
6   What must an offer be?
7   What happens before agreement is reached?
8   What is a legally binding agreement?
9   This is not an offer.

Figure 4.1

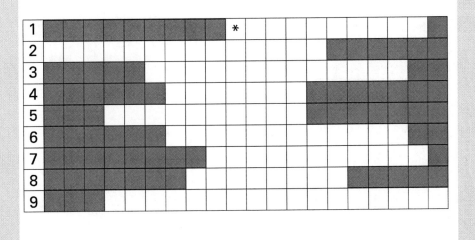

Feedback on page 49

4.3   Termination of offer

Offers can terminate in different ways, but once they end they cannot be resurrected. These are the most common ways that offers come to an end.

- Rejection: the offeree can reject the offer outright. This will then be an end to the matter.
- Acceptance: the offeree can accept the offer unconditionally. An agreement then exists.

- Counter-offer: if the offeree replies with suggested changes to the original offer, then this will be a counter-offer. The counter-offer will now be the only 'offer' in existence as, once a counter-offer is made, it terminates the original offer. (Counter-offers are also considered in section 4.4 below.)
- Revocation: if the offeror changes their mind and no longer wishes their offer to be open, they can take it back by revoking it. Revocation is only possible until the offer is accepted. Once acceptance takes place the offer cannot be revoked. In addition if the offeror wishes to revoke their offer the revocation is not valid until the offeree receives actual notice of the revocation whether it be from the offeror or via a reliable third party.
- Time: an offer that is stated to be open for a particular time will automatically end when that time expires. If no time is specified when an offer is made, then it will expire after a reasonable time.

Learning activity 4.3

Draw a diagram to summarise the ways that offers can terminate.

Feedback on page 50

Now complete this self-assessment question.

Self-assessment question 4.3

Answer the following questions by saying if the statements are true or false.

1   If an offer is unconditionally accepted by the offeror an agreement exists.
2   If the offeree rejects the offer no agreement will be made.
3   If an offer is terminated, in some circumstances it could still become part of an agreement.
4   If no time period is specified in an offer then it will remain open indefinitely until it is accepted.
5   Revocation can only be communicated by the offeror.

Feedback on page 51

4.4 Acceptance

There must be clear and unqualified acceptance of the terms of the offer. Unless the acceptance is unconditional it will be a counter-offer and it will destroy the original offer. In the case of *Hyde* v *Wrench* [1840] it was established that once destroyed, the offer cannot be revived.

It does not matter whether the offeree uses the words that they 'accept' when replying to the offer as sometimes counter-offers can be disguised as something that is worded like an acceptance but which does not unconditionally accept the offer. Sometimes when it appears that the offeree is accepting the offer they are actually making a counter-offer, which destroys the original offer.

If, however, the offeree requests information from the offeror, this cannot be treated as a counter-offer and the original offer will still be open to acceptance.

4

Learning activity 4.4

State whether the following are examples of acceptance or counter-offers.

1   Balls Ltd offers to sell 1,000 balls to Sports Centre Ltd at a discount price of £50 per 100 for delivery within 14 days. Sports Centre Ltd accepts the offer but wants the balls delivered the same afternoon.
2   Office Ltd is in negotiations with Clean It Ltd for a new cleaning contract for their offices. Clean It Ltd has offered a daily weekday cleaning service 6–8 pm at a cost of £1,000 per month per site. Office Ltd accepts the offer saying that they expect cleaning on Saturdays to be included too.
3   On Monday, Mouldings Ltd offers to supply to Frames Ltd 100 UPVC window frames as per a schedule setting out dimensions of the different windows and the price per unit. They state the offer is open for seven days. On Thursday, Frames Ltd email Mouldings Ltd asking if they make UPVC windows in colours other than white.

Feedback on page 51

Now complete this self-assessment question.

Self-assessment question 4.4

Fill in the missing words in the paragraph below.

There has to be _____ acceptance of an offer by the _____ for an agreement and thereafter a _____ to be formed. Where the purported acceptance is actually changing part of the original offer, this will be a _____ and it will _____ the original offer. Once the original offer is destroyed it cannot be _____, as is seen in the court's decision in _____ v _____.

Feedback on page 51

4.5   Communication of acceptance

In section 4.3 above you saw that for an offer to be capable of acceptance it must be communicated to the offeree. The same also applies as a general rule to acceptance (apart from the postal rule as you will see later). For acceptance to be effective it must be communicated.

Acceptance is often communicated in writing or verbally, but situations involving silence or conduct may also arise.

4

Silence

Silence alone cannot amount to acceptance even if the offeror stipulates this. This can be seen in the case of *Felthouse* v *Bindley* [1862].

Conduct

Acceptance can be by conduct. If conduct is silent that can amount to acceptance, as in the case of *Brogden* v *Metropolitan Railway Company* [1877].

By making a unilateral offer as in the *Carlill* case, the offeror is waiving their right for acceptance to be communicated.

There have also been some cases where the courts have been unable to identify the separate elements of offer and acceptance although the judges have been prepared to hold that a contract has come into existence. This happened in the case of *Trentham Ltd* v *Archital Luxfer* [1993].

Methods of communication

Communication can be by an instantaneous method such as telephone, telex, fax or internet, in which case these methods follow the general rule and acceptance must be received by the offeror.

If, however, acceptance is to be posted, this is an exception to the general rule. Acceptance is deemed to be communicated when you put your letter of acceptance into the post even if it never arrives and the offeror does not receive actual notice of your acceptance. Obviously this could cause problems if the offeror is unaware that you have validly accepted their offer by posting them a letter, and before the letter is delivered they sell the goods to another person, as happened with the sale of some wool in the case of *Adams* v *Lindsell* [1818].

Learning activity 4.5

Identify relevant cases on communication of acceptance; briefly identify the relevant facts and then explain the legal principle involved

Feedback on page 51

Now answer this self-assessment question.

Self-assessment question 4.5

Answer the following questions by identifying which, if any, of the statements are correct.

1   For acceptance to be effective:
    (a)   it must always be communicated
    (b)   it must be communicated in writing
    (c)   it must be communicated unless it is sent by post.

(continued on next page)

Self-assessment question 4.5 *(continued)*

2.

(a) Silence alone can amount to acceptance.

(b) Silent conduct can amount to acceptance.

(c) In *Brogden* v *Metropolitan Railway Company* [1877] the court held that silent conduct can amount to acceptance.

Feedback on page 52

4.6 Framework and call-off contracts

Learning activity 4.6

List any framework or call-off contracts in which your organisation is involved and describe the differences between them. If you are not involved in such contracts, would there be any opportunities for your organisation to be involved in such contracts in the future?

Feedback on page 52

Frameworks are freestanding documents, which set out agreements to provide goods and/or services on specified terms. They are used in situations where the parties anticipate doing business with each other in the future, but they want to agree the terms now on which that future business will be done.

In a framework arrangement there is no contractual commitment for a particular quantity, nor is there even any commitment to purchase at all. Usually, the framework arrangement includes any agreed specifications, prices, delivery arrangements and terms and conditions of contract that would apply to any contract entered into in the future. In a framework agreement, however, you would have a contractual commitment to purchase a particular quantity or value of goods and/or services although this could be set out as a specified range that is no less than the minimum specified and no more than the maximum specified.

Framework arrangements or agreements can be fixed term, fixed quantity or 'insurance'. Fixed-term arrangements usually give an estimate of the goods and/or services to be supplied. Fixed quantity arrangements give greater reassurance that the estimated quantities of goods and frequency of services will be required. Insurance arrangements deal with services with a fixed annual cost regardless of the frequency of the service required.

Call offs or call-off contracts are the names commonly given to the purchase orders submitted against the framework arrangement or agreement. In practice, framework arrangements are sometimes inappropriately referred to as call-off contracts too, even though they are not contracts. The purchase orders (call offs) are offers made by the purchaser. The supplier then has the choice of accepting the offer and supplying the goods/services ordered according to the terms and conditions already agreed in the framework agreement, or, if the supplier is no longer willing to abide by the terms agreed in the framework agreement, he can reject the offer and no contract will be formed.

4

Depending on the size of the framework agreements and the individual call offs, in the public sector the contract might be caught by the thresholds under the EU Procurement Directives. The total value of the goods/services supplied under the framework must be considered. The call offs cannot be considered separately, but if over the thresholds, provided the framework agreement has been dealt with according to the directives and advertised in the Official Journal of the European Union (OJEU), the call offs do not need to be advertised individually. The EU Procurement Directives will be considered in more detail in study session 18.

Self-assessment question 4.6

Compare and contrast framework and call-off contracts.

Your answer should be around 200 words. You should refresh your memory about the best way to answer essay questions in appendix 5, Advice on answering examination questions.

Feedback on page 52

Revision question

Now try the revision question for this session on page 238.

Summary

In this session you considered:

- the English legal system and identified the sources of law which are referred to in this course, namely case law, statute, statutory instruments and EU law
- basic principles of the law relating to contract formation
- the elements of a contract (and you studied two of them)
- offer
- acceptance
- the formation of framework contracts.

In study session 5 you will study the remaining elements of a contract – consideration and intent.

Suggested further reading

Carter and Kirby (2006). You could read the chapters on framework agreements and on legal issues including duress and undue influence, misrepresentation and mistake.

Griffiths and Griffiths (2002). You should read the chapter on contract formation.

Wyborn (2000). You could read the sections on agreements, duress and undue influence, misrepresentation, and mistake.

Feedback on learning activities and self-assessment questions

Feedback on learning activity 4.1

During the last week you may have entered into many agreements with different individuals and organisations either at work involving the supply of goods and/or services, or you may have bought personal items of food, clothing, fuel for your vehicle or tickets for public transport. You may have agreed to meet friends socially or visit relatives; or lend your neighbour some tools. The agreements which are contracts are likely to include your organisation's purchases of goods and services, and your personal shopping for food, clothes, fuel and tickets; these are more formal, are made with 'strangers' and involve payment. The agreements which are unlikely to be contracts are your 'favour' for your neighbour and your social arrangements which are with family and friends; these are more informal and did not involve payment. You may have found that you are entering into contracts more often than you realised. In this session and in study session 5, you will consider this further and discover how contracts are formed.

Feedback on self-assessment question 4.1

Your explanation of what a contract is should have included a definition explaining that a contract is an agreement, enforceable by law, between two or more persons, to do or to abstain from doing some act or acts.

Feedback on learning activity 4.2

1   Invitation to treat. In the *Argos* case, its website had advertised £300 televisions for £3 and the advertisement on the website was an invitation to treat.
2   Invitation to treat. In *Grainger and Son* v *Gough* [1896] a price list that had been circulated by a wine merchant was held to be an invitation to treat and not an offer.
3   Invitation to treat. In *Fisher* v *Bell* [1961] a shopkeeper displayed a flick knife for sale in his shop window. The court had to decide if this amounted to an offer to sell it or something else. The court held that it was an invitation to treat.
4   Invitation to treat. In *Pharmaceutical Society of Great Britain* v *Boots Cash Chemists (Southern) Ltd* [1953] the court held that goods displayed on a shelf are an invitation to treat. The purchaser makes the offer when the goods are taken to a checkout.
5   A supply of information. In *Harvey* v *Facey* [1893] there was an exchange of telegrams between the parties. The court held that the respondent's reply was merely a statement of the minimum price he would accept if he decided to sell, not an offer.

Feedback on self-assessment question 4.2

You should have completed the word quiz as shown in figure 4.2 showing 'agreement' as the mystery word.

Figure 4.2

1									A*	C	C	E	P	T	A	N	C	E
2	D	I	S	P	I	A	Y	O	F	G	O	O	D	S				
3						A	D	V	E	R	T	I	D	R	M	E	N	T
4					O	F	F	E	R	O	R							
5			U	N	I	L	A	T	E	R	A	L						
6						C	O	M	M	U	N	I	C	A	T	E	D	
7							N	E	G	O	T	I	A	T	I	O	N	
8						C	O	N	T	R	A	C	T					
9				I	N	V	I	T	A	T	I	O	N	T	O	T	R	E	A	T

Feedback on learning activity 4.3

Figure 4.3

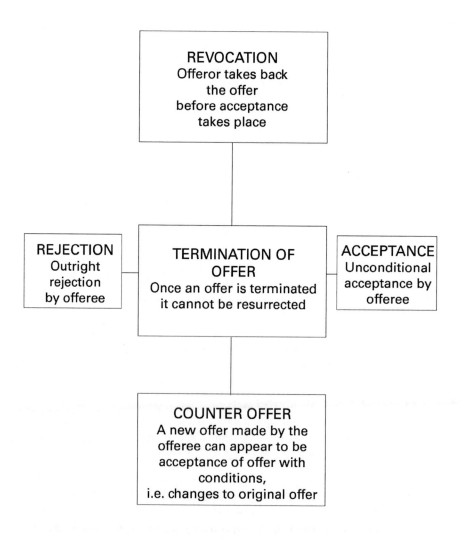

REVOCATION
Offeror takes back
the offer
before acceptance
takes place

REJECTION
Outright
rejection
by offeree

TERMINATION OF
OFFER
Once an offer is terminated
it cannot be resurrected

ACCEPTANCE
Unconditional
acceptance by
offeree

COUNTER OFFER
A new offer made by the
offeree can appear to be
acceptance of offer with
conditions,
i.e. changes to original offer

Feedback on self-assessment question 4.3

1   False. It is the offeree who would accept an offer. The offeror makes the offer. The statement would be true if the word offeror was replaced by offeree.
2   True.
3   False. If an offer terminates it cannot be revived.
4   False. If no time is specified in the offer it will terminate after a reasonable time.
5   False. The offeree can receive actual notice of the offeror's revocation from the offeror or a reliable third party.

Feedback on learning activity 4.4

1   This is a counter-offer as although Sports Centre Ltd is accepting the offer, they are not unconditionally accepting all of the terms of the original offer.
2   This is a counter-offer. If Office Ltd purport to accept the offer but then want to have one additional day's cleaning each week included then this is not unconditional acceptance of Clean It Ltd's offer.
3   There is no acceptance in this example but there is no counter-offer either. Frames Ltd made a request for information so the original offer by Mouldings Ltd was still open to Frames Ltd.

Feedback on self-assessment question 4.4

There has to be unconditional acceptance of an offer by the offeree for an agreement and thereafter a contract to be formed. Where the purported acceptance is actually changing part of the original offer, this will be a counter-offer and it will destroy the original offer. Once the original offer is destroyed it cannot be revived, as is seen in the court's decision in *Hyde* v *Wrench* [1840].

Feedback on learning activity 4.5

The cases which you could use are listed below. The important thing in this activity is to ensure that you understand the legal principle involved and can summarise the relevant facts.

* *Felthouse* v *Bindley* [1862]. The plaintiff was negotiating the purchase of a horse from his nephew and he wrote to his nephew saying that if he heard nothing further he would assume he could buy the horse. The nephew mentally accepted that his uncle would buy the horse but did nothing to communicate his acceptance. The animal was then sold to a third party by the auctioneers dealing on behalf of the nephew. The court held that the nephew's mental acceptance did not constitute contractual acceptance.
* *Brogden* v *Metropolitan Railway Company* [1877]. The plaintiff supplied coal to the defendant on a written annual contract. A new contract was sent to the plaintiff who amended it (counter-offer) and returned it to the defendant who filed it and forgot about it, but they accepted deliveries in keeping with the new amended contract until a dispute

brought the matter before the court. The court held that the defendants had accepted the new amended contract by their silent conduct.

- *Trentham Ltd* v *Archital Luxfer* [1993]. The plaintiffs, the main building contractors on a project, were negotiating a subcontract with the defendants, but work began before their negotiations were completed. Allegations were made that the defendant's work was defective, but when the defendant tried to argue that no contract existed (as there was no acceptance) to avoid the claims made against it, the court found there had been acceptance by conduct.
- You could also use *Carlill* v *Carbolic Smoke Ball Company* [1893] and *Adams* v *Lindsell* [1818].

Feedback on self-assessment question 4.5

1   The correct answer is (c).
    Answer (a) is not correct because if acceptance is sent by post, posting it means that the acceptance is effective even if it never arrives at its destination.
    Answer (b) is not correct as it does not have to be in writing, it could be oral or even by conduct.
2   Answers (b) and c) are correct.
    Answer (a) is wrong because silence alone cannot amount to acceptance, although silent conduct could be seen as acceptance.

Feedback on learning activity 4.6

You may use framework agreements to order supplies as and when required by calling off your requirement. These may be for consumables in your office or for goods or services in your organisation. You may have noticed various differences from a practical point of view in relation to the timing; the framework arrangement may be in place for a long time whereas the call offs are individual orders for the present requirement. You may have noticed that whereas the frameworks have detailed terms and conditions, the call offs may be quite simple documents.

If you are unfamiliar with framework arrangements and call-off contracts you could look at some of the local government websites or the DTI website to get some idea of what framework arrangements/call-off contracts can be used for.

Feedback on self-assessment question 4.6

You should answer this question in the form of a short essay. First of all you could explain what frameworks and call offs are by way of an introduction.

You should then consider whether there is anything they have in common and then deal with the various points where they are different.

You could mention that they can be used by the public and private sectors in respect of goods and/or services, and explain that the framework contains detailed terms and conditions which have been negotiated sometimes at quite a high level in an organisation, whereas the call offs can be relatively simple documents and can be used by people at a lower level in the organisation. You could also mention that whereas frameworks do not show a contractual commitment, call offs are actual offers which if accepted will lead to binding contracts being made.

4

Contract formation – consideration and intention

'A verbal contract isn't worth the paper it's printed on.'
(Samuel Goldwyn (1882–1974), Polish-born American movie producer and founder of Metro-Goldwyn-Mayer)

5

Introduction

In this study session you will continue to study the elements of a valid contract. First of all you will examine consideration and the concept of the contractual promise. You will then consider whether the parties have the intention to create legal relations. After that you will move on to study the issues relating to the doctrine of privity and third-party rights, before considering whether the parties have the legal capacity to enter into a contract. You will have the opportunity to develop your skills in answering problem questions on the topics covered in this session.

Session learning objectives

After completing this session you should be able to:

5.1 Define 'consideration' in the context of contract formation and explain its main principles.
5.2 Identify the legal presumptions in intention and explain their application to the formation of contracts.
5.3 Explain who has the right to sue on contracts.
5.4 Explain the meaning of capacity in the formation of contracts.

Unit content coverage

This study session covers the following topic from the official CIPS unit content document.

Learning outcome

Describe and apply the legalities linked to the formation of contracts.

Learning objectives

2.1 Identify and apply the legal aspects relating to the formation of contracts.
  • Consideration
  • Intention to create legal relations
  • Capacity
  • The contractual promise

3.3 Discuss and apply:
  • Key legislation relating to contracts
    – Contracts (Rights of Third Parties) Act

5

Prior knowledge

Study session 4

___

Resources

Appendix 2, Case law, appendix 3, Legislation and appendix 5, Advice on answering examination questions.

___

Timing

You should set aside about 6 hours to read and complete this session, including learning activities, self-assessment questions, the suggested further reading (if any) and the revision question.

___

5.1 Consideration

As you saw in study session 4, consideration is one of the essential elements of a contract – if there is no consideration, there can be no contract. Consideration carries with it the idea that in a contract, a deal is made, a bargain is struck. Consideration is something of value in the eyes of the law, which constitutes the price for which the promise of the other party is bought. It is that which is actually given or accepted in return for a promise. For example, company A receives £1,000 and in return promises to deliver goods to company B. The consideration for the promise of delivery is £1,000. It is not just money, goods and services that are of value, promises are also of value. Contracts are based on promises, hence the idea of the contractual promise.

Learning activity 5.1

Think about five procurement contracts in which your organisation has recently been or is currently involved. For each of the contracts state what consideration has been given by your organisation/the other organisation.

Feedback on page 65

There are various rules of consideration that have been developed by the courts.

Consideration must be sufficient but need not be adequate

The distinction between sufficiency and adequacy is important. In the context of contract law, if consideration is sufficient it means it is of a type that the law recognises as being capable of having value, for example money. Adequacy, on the other hand, is about the value or the amount of the consideration. The law is not interested in how good a deal you have made, as long as it is clear that you have made some kind of deal. For example if company X agrees to sell plant and machinery for £1, this agreement will be enforceable as the consideration is money, which is recognised as a category, which is capable of having value. Clearly £1 is unlikely to be equal in value to the plant and machinery being given in exchange, but the law will not concern itself with whether the true market value is being paid; that is a matter for the parties to the contract to decide upon themselves.

However, there are some circumstances when the courts will find that there is no valuable consideration and therefore no contract because the consideration given is insufficient. This could be because the alleged consideration involves the party doing something that they are already obliged to do as follows:

- Performance of existing public duties. If you are already obliged to do something because of an existing public duty, it cannot be sufficient consideration for a contract as in *Collins* v *Godefroy* [1831].
- Performance of existing contractual duties. If you are already obliged to do something because of an existing contractual duty then it will not be sufficient consideration in a new contract. In *Stilk* v *Myrick* [1809] and *Hartley* v *Ponsonby* [1857] this point was considered. Both cases involved ships being sailed back to port with reduced crews, but in *Stilk* v *Myrick* [1809] the claim failed as the court took the view that the sailor was already contractually bound to sail the ship home. In *Hartley* v *Ponsonby* [1857] the judge took the view that the sailor was doing a different, more hazardous job than he originally contracted for and so should receive the additional wages. This point is also illustrated by the more recent case of *Atlas Express Ltd* v *Kafco (Importers) Ltd* [1989] where a haulier tried to increase the price on a contract that was already agreed. The purchaser reluctantly agreed to the increase, but as the haulier was only providing the service that he had originally contracted to do, the court found that the haulier provided no additional consideration for the increased contract price and so the variation of the contract was not valid.
- Part payment of a debt. If you only pay part of a debt, it cannot usually be considered sufficient consideration to settle the debt in full. In *D&C Builders* v *Rees* [1965] the defendant made a part payment in cash, but this was held to be insufficient to settle the debt. If, however, the payee requests payment to be made at an earlier date, in a different place or in a different form, although less than the full amount is being paid, the payee is receiving the benefit of the different arrangement they have requested and in such circumstances payment of a lesser sum could be sufficient.

Past consideration is no consideration

When the consideration is related to past actions, the law will not enforce a promise. Any consideration given in these circumstances will be as an ex gratia payment made after the agreement. It will not be part of the contract and so will not be enforceable, as in *Re McArdle* [1951] where the Court of Appeal held that as the promise to reimburse was made after the work was done the recipient of the promise could not enforce it. If, however, the defendant requests the work to be done, as in *Lampleigh* v *Braithwait* [1615] (request to obtain a royal pardon), or there is a reasonable assumption that

5

payment will be made, as in *Re Casey's Patents, Stewart v Casey* [1892] (claimant managed the royalties from some patents), the promisee (party receiving the benefit of the promise) can sue to enforce the promise of payment even if it is made after the work is done.

Consideration must move from the promisee

Only someone who provides consideration for the contractual promise can enforce the contract. This rule is shown in the case of *Tweddle v Atkinson* [1861].

This rule of consideration follows the principle of privity of contract, that only someone who is a party to the contract can sue or be sued on it. There have been some changes to this old rule by the Contract (Rights of Third Parties) Act 1999 which you will examine in section 5.4 below.

Self-assessment question 5.1

Explain, referring to appropriate cases, what is meant by the following principles of consideration:

- Consideration must be sufficient but need not be adequate.
- Performance of an existing public duty is insufficient consideration.
- Performance of an existing contractual duty is insufficient consideration.
- Part payment of a debt is insufficient consideration.
- Past consideration is no consideration.
- Consideration must move from the promisee.

When answering this question you should refer to appendix 2, Case law, which sets out information about the cases mentioned in this session.

Feedback on page 65

5.2   Intention to create legal relations

In order to decide if the parties have intention to enter into a legal relationship, the law uses two presumptions that can be rebutted by evidence to the contrary. The burden of overturning the presumption lies with the person seeking to adduce such evidence. One of the presumptions applies to social/domestic agreements and the other to business/commercial agreements. In order to apply the rules on intention to a particular agreement therefore, you must first decide whether it is a domestic/social situation or a commercial one. This distinction is important as the law treats agreements in these two broad categories very differently.

Where the agreement is of a social or domestic nature the law presumes that the parties had no intention to create legal relations unless evidence is produced to the contrary. In *Coward v Motor Insurance Bureau* [1963], the court held that it was a social arrangement and in the absence of evidence to the contrary there was no intention to create a legal relationship. In

Simpkins v *Pays* [1955] the court held that the presumption was rebutted by the evidence and there was intention to create a legal relationship.

Where the agreement is of a business or commercial nature there is a strong presumption that the parties did intend to create a legal relationship. This presumption can be rebutted but very strong evidence is required to do this. One way to rebut it would be to have a robust express statement to the contrary, but this may not succeed when there has been a working arrangement.

In *Rose & Frank Co.* v *J R Compton & Bros Ltd* [1925] the defendant was obliged to fulfil the orders it had received, but it was not obliged to fulfil future orders because the marketing arrangement specifically said that there was no intention for it to have legal consequences.

If the clause that an organisation relies upon to rebut the presumption is ambiguous, then it is up to the organisation to prove that the clause is effective. If it fails, the presumption stands, as was the case in *Edwards* v *Skyways Ltd* [1964], where the presumption was not overturned and there was therefore an intention to be legally bound.

Advertisements are the one exception that statements made in a commercial setting will be presumed to show intention to be legally bound. In order to protect advertisers who make flamboyant claims about the products they are advertising, the law assumes there is no legal intention to be bound. They are 'mere puffs' to puff up the product. Some advertisements have wildly outrageous claims and the more extravagant the claim the safer the advertiser is that a disappointed purchaser will not be able to prove there is a legal intention to be bound. It is possible of course that an advertisement can show an intention to be legally bound if there is evidence to substantiate this, as in the case of *Carlill* v *Carbolic Smoke Ball Co.* [1892]. Here the defendants argued that the advertisement was 'mere puff' and so there was no intention to be bound. The Court of Appeal disagreed however, and said there was evidence to rebut the presumption. The defendant had shown its intention to be bound when it said it was putting £1,000 on deposit to compensate users of the product.

Learning activity 5.2

Complete the following table (missing text denoted by '…') by identifying the relevant facts, legal principles and case names.

Table 5.1

Name	Relevant facts	Legal principle
Simpkins v *Pays* [1955]	…	…
…	…	The Court of Appeal found that each of the orders given and accepted constituted

(continued on next page)

5

Learning activity 5.2 *(continued)*

Name	Relevant facts	Legal principle
		an individual contract, and the defendant was obliged to fulfil the orders it had received but it was not obliged to fulfil future orders because the marketing arrangement specifically said that there was no intention for it to have legal consequences.
...	The plaintiff's husband usually got a lift to work with a colleague and contributed towards the petrol. The men were killed in a car accident and the widow sued the Motor Insurance Bureau.	...
Edwards v *Skyways Ltd* [1964]	...	...
Carlill v *Carbolic Smoke Ball Co.* [1892].	...	...

You should use appendix 2, Case law as a case-law resource for answering this question.

Feedback on page 66

Now complete this self-assessment question.

Self-assessment question 5.2

Answer the following questions to complete the horizontal words. Once the quiz is completed you should discover the mystery vertical word.

1 Name the plaintiff in a social case.
2 What does the law use to decide whether there is intention?
3 A word to describe the answer to question 2.
4 This is not social.
5 By using this you can persuade the court that 2 does not apply.
6 One of the two categories relevant for intention.
7 The lucky plaintiff who read an advertisement.
8 The successful widow plaintiff.
9 The defendant in a case where there was no intention to be bound in respect of future rights.

(continued on next page)

Self-assessment question 5.2 *(continued)*

Figure 5.1

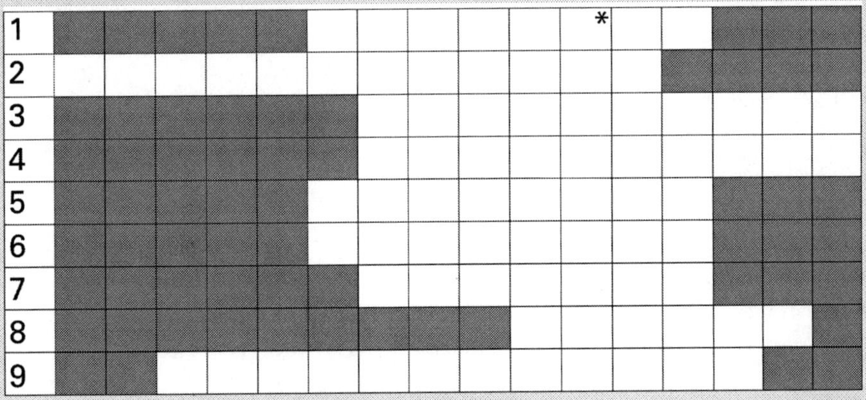

Feedback on page 67

5.3 Privity and third-party rights

Learning activity 5.3

Using your own experience and discussions with colleagues, consider any third parties with which your organisation is involved. If there are no contracts involving third parties, are there situations where you may be involved with them in the future? Have there been any occasions when difficulties have arisen with third parties? How has your organisation resolved those difficulties? If you have not experienced difficulties with third parties, can you recognise any areas where difficulties may arise in the future?

Feedback on page 67

You may remember reading about privity of contract in section 5.1 above. The **doctrine of privity of contract** is that only a party to a contract can sue to enforce the contract or be sued on it. The application of the doctrine of privity can be seen in *Dunlop Ltd* v *Selfridges Ltd* [1915]. The plaintiff, a tyre manufacturer, sold tyres to a wholesaler (W) and inserted clauses into the contract to ensure the ultimate retail tyre price was fixed. W included the same clauses in its contract with the defendant, a retailer, but the defendant still sold the tyres below the price specified by the plaintiff. When the plaintiff tried to sue the defendant the court held that the plaintiff had no contract with the defendant and so could not sue.

This principle has given rise to many practical difficulties and so the law has developed ways to deal with the problems caused by privity, one of which relates to subcontractors. A **subcontractor**, from a legal perspective, is someone that you do not have a direct contractual relationship with; they are a third party. Often, the purchaser cannot sue or be sued by the subcontractor (third party), as their contract is with the main contractor.

5

From the purchaser's point of view, to get round this problem if they are in a strong position when the contract is negotiated, the purchaser can insist on a clause being inserted into the contract holding the main contractor liable for any breaches by the subcontractor. However, if, as is often the case, the purchaser cannot insist upon such a clause, then as a result of the privity rule, if the subcontractor is in breach the purchaser will not be able to sue him in contract.

If you consider the situation from the third party's point of view, however, they are not party to the contract and may not even be involved in the transaction when the contract is made between the purchaser and main supplier/contractor. Consequently the third party may have little or no influence on the terms of the main contract. If a problem arises and the third party needs to sue the purchaser, then due to the doctrine of privity they will be unable to do so as they are not a party to the main contract between the main supplier/contractor and the purchaser.

Parliament tried to address this problem in an effort to bring this area of English law in line with the law of other European systems with the Contracts (Rights of Third Parties) Act 1999, which provides rules by which third-party rights can be granted in the main contract. The Act can insert clauses into contracts to give rights to a third party who could then enforce them through the courts. Some of the important sections of the Act can be examined in more detail in appendix 3, Legislation. Briefly, however, section 1 Contracts (Rights of Third Parties) Act 1999 explains that the third party has a right to enforce a contract term if the contract provides for this or if a term of it purports to give a benefit the third party. The third party must be identified by name or must belong to a class of people identified in the contract. The third party's right to enforce their rights under the contract are subject to the terms and conditions of that contract but they do have the whole range of remedies available should they wish to seek them. In addition, as well as suing to enforce their rights, they can also take advantage of any exclusion/limitation clauses in the contract. You will be taking a detailed look at exclusion clauses in study session 12.

Self-assessment question 5.3

Write a memo to your head of department briefly explaining the impact of the Contracts (Rights of Third Parties) Act 1999 on subcontracting situations.

Limit your memo to 150 words.

Feedback on page 68

5.4 Capacity

Problems can arise where one party does not have capacity but the other party is unaware of this. It is important to know whether any resulting contract can be enforced and what can be done to avoid such problems arising.

Learning activity 5.4

In your organisation which individuals have authority to contract on its behalf? Do they all have the same level of authority or not? Consider the organisations with which your organisation does business. Which people have authority to enter into contracts?

Have you or any of your colleagues come across any situations where problems were caused because the individuals who entered into contracts on behalf of their organisations did not have authority to do so? If so, can you think of any practical steps that could have been taken to avoid the problem (apart from not entering into the contract!)? You should return to this part of the activity at the end of section 5.4 to see whether you have learnt about any practical steps which might be helpful.

Feedback on page 68

The general rule is that the law assumes that the parties to a contract are legally competent to enter into that contract, or in other words, that they have the *capacity* to do so. There are certain groups whose members may not have liability, such as minors (those under 18 years of age), mentally disordered persons and those in a state of drunkenness when the contract is made. This area of law has limited application in procurement contracts.

The rules relating to capacity are different for different types of individuals and organisations. With sole traders they are treated as individuals in the eyes of the law. Their business does not have a separate identity. Partnerships do not have a separate legal identity either, so when you enter into a contract with a partnership, your contract is with the individuals who are the partners in the firm. However, companies are very different. The law recognises companies as having legal personality in their own right, which is quite separate from the individuals involved in the company as directors, for example.

A company has the capacity to enter into a contract provided its actions fall within the provisions of its objects clause in the memorandum of association, a document that is registered at the time the company is incorporated (that is, formed). The objects clause sets out the areas of business in which the company will be involved, and if the company enters into any contracts which are beyond the scope of its powers then those contracts will be void. This is called the doctrine of *ultra vires* and it limits the power of a company to enter into contracts beyond its powers. Although it was intended to protect investors, creditors and third parties dealing with the company, this protection is very much reduced now as the doctrine has been significantly affected by the Companies Acts 1985 and 1989, which allow companies to have very broadly worded objects clauses. Purchasers can

5

assume that the company has authority to act unless one of the following exceptions applies:

- the purchaser has received notice that the company does not have authority
- the purchaser knows of a restriction in the objects clause at the time the contract is made
- the purchaser is dealing with a local authority. Under Local Government (Contracts) Act 1997, it is bound by any contracts where it has given a valid certificate as to its capacity
- the purchaser is not dealing with a normal registered company but a different type of company set up as a charitable or trust company
- the purchaser is not dealing with a company at all but some other category of organisation such as an institute formed by royal charter or a university.

To avoid problems when contracting with the more unusual organisations it is good practice to ask the organisation about its capacity to contract and find out which individuals in the organisation have authority to enter into contracts on its behalf.

Another consideration concerns individual staff in the company. You need to be aware who has authority to act. The usual rule is that any officer of the company has ostensible authority. These individuals could therefore be the directors and company secretary, buyers and purchasing officers, managers, but the authority will diminish further down the chain of command. The authority in your organisation should also be in keeping with what you would expect to find in your particular industry and it should be appropriate to the level at which that individual is in the organisation.

Self-assessment question 5.4

Read the following sentences and state whether the statements are true or false.

1   Only the managing director of a company has authority to enter into a contract on the company's behalf.
2   Purchasers can always assume local authorities have authority to enter into any contract.
3   A company has authority to enter into contracts on matters that are outside the scope of its objects clause.
4   Companies have very broadly drafted objects clauses.
5   Minors always have capacity to enter into contracts.

Feedback on page 68

Revision question

Now try the revision question for this session on page 238.

Summary

In this session you studied the legal principles relating to:

- consideration and how the courts apply the principles relating to this
- intention to create legal relations with domestic/social agreements and commercial agreements and the presumptions made by the courts which can be rebutted with evidence to the contrary
- privity and the problems it creates with regard to third-party rights
- capacity of various parties to enter into contracts.

You also had an opportunity to develop skills in applying legal principles to given practical situations.

In study session 6 you will be studying one of the areas that can create practical problems with purchasing in the formation of contracts – battle of the forms.

Suggested further reading

Griffiths and Griffiths (2002). You should read the chapter on contract formation.

Wyborn (2000). You could read the sections on consideration, capacity and *ultra vires*, and privity of contract.

Feedback on learning activities and self-assessment questions

Feedback on learning activity 5.1

Your answers are likely to include money, items or goods supplied, or services provided. They may also include promises to pay, promises to deliver goods and promises to provide services. Consideration could be your organisation promising not to take action to enforce their rights in return for the other organisation giving a promise to do something by a particular date.

Feedback on self-assessment question 5.1

Where reference is made to cases in your answer you should give the case name and legal principle. You may also briefly refer to the facts. In the feedback below, your attention is drawn to relevant cases to which you should refer.

- Consideration must be sufficient but need not be adequate. If consideration is sufficient it means it is of a type that the law recognises as being capable of having value, for example money. Adequacy, on the other hand, is about the value or the amount of the consideration.
- Performance of an existing public duty is insufficient consideration. If you are already obliged to do something because of an existing public duty, it cannot be sufficient consideration for a contract, as in *Collins* v *Godefroy* [1831].

5

- Performance of an existing contractual duty is insufficient consideration. If you are already obliged to do something because of an existing contractual duty then it will not be sufficient consideration in a new contract. In *Stilk* v *Myrick* [1809] and in *Hartley* v *Ponsonby* [1857] this point was considered.
- Part payment of a debt is insufficient consideration. If you only pay part of a debt it cannot usually be considered sufficient consideration to settle the debt in full. In *D&C Builders* v *Rees* [1965] the defendant made a part payment in cash, but this was held to be insufficient to settle the debt. There are some circumstances where payment of a lesser sum could be sufficient consideration to settle the debt in full.
- Past consideration is no consideration. When the consideration is related to past actions, the law will not enforce a promise. Any consideration given in these circumstances will be as an ex gratia payment made after the agreement. It will not be part of the contract and so will not be enforceable, as in *Re McArdle* [1951].
- Consideration must move from the promisee. Only someone who provides consideration for the contractual promise can enforce the contract. This rule is shown in the case of *Tweddle* v *Atkinson* [1861].

Feedback on learning activity 5.2

Table 5.2

Name	Relevant facts	Legal principle
Simpkins v *Pays* [1955]	The defendant owned a house where she lived with her granddaughter and the plaintiff, who was a paying lodger. They regularly entered a newspaper competition, the entry being submitted in the defendant's name. All three contributed to it although there was no regular arrangement about paying for it or posting it. When the parties won, the defendant refused to pay the lodger his share, claiming there was no intention to create a legal relationship.	The court held that there was sufficient mutuality in the arrangements to establish a legally binding commitment to share any prize money.
Rose & Frank Co. v *J R Compton & Bros Ltd* [1925]	The defendants agreed to supply paper to the plaintiffs. A written marketing arrangement was made which included a clause stating, 'this is not a legal agreement and shall not be subject to the law courts'. Before the end of the agreed arrangement period, the defendants refused to complete orders and terminated the arrangement without giving proper notice.	The Court of Appeal found that each of the orders given and accepted constituted an individual contract, and the defendant was obliged to fulfil the orders it had received but it was not obliged to fulfil future orders because the marketing arrangement specifically said that there was no intention for it to have legal consequences.
Coward v *Motor*	The plaintiff's husband usually got a lift to work with a colleague and contributed towards the petrol. The men were killed	The court held that it was a social arrangement and in the absence of

(continued on next page)

Table 5.2 *(continued)*

Name	Relevant facts	Legal principle
Insurance Bureau [1963]	in a car accident and the widow sued the Motor Insurance Bureau.	evidence to the contrary there was no intention to create a legal relationship.
Edwards v *Skyways Ltd* [1964]	The defendant made the plaintiff redundant. In negotiations about his pension entitlement, he agreed to receive a refund of his contributions and an ex gratia payment in respect of the contributions that the employer made into the pension scheme. The defendants then refused to make the ex gratia payment.	The court held that the words 'ex gratia' did not negate the existence of a contract, they simply meant the defendants were not admitting to any prior liability. As a result of this they had not overturned the presumption and there was therefore an intention to be legally bound.
Carlill v *Carbolic Smoke Ball Co.* [1892]	The defendants argued that the advertisement was 'mere puff' and so there was no intention to be bound.	The Court of Appeal held that the presumption was rebutted. The defendant showed its intention to be bound when it said it was putting £1,000 on deposit to compensate users of the product.

Feedback on self-assessment question 5.2

Figure 5.2

1							S	I	M	P	K	I*	N	S			
2		P	R	E	S	U	M	P	T	I	O	N	S				
3								R	E	B	U	T	T	A	B	L	E
4								C	O	M	M	E	R	C	I	A	L
5							E	V	I	D	E	N	C	E			
6								D	O	M	E	S	T	I	C		
7								C	A	R	L	I	L	L			
8										C	O	W	A	R	D		
9			R	O	S	E	&	F	R	A	N	K	C	O			

The mystery word is intention.

Feedback on learning activity 5.3

Your organisation may be involved in many contracts where a third party is involved in supply. There are various kinds of difficulties which could arise, for example there could be delays in supply of goods or services, or there could be defects in the goods supplied, or perhaps there could be defective performance of services.

If these situations arise your organisation may deal with them by using indemnity clauses to make the third party liable through the parties with whom you contract. You will be considering indemnities in study session 11.

Feedback on self-assessment question 5.3

In your memo you should be able to set out the main points covered in this section. Initially you should explain the rule of privity in order to explain the difficulties that exist when third parties are involved in contractual situations. You should then comment on the main provisions of the Act and explain what difference this will make to the situation with third parties.

Feedback on learning activity 5.4

You may have several individuals in mind who have authority in your organisation to contract for the purchase/supply of goods and services. You may well have authority to do so yourself. It is unlikely that out of the people you have listed they all have the same authority unless they are all doing the same type of job. If you have a range of individuals at different levels on your list, it is likely that the senior people will have authority to enter into larger-value or more complex purchases than the junior people.

Feedback on self-assessment question 5.4

1   False. As explained in the text, there are many people in an organisation who have authority to contract on behalf of the company. The directors/company secretary will have the highest authority to do so.
2   False. Companies have very widely drafted objects clauses so they are not restricted in what they can do.
3   False. Such contracts would be *ultra vires*.
4   True.
5   False. Minors do not always have capacity to enter into contracts, but there are a few exceptions.

Battle of the forms

6

One does not like hot, the other does not like cold, make it tepid to make an agreement.
(Malagasy proverb)

Introduction

In this section you will be studying the 'battle of the forms', what it is and how it can determine which of the parties' standard terms and conditions will bind the contract. You will also think about how the battle of the forms could be avoided and you will consider given situations and apply the legal rules. Finally, you will consider e-contracts and how the battle of the forms relates to them.

Session learning objectives

After completing this session you should be able to:

6.1 Explain what is meant by the 'battle of the forms'.
6.2 Apply the legal principle in battle of the forms in a given situation.
6.3 Identify how the procurement function can avoid battle of the forms situations arising.
6.4 Analyse the formation of e-contracts.

Unit content coverage

This study session covers the following topic from the official CIPS unit content document.

Learning outcome

Identify a range of legal aspects in relation to the contracting process.

Describe and apply the legalities linked to the formation of contracts.

Learning objective

2.2 Discuss the legalities and commercial considerations linked to the battle of the forms.
 • The exchange of suppliers' and purchasers' terms in the contract formation process.
 • Counter-offers and acceptance.
 • Precedent set by case law on contract formation.
 • The creation of e-contracts.

Prior knowledge

Study sessions 4 and 5.

Resources

Appendix 2, Case law and appendix 5, Advice on answering examination questions.

Timing

You should set aside about 5 hours to read and complete this session, including learning activities, self-assessment questions, the suggested further reading (if any) and the revision question.

6.1 Battle of the forms

In study session 4 you studied the roles of offer, acceptance and counter-offer. In this session you will be considering these elements in the context of organisations' use of standard terms and conditions (st&c). Organisations do not negotiate each and every term in every contract they make. Instead, in the business world, organisations use standard terms that they will want to apply to all contracts that they enter into. Obviously these terms and conditions will obtain the contractual advantage for the particular organisation, whether it is the purchaser or the seller, in that contract. The problem arises when two organisations are trying to ensure their st&c will govern the contract. This is known as the 'battle of the forms'.

One of the organisations makes an offer on its st&c, but when the other organisation 'accepts' on its own st&c this is actually a counter-offer. The effect of the counter-offer is to extinguish the original offer and the counter-offer is therefore the only 'offer' capable of acceptance. Sometimes the battle of the forms can go through several steps as each organisation replies to the other making new counter-offers as neither wants to contract on the other's terms until finally the buyer accepts the goods which are accompanied by a document containing the seller's st&c and the battle is won. The contract is on the seller's st&c.

Learning activity 6.1

Investigate whether your organisation has, or is involved in, a battle of the forms situation. Is your organisation the buyer or the seller? What are the implications of this distinction?

Feedback on page 77

The court considered the battle of the forms in the case of *Butler Machine Tool Co.* v *Ex-Cell-O Corporation* [1979]. The plaintiff offered to sell machinery (on its own st&c) to the defendant. The st&c contained a price variation clause allowing the seller to charge the price applicable at the time of delivery. The defendant ordered the machinery on its own st&c which had no price variation clause but which had a 'tear off and return' acknowledgement slip. The plaintiff returned the slip indicating its acceptance of the defendant's st&c. When the machinery was delivered, the plaintiffs tried to charge the price applicable at the time of delivery. There had been a price increase since the order was placed. The court held that as the plaintiff had accepted the defendant's st&c the price variation clause did not apply to the contract.

In *BRS* v *Arthur B Crutchley Ltd* [1968], the plaintiffs delivered whiskey to the defendants for storage. Their driver gave the defendant the delivery note, which said it incorporated the plaintiff's terms. The defendants stamped the note that the goods were received under their terms and conditions. The court held that this was a counter-offer, which the plaintiffs accepted by conduct when they handed over the whiskey. The contract was made on the defendant's terms and conditions.

In the battle of the forms, it is usually the person who 'fires the last shot' who wins. However, the facts of each case must be considered carefully. Sometimes the situation is not very clear-cut.

Self-assessment question 6.1

Explain how acceptance can take place with the battle of the forms.

Feedback on page 78

6.2 Applying: a battle of the forms

Learning activity 6.2

What are the signs to look for when recognising situations which can result in battle of the forms?

Feedback on page 78

When contracts are being negotiated there are various documents which can go back and forth between the parties, such as catalogues, price lists, order form, acknowledgement, confirmation, despatch note, delivery note and invoice. Each one of these documents will have a particular status in law. Table 6.1 shows what these documents would usually be in terms of legal status.

Table 6.1

Document	Status	Whose st&c apply?
Catalogue/price list	Invitation to treat	Seller's
Order	Offer by purchaser	Purchaser's
Acknowledgement/confirmation	Counter-offer	Seller's
Despatch/delivery note	Counter-offer	Seller's
Signature on delivery/conduct of purchaser	Acceptance	Seller's

There are various scenarios where these documents would play a part in the battle of the forms. In section 6.1 above you saw how the courts applied the rules in *Butler Machine Tool Co.* v *Ex-Cell-O Corporation* [1979]; now you will consider some scenarios and consider how the courts would deal with the parties. You must remember, every case turns on its own facts. The following examples will take you through different situations.

Table 6.2 Example 1 – battle of the forms does not apply

Document/conduct	Status	Whose st&c apply?
Purchaser's order requesting S to reply on P's acknowledgement slip or by letter	Offer	Purchaser's st&c
Seller's acceptance letter of P's terms sent or P's acknowledgement slip returned	Acceptance	Purchaser's st&c

Contract is made on purchaser's st&c.

Table 6.3 Example 2 – battle of the forms applies

Document/conduct	Status	Whose st&c apply?
Purchaser's order requesting S to reply on P's acknowledgement slip or by letter	Offer	Purchaser's st&c
Seller's acceptance letter with S's st&c	Counter-offer	Seller's st&c
S delivers goods	Acceptance of goods by P	Seller's st&c

Contract is made on seller's st&c.

Table 6.4 Example 3 – battle of the forms applies

Document/conduct	Status	Whose st&c apply?
Purchaser's order requesting S to reply on P's acknowledgement slip or by letter	Offer	Purchaser's st&c
Seller is silent. No letter or acknowledgement	–	–
S delivers goods without S's st&c being on delivery note	Acceptance of S by delivering goods	Purchaser's st&c

Contract is made on purchaser's st&c.

Table 6.5 Example 4 – battle of the forms applies

Document/conduct	Status	Whose st&c apply?
Purchaser's order requesting S to reply on P's acknowledgement slip or by letter	Offer	Purchaser's st&c
Seller is silent. No letter or acknowledgement	–	–
S delivers goods and informs P that S's st&c are on delivery note	Counter-offer	Seller's st&c
P accepts goods with S's st&c on delivery note	Acceptance	Seller's st&c

Contract is made on seller's st&c.

If you are a purchaser it is important that you establish whose st&c will apply to the contract if you accept the goods.

Self-assessment question 6.2

Parker Ltd has discovered defects in goods supplied by Brick Ltd that they have used in their production line. In correspondence between the companies Brick Ltd allege the contract is on their standard terms and conditions, which are not favourable to Parker Ltd over the defective goods. Parker Ltd is surprised as it assumed that the contract was made on its standard terms. The head of purchasing is investigating the matter and discovers that the order Parker Ltd sent to Brick Ltd contained Parker Ltd's standard terms and conditions. Brick Ltd sent an acknowledgement of the order on its standard terms and conditions. Brick Ltd's delivery note which accompanied the goods delivered to Parker Ltd contained Brick Ltd's standard terms and conditions.

Advise Parker Ltd.

You may wish to read through the relevant information about answering problem questions in appendix 5, Advice on answering examination questions before answering this question.

Feedback on page 78

6.3 Avoiding: a battle of the forms

Learning activity 6.3

Investigate the procedures and systems in place in your organisation for entering into contracts. Consider whether they would permit battle of the forms to occur.

Feedback on page 79

You have seen how easy it is to become involved in the battle of the forms and, if you are the purchaser, how easy it is for you to lose the battle. The implications of losing can be serious as you will be contracting on the other party's st&cs which will not be favourable to you. The best solution for purchasers therefore is to avoid becoming involved in the battle of the forms at all. There are several ways that you can do this.

Proper management of contract documentation

You could create a set of standard terms and conditions in advance which will cover all future dealings between you and your supplier before you actually start to agree individual transactions. The terms and conditions that

73

you agree could be yours or theirs or a combination of both sets. They will form a framework agreement (see section 4.6).

Tendering is another way to avoid the battle of the forms. With the tendering process it is the buyer who controls the terms of the contract. The buyer will set out the terms of the tender which they are inviting from suppliers. If any supplier fails to comply with what is specified, the buyer can reject that tender. Tendering is considered further in study session 17.

Many e-contracts are made by purchasers buying goods from websites where, in order to complete the purchase, the purchaser must click acceptance of the seller's terms and conditions before the contract can be made. Consequently, in such cases the battle of the forms is avoided. These contracts are considered in detail in section 6.4 below.

Self-assessment question 6.3

Word quiz

Answer the following questions to complete the horizontal words. Once the quiz is completed you should discover the mystery vertical word.

1   This party 'fired the last shot'.
2   Who usually loses the battle of the forms?
3   A soft way to avoid the battle of the forms.
4   They did not include a price variation clause.
5   Agreements which avoid battle of the forms.
6   This can be used to avoid battle of the forms.

Figure 6.1

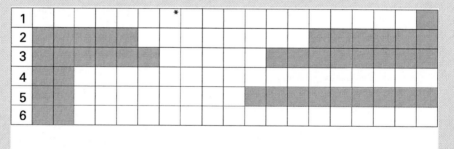

Feedback on page 79

6.4 E-contracts

You may come across different definitions relating to aspects of e-business, but in this course you should use the CIPS definitions below for e-sourcing, e-procurement and e-commerce.

- E-sourcing is using the internet to make decisions and form strategies regarding how and where services or products are obtained.

- E-procurement is using the internet to operate the transactional aspects of requisitioning, authorising, ordering, receipting and payment processes for the required services or products.
- E-commerce includes e-procurement as well as use of the internet to build more collaborative ways of working between the customer and supplier, and within companies themselves.
- E-contracts are contracts made using electronic communication on the internet and using email.

You may wish to reread sections 5.2, 5.3 and 5.4 to refresh your memory about the legal principles involved in agreements (invitation to treat, offer, counter-offer and acceptance).

Learning activity 6.4

Visit several supplier websites. Examine them from a contractual point of view. For each website consider the steps in forming contracts between the seller and the purchaser. Are the steps the same for each of the sites? Why is this?

Feedback on page 79

As a purchasing professional, you may already use the internet or email to purchase goods, or your organisation may do so in the future. Therefore it is important to know how e-contracts are formed.

E-offers and e-acceptance

The legal principles applicable to contract formation that you have studied in study sessions 4, 5 and here, apply equally to e-contracts. Like any other contract, an e-contract requires the essential elements of offer, acceptance, consideration and intention to enter into legal relations.

To understand how e-contracts are formed, you must consider how the steps in contract formation (invitation to treat, offer, counter-offer and acceptance) relate to purchases using electronic communication.

Firstly, you need to consider the information on the website carefully – look at the general information as well as any standard terms and conditions.

If the website is offering goods for sale which can be bought by purchasers 'clicking' acceptance on the website, then the website is making an offer which the purchaser is accepting, and any subsequent email sent by the supplier to the purchaser may well be just a confirmation of the contract which has already been formed.

If the website simply advertises the supplier's goods or acts like a shop window, displaying the goods and inviting offers from potential purchasers, then maybe it is just an invitation to treat in the same way that the courts have held advertisements and displays to be invitations to treat in non

6

e-contract cases such as *Partridge* v *Crittenden* [1968] and *Fisher* v *Bell* [1961]. If this is what the website is doing, it is advisable for them to make it clear that they are merely inviting offers from potential customers.

As you know, it is possible to have a series of offers and counter-offers before one of the parties finally accepts in non e-contract situations. The same thing could happen if the parties were contacting by way of email.

Battle of the forms and e-contracts

If an offer is made electronically, the purchaser must know before or at the time of acceptance what the seller's terms and conditions are. Battle of the forms situations could, however, arise where contracts are made using emails and the same safeguards should be put in place as with non e-contracts.

On the internet, the terms and conditions would usually be on the website, so purchasers could read them and click to confirm their consent. However, suppliers can take further steps to ensure that buyers must consent to their terms and conditions by ensuring that prospective purchasers cannot purchase any goods unless they have already clicked their consent to the supplier's standard terms and conditions of contract.

By having such a website design, suppliers can ensure that their standard terms and conditions must apply to any contract and can avoid the battle of the forms situation arising, as prospective purchasers unwilling to accept the supplier's standard terms and conditions simply would not be able to proceed to purchase any goods.

Electronic signatures

The Electronic Communications Act 2000 permits contractual negotiations and documents to be exchanged by email and permits the electronic signature to be used to confirm that the email is authentic.

Self-assessment question 6.4

As a purchasing professional, you have visited various suppliers' websites to access data about office equipment required by your company. An appropriate supplier has been identified and now you are about to visit the supplier's website to purchase the required items. Consider the following questions in the light of the steps in the contract formation:

* What information is on the supplier's website?
* What would your communication be if you ordered goods from the website?
* The supplier received your website order but was unable to supply the items requested. The supplier then emailed you informing you of this and suggesting alternative products. What would the supplier's email be?

Feedback on page 79

Revision question

Now try the revision question for this session on page 238.

Summary

In this session you have examined what battle of the forms is and how the courts deal with such situations. Having studied this session you should be able to:

- Explain what battle of the forms is, that it occurs where two parties each with st&cs try to ensure their terms bind the contract. Often it is the person who 'fires the last shot' who will win the battle.
- Apply the legal principles to given situations to discover whether battle of the forms has arisen.
- Recognise how battle of the forms can be avoided by proper contract management, setting up an agreed set of terms and conditions ahead of the contract (framework agreements), tendering and e-contracts.
- Apply your knowledge of the steps in contract formation and to e-contracts. You should be able to recognise offer and acceptance in e-contracts, and understand the impact of the battle of the forms on e-contracts.

And finally, having understood the processes involved in e-contracts, you should be able to examine the implications of e-contracting on procurement.

Suggested further reading

Griffiths and Griffiths (2002). You should read the sections on battle of the forms and electronic commerce.

Singleton and Lawson (2002). You could read the sections on battle of the forms.

Wyborn (2000). You could read the sections on battle of the forms and electronic commerce.

Feedback on learning activities and self-assessment questions

Feedback on learning activity 6.1

It is very easy in practice to become involved in battle of the forms situations. You may have been able to see exactly why it has come about in your organisation. This should help you to avoid the same pitfalls. It is important to avoid a battle of the forms situation arising especially if you are the buyer. As you will see, usually the contract is made on the last set of st&c to be sent from one party to the other. No matter what has gone on before, the last document will often be the delivery note which accompanies the goods. This will usually contain the seller's st&c and so they will bind the contract if the purchaser accepts the goods.

Feedback on self-assessment question 6.1

Acceptance usually takes place in negotiations for a contract when one party indicates to the other that they unconditionally accept the other's offer. Often this is done in writing.

In the battle of the forms, often acceptance takes place when the purchaser accepts the goods. The goods are usually delivered and signed for, but if they are not capable of inspection at that time to ensure conformity to the order then acceptance is likely to take place when the goods are accepted by the purchaser's conduct. This may include paying for the goods, using the goods or doing anything which prevents the supplier from having the goods back in the form in which they were delivered.

Feedback on learning activity 6.2

Signs that may alert you to a battle of the forms situation include the following:

- the parties do not have any agreed terms and conditions already in place prior to the contract
- the parties each have standard terms and conditions which they are trying to make the contract upon
- absence of the parties using negotiation and agreeing terms for inclusion in a single contract document
- there are various documents/letters passing between the parties.

Feedback on self-assessment question 6.2

In order to decide if Parker Ltd can rely on its own favourable st&cs you must decide whose terms bind the contract. Here the contract was formed in a battle of the forms situation. You should explain that and its implications for Parker Ltd.

Your answer should identify the battle of the forms situation where neither party to the contract has obtained unconditional acceptance of its own terms and conditions of sale before entering into a legal agreement. The law states that where no definite set of terms has been agreed, the last set of terms and conditions to be received will often apply. In this case, Brick Ltd's were the last to be received. They were printed on the delivery note which accompanied the delivery of goods. Unconditional acceptance of Brick Ltd's st&cs by Parker Ltd is implied by their conduct in using the goods. There is a legally binding contract on Brick Ltd's standard terms and conditions. You should also refer to case law, for example, *Butler Machine Tool Co. Ltd* v *Ex-Cell-O Corporation* [1979]. An excellent answer might also refer to cases such as *Hyde* v *Wrench* [1840] (counter-offers), and *Brogden* v *Metropolitan Railway Co.* [1877] (acceptance by conduct).

As the contract has been made on Brick Ltd's st&cs, Parker Ltd's own more favourable st&cs have no bearing on the contract and so Parker Ltd cannot rely on them.

Feedback on learning activity 6.3

You may be able to avoid battle of the forms if:

- you have a well-organised office
- staff are competent
- there are effective and efficient office procedures in place
- you use a tendering procedure
- you use a framework agreement.

In the rest of this section you will be considering these points and others in considering how to avoid battle of the forms.

Feedback on self-assessment question 6.3

Figure 6.2

1	A	R	T	H	U	R	B*	C	R	U	T	C	H	L	E	Y	L	T	D
2						P	U	R	C	H	A	S	E	R					
3						T	E	N	D	E	R								
4		E	X	C	E	L	L	O	C	O	R	P	O	R	A	T	I	O	N
5		F	R	A	M	E	W	O	R	K									
6		C	O	N	T	R	A	C	T	M	A	N	A	G	E	M	E	N	T

The mystery word is Butler.

Feedback on learning activity 6.4

When considering the steps involved in purchasing by electronic means, you need to think back to your studies of invitation to treat, offer, counter-offer and acceptance and consider what legal step is taken each time an event or action takes place. That way you will be able to analyse the formation of contracts.

You are likely to find that the websites are mostly, if not all, the same. That is usually the case as suppliers will try to ensure their terms govern the contract by having a box that must be clicked.

Feedback on self-assessment question 6.4

You need to consider the information on the website carefully. Look at the general information as well as any standard terms and conditions on the website.

- Is the website advertising the supplier's goods or acting like a shop window, displaying the goods and inviting offers from potential purchasers? If so, it may be regarded as an invitation to treat, just as advertisements and displays have been held to be invitations to treat by the courts in non e-contracts in cases such as *Partridge* v *Crittenden* [1968] and *Fisher* v *Bell* [1961]. If this is the case, it is advisable for websites to make it clear that they are merely inviting offers from potential customers.

Is the website offering goods for sale which can be bought by purchasers 'clicking' acceptance on the website? If this is the case, then the website is making an offer which is capable of acceptance.

- If the website is clearly an invitation to treat inviting offers, then your communication would be an offer which the supplier could accept if it wished to enter into a contract with you.

If the supplier is making an offer on the website then your communication would be an acceptance and a contract would be formed.

- If the supplier, upon receipt of your offer to purchase, realised he could not supply what you wanted and instead suggested an alternative item for you to purchase, this would be a counter-offer that you could accept or reject. If offer and acceptance had already occurred, a contract would exist which the supplier would be obliged to fulfil. If the supplier could not supply the goods according to the contract, it would be in breach of contract and you could sue.

Study session 7

Effectiveness of supply agreements

Introduction

In this session you will study the various factors that can play a part in making supply agreements effective or not. You will also consider the evaluation of effectiveness of supply agreements and how their differences can mean that their effectiveness can be viewed in different ways.

'Efficiency is doing things right; effectiveness is doing the right things.'
(Peter F Drucker (1909–2005), American educator and writer)

Session learning objectives

After completing this session you should be able to:

7.1 Identify matters that affect the effectiveness of supply agreements.
7.2 Evaluate the effectiveness of supply agreements.

Unit content coverage

This study session covers the following topic from the official CIPS unit content document.

Learning objective

3.1 Analyse and discuss the effectiveness of a supply agreement.
 • Contractual obligations
 • Contract termination

Prior knowledge

Study sessions 1 – 6.

Timing

You should set aside about 4 hours to read and complete this session, including learning activities, self-assessment questions, the suggested further reading (if any) and the revision question.

7.1 Effective supply agreements

Learning activity 7.1

Interview as many purchasing professionals as you can from your organisation, from other organisations or from your CIPS tutor group. Find

(continued on next page)

Learning activity 7.1 *(continued)*

out their opinion of what makes a supply agreement effective. Ask them to give you an example of an agreement that they considered was effective and one that was not with reasons for their choice. Make a note of their comments. You may wish to summarise the information in a table.

Feedback on page 87

What does 'effectiveness' mean?

As you saw above, effectiveness can be doing the right things. Effectiveness can also be defined as success in producing a result.

In reality whether a supply agreement is effective depends on whether it does what it is supposed to do, whether it produces results, or more importantly whether it produces the right results. Throughout the process of contract development the purchasing professional can work to ensure the effectiveness of the supply agreement, to ensure that the right results are produced.

Objectives

As you saw in study session 2, purchasing can be defined by the 'rights' of purchasing, namely purchasing inputs of the right quality, in the right quantity, from the right source, which are delivered to the right place at the right time for the right price.

This definition sees purchasing in terms of objectives. When objectives are considered from the perspective of a purchasing department, they must be functional and so they are tactical, short term and specific. As the 'rights' of purchasing are not always all compatible, when a purchasing department is considering its objectives for a particular contract, it must weigh up all the 'rights' and decide which of the irreconcilable rights it wishes to focus upon, for example a low price rather than an early delivery, or high quality rather than a low price.

There may also be changes in the importance of certain objectives to the organisation with different categories of procurements. In study session 1 you studied the various categories of procurements, such as capital equipment, production materials used in manufacturing (raw materials, semi-finished goods and component parts and assemblies), consumables and maintenance, repair and operating (MRO) supplies, resale goods and services. With regard to objectives, some will be common to various contracts, but others will be different. The objectives when purchasing a high-value piece of specialist machinery are likely to be very different to the ones for the purchase of office consumables like standard photocopying paper. It is only by focusing clearly on what the appropriate objectives are for a particular contract that the purchasing department can set the scene for an 'effective' supply agreement. The objectives must be specific, measurable, achievable, realistic and timed. These objectives will be referred to later in the process when the effectiveness of the supply agreement is being evaluated, as you will see in section 7.2 below. It is important therefore that the objectives of the supply agreement are clearly and accurately defined.

Defining the need – specifications

As you saw in study sessions 1 and 2, the need must be clearly defined in the specification. The specification is an important part of ensuring that supply agreements are effective. Again here the purchasing professional plays a part in the specification process. If the need is not clearly identified and the specification is not well prepared then the implications can be that costs are wasted through over-specification, unnecessary additional requirements, using branded items, and elaborate packaging for example. All of these factors could result in additional costs which do not achieve the objective of the 'right' price as the value-added element would be reduced. This would affect how effective the supply agreement is.

Negotiating the contract

Whether or not a supply agreement is effective is also dependent on the 'deal' that is negotiated between the parties. Practical matters such as quantities, pricing and delivery arrangements to mention a few will need to be carefully considered, discussed and agreed in negotiation.

In addition, the 'legal' aspects of the various obligations that the parties may have one against the other in relation to delivery, payment and quality levels as well as agreement relating to issues such as how the agreement will end, and how disputes will be dealt with, will all need to be agreed. You will study the various terms that appear in contracts in study sessions 8 to 13. These agreed terms form the basis of the contract. Therefore it is important that they are well considered and the purchasing team negotiates well to ensure that the contract agreed for the supply of the goods or services will be an effective one which will do the right things.

If the supplier failed to meet its obligations under the contract the purchasing organisation would be able to enforce the contract to ensure its rights were protected and the supplier met its obligations or was required to compensate for losses caused. This too is an aspect of the effectiveness of a supply agreement, that is, to be an agreement that the parties can feel confident will do the right thing. However, if it is poorly drafted it would not be as effective.

Commercial relationships

Once your supply agreement has been negotiated and the contract agreed, it will then be performed. At this stage its effectiveness can be affected by your commercial relationship with the supplier. If you do not develop the appropriate relationship for that particular contract its effectiveness could be reduced.

Kraljic (1983: 110) identified the two variables of risk and spend as determining the type of commercial relationships that should be formed for supply agreements. Using these two criteria all procurements can be assigned to one of the categories in figure 7.1. The vertical axis represents the supply risk and the horizontal axis represents the relative spend.

The organisation's procurements (and consequently the suppliers who supply them) can then be assigned to one of the four boxes labelled as bottleneck, strategic, non-critical and leverage items. Once assigned, this indicates the style of commercial relationship which is appropriate for that supply agreement.

- Bottleneck items: these items are high risk but low spend. The seller is often in a powerful position and the buyer must behave accordingly.
- Strategic items: these items are high risk and high spend. These inputs are critical to the purchasing organisation and it has a high spend. Here the purchaser should work closely with the seller to drive costs down and quality up.
- Non-critical items: these items are low risk and low spend. These are everyday items that can be easily sourced. Time and effort expended by the purchaser is unlikely to bring any benefit to the organisation.
- Leverage items: these items are low risk and high spend. Usually there will be many suppliers and the main focus is on price.

Figure 7.1: Commercial relationships matrix based upon the criteria of risk and spend

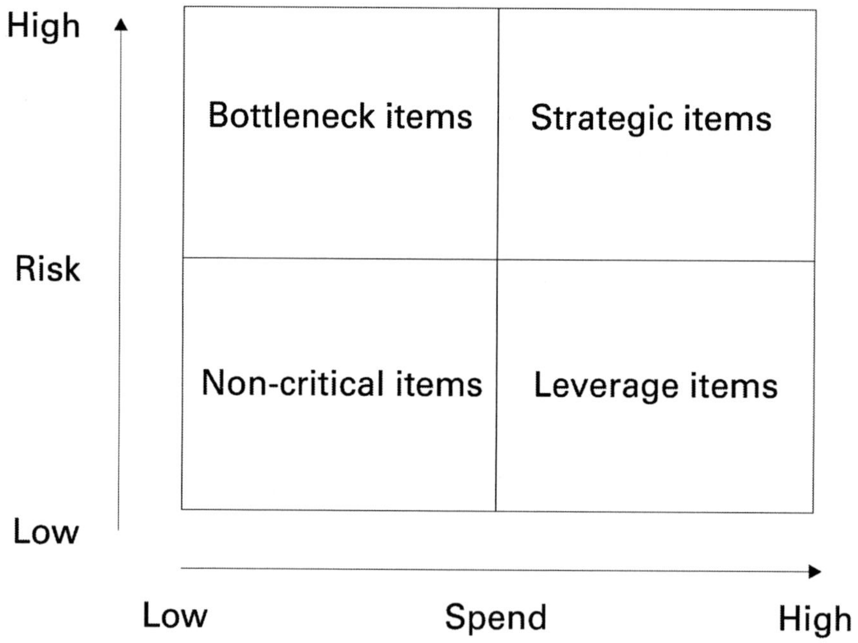

If a purchasing professional did not try to develop the right type of relationship then the effectiveness of the ultimate contract would be affected. For example, if instead of developing a close relationship with a strategic supplier a purchaser paid insufficient attention to the relationship it is likely that the quality levels achieved may not be as high and the price may not be as low.

Self-assessment question 7.1

Identify the stages in the development of a contract where the purchasing professional can work to ensure the effectiveness of the agreement and explain their role in each of these stages.

(continued on next page)

Feedback on page 87

Self-assessment question 7.1 (continued)

Your essay should be approximately 750 words.

You could use the information in appendix 5, Advice on answering examination questions as guidance on how best to approach essay questions.

7.2 Evaluating the effectiveness of supply agreements

Learning activity 7.2

How are supply agreements evaluated in your organisation?

Feedback on page 88

7

In section 7.1 above you considered what the purchasing professional can do to ensure that supply agreements are effective. In this section you will consider the evaluation of supply agreement effectiveness.

As a purchasing professional you may need to evaluate how effective a supply agreement is in order to compare it with other agreements, or you may wish to evaluate it to ascertain whether it meets original expectations. In reality, how effective a supply agreement is depends on various things – as you saw in section 7.1 above, for example, the specifications, the matters agreed in negotiations and the contractual terms. In order for there to be any assessment of how well the agreement has achieved its objectives, the performance of the agreement needs to be measured. In study sessions 2 and 3 you considered measuring performance in respect of compliance to specifications (section 2.3), and key performance indicators (section 3.2), and in order to evaluate a supply agreement these and any other relevant aspects of the supply agreement must be monitored throughout the performance of the agreement, measurements recorded and 'scored' in accordance with a scoring system, in order to make analysis and comparison of agreements possible.

During the performance of the contract with ongoing monitoring, 'measuring' and scoring analysis can be used to assess how close to or far from achieving the contract objectives the organisation actually is. Once this process has ended, the contract has been fully performed, appropriate monitoring has occurred and 'measurements' have been recorded and scored and analysed, the final picture can be ascertained. This will reveal how big or small the gap is between on the one hand the objectives and on the other hand what has actually been achieved, and the reality of the actual situation will be known. The organisation then needs to decide how that gap, which prevented it from achieving its objectives in this particular supply agreement, can be closed so that improvements can be made for the future. An organisation can take steps to close the gap by good contract management and you will return to this when you study study session 20 at the end of the course book.

Figure 7.2 summarises the process of evaluating the effectiveness of supply agreements from the initial setting of objectives through the process leading to the achievement of those objectives by contract development including drafting specifications, negotiating the deal and agreeing the contract terms. It then shows the stage of evaluation to assess the effectiveness of the agreement to see if it has achieved its objectives and indicates the gap between the objectives and the actual achievement or lack of achievement which the organisation can work to close through the process of contract management.

Figure 7.2: Evaluating and controlling the effectiveness of supply agreements

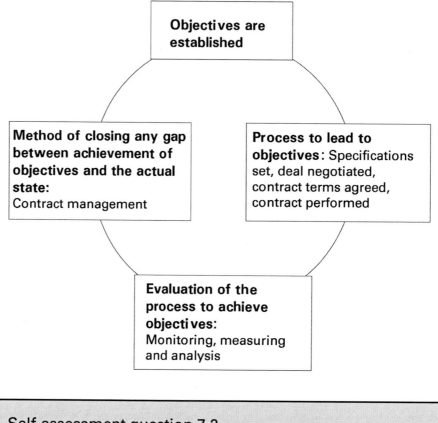

Objectives are established

Process to lead to objectives: Specifications set, deal negotiated, contract terms agreed, contract performed

Evaluation of the process to achieve objectives: Monitoring, measuring and analysis

Method of closing any gap between achievement of objectives and the actual state: Contract management

Self-assessment question 7.2

Complete the missing words in the paragraph below.

In order to evaluate a supply agreement, compliance to _____, key _____ and any other relevant aspects of a supply agreement must be _____ during performance of the agreement. The measurements must be _____ and scored and the results analysed.

The analysis can be used to assess how far from achieving its _____ the agreement is. Once the organisation knows how large or small the gap is between where it is and where it should be to achieve its _____, for repeated or similar contracts in the future it can take steps to close the ___ by means of implementing good _____ _____.

Feedback on page 88

Revision question

Now try the revision question for this session on page 239.

Summary

In this study session you have studied:

- Effective supply agreements – you considered various matters which are relevant for ensuring that supply agreements are effective.
- Objectives, defining the need and specifications.
- Negotiating the contract and agreeing the contract terms.
- Commercial relationships.
- Evaluation of supply agreements – you considered the process of evaluation as a way of deciding how effective a supply agreement is, namely whether it has achieved its objectives.
-

Feedback on learning activities and self-assessment questions

Feedback on learning activity 7.1

Look at the types of agreement given as examples and then look at the reasons given for agreements being effective or not. Try to see if there are any common trends in the information you have obtained. Are there any common reasons why they are effective or not? If there are no common factors, look at the range of reasons given.

Feedback on self-assessment question 7.1

In your answer you should identify the areas of setting objectives for the contract, preparing appropriate specifications, negotiating the contract and developing the appropriate commercial relationship with the supplier.

Your essay should also include explanation of the role that the purchasing professional plays at each of these stages and could refer to matters such as those set out below. To illustrate your answer you could also refer to any examples you have from your own experience of where you have played a part in achieving an effective agreement for your organisation. The purchasing professional should:

- Set clearly and accurately defined objectives which are specific, measurable, achievable, realistic and timed (SMART), decide which of the 'rights' of purchasing is to prevail in the event that there are irreconcilable rights and ensure that the objectives set are appropriate for the type of procurement being sourced
- Ensure that there is a clearly defined specification which has not only its technical aspects well covered but also the commercial aspects such as ensuring that the need is accurately defined, and that, for example, there is no over-specification or unnecessary use of brands

- Ensure that the contract is negotiated well to obtain not only the best deal in terms of price/quality aspects, but also that the contract incorporates appropriate terms from a legal perspective to ensure that the contract can be enforced if necessary and the purchasing organisation has the necessary protection if the contract is breached by the supplier
- Ensure that an appropriate relationship for the contract is developed with the supplier. The type of relationship which is appropriate in a particular case can be analysed using the criteria of risk and spend and classifying the commercial relationship as one of the types of relationships recognised by Kraljic, and dealing with it accordingly.

Feedback on learning activity 7.2

If you are not involved in the process of evaluation yourself you should have had an opportunity to talk to colleagues who are. It would be useful for you to have some idea of what is measured when evaluation takes place and how your department compares different supply agreements. You may find that you have a sophisticated system to use or you may have quite a simple one, but the principles should be the same.

In section 7.2 you will consider evaluation of the effectiveness of supply agreements a little further.

Feedback on self-assessment question 7.2

In order to evaluate a supply agreement, compliance to specifications, key indicators and any other relevant aspects of a supply agreement must be monitored during performance of the agreement. The measurements must be recorded and scored and the results analysed.

The analysis can be used to assess how far from achieving its objectives the agreement is. Once the organisation knows how large or small the gap is between where it is and where it should be to achieve its objectives, for repeated or similar contracts in the future it can take steps to close the gap by means of implementing good contract management.

Classification of contract terms

Introduction

In this session you will begin to look generally at the terms in a contract and begin to consider some of the ways that contract terms are classified with a view to being able to apply that knowledge in practical situations.

Session learning objectives

After completing this session you should be able to:

8.1 Explain the classifications of statements and contractual terms.
8.2 Identify and explain what is meant by a 'condition' and a 'warranty' and the effect each of these will have on breach of contract.
8.3 Identify and explain what is meant by an 'innominate term' and the effect this will have on breach of contract.

Unit content coverage

This study session covers the following topic from the official CIPS unit content document.

Learning outcome

Identify a range of legal aspects in relation to the contracting process.

Explain the impact of both implied and express terms in contracts.

Recognise the remedies for breaches of contracts and draft terms to cover such risks.

Learning objective

3.2 Recognise different contract terms and their impact on any breach of contract.
- Conditions.
- Warranties.
- Innominate terms.

Prior knowledge

Study sessions 4 – 7

Resources

Appendix 2, Case law.

Timing

You should set aside about 5 hours to read and complete this session, including learning activities, self-assessment questions, the suggested further reading (if any) and the revision question.

8.1 Different classifications

Learning activity 8.1

Reflect upon your own professional practice and consider all of the different statements you may hear or read, about products or services that you may be considering as potential acquisitions for your organisation. Then consider the statements that you receive in writing or orally during negotiations. Have any of these statements been incorrect? What did you do or could you do if this happened?

Feedback on page 97

As a purchaser you might see advertisements for goods or services that you may consider purchasing for your organisation. When you negotiate purchases on behalf of your organisation there are certain matters which must be discussed, as you saw in study session 1 when you considered the role of the purchasing professional in procuring goods and services. These pre-contractual discussions are a normal part of the purchaser's role in developing contracts. Not all of the statements that are made in those negotiations or indeed the statements made in advertisements will find their way into the contract.

The pre-contractual statements are divided into three groups. It is important to know which group statements belong to as some are legally binding and others are not.

- Advertising 'puffs' are the exaggerated statements found in advertisements, which are clearly not intended to be relied upon, for example 'just like mother bakes' when applied to apple pie. These statements have no legal effect and can be ignored for contractual purposes.
- Representations are factual statements that are made during the pre-contractual stage by one of the parties to the other, and by which that other party is induced to enter into the contract. If such a statement is false then it will be a misrepresentation. A representation has legal effect and if it is false, it can give rise to a claim for misrepresentation to the party who relies upon it, and in some circumstances a claim under criminal law under the Trade Descriptions Act 1968.
- Contractual terms are the third category. These may have their origin in statements made during discussions as the pre-contractual negotiations progressed but then the content of those statements was incorporated as

terms of the contract when it was finally agreed. Contractual terms are legally binding and if a party fails to comply with its obligations under the terms of the contract, then that party will be in breach of contract and could be sued by the other party.

As you can see, it is important that you are able to recognise what a statement is in terms of the above groups. If advertising puff is incorrect there is no cause of action; if a false representation is made then an action will lie in misrepresentation; if, however, a contractual term has not been complied with then an action will lie for breach of contract.

This distinction between representation and contract terms is vital as the remedies for breach of contract differ in certain aspects from the remedies for misrepresentation. Consequently it is possible that if a claim is brought it could fail if the statement was found to be in one category rather than the other. To assist in deciding whether statements are representations or terms, the common law has developed guidelines to establish the status of the statement as a term or as a representation.

- The timing of the statement. If there is a marked gap between the time the statement is made and when the contract is put into writing, the courts are likely to find it is merely a representation as in the case of *Routledge* v *McKay* [1954] in which the parties, who were private individuals, discussed the sale of a motorbike. The defendant said, in reliance on the vehicle registration document, that the bike was a 1942 model. A week later when the written contract was drawn up it did not mention the year of the bike and it was later discovered that it was a 1930 model. The court held that due to the length of time between the discussion and the preparation of the written contract, the statement about the bike being a 1942 model was a representation not a term and the claim failed.
- Whether the statement is later put in writing in the contract. This is also illustrated by *Routledge* v *McKay* [1954]. Here the term was not later put into writing in the contract, therefore the court concluded that it was a representation and not a term.
- The importance of the term to the parties. If a party would not have entered into the contract but for the statement, then the courts are likely to find that it is a term and not a representation as in *Bannerman* v *White* [1861] in which, during negotiations for the purchase of hops, the buyer asked if they had been treated with sulphur, adding that if they had he would not even bother asking the price. The seller said none had been used in their cultivation and a contract was entered into. Some sulphur had in fact been used on the hops and when the buyer found out he refused to pay for them. The court held that the false statement about the hops was not a representation, a pre-contractual inducement, but an important description of the goods and therefore a term of the contract. The buyer would not have purchased them had he known the truth.
- The relative expertise of the parties. If the person making the statement has special knowledge or skill, the courts are likely to find that the statement is a term of the contract because of the implication that there is no need to check the accuracy of the statement. In *Oscar Chess Ltd* v *Williams* [1957], the defendant (an ordinary individual) sold a car to

8

the plaintiff (a motor trader) stating that it was a 1948 model (as stated on the vehicle registration document) when in fact it was a 1939 model. The court of appeal held that this was not a contractual term merely a representation, so there was no breach of contract. In this case the buyer was in a better position to check the year of the car than the seller was. In a similar case, however, the court found that a statement made was a term of the contract. In *Dick Bentley Productions Ltd* v *Harold Smith (Motors) Ltd* [1965], a car dealer sold a car stating its mileage to be 20,000 since a replacement engine when in fact it was 80,000. The plaintiffs bought it and later found out that the statements about the car were false. The court of appeal held that the defendant's statement was a term of the contract and they were liable for the breach. The defendants, who had special knowledge as car dealers, were in a better position to know the truth about the car than the plaintiffs.

As you have seen in this session, statements and contract terms can be classified. One possible classification of contract terms is to divide them into two groups, namely express and implied terms. Express terms of a contract are terms which either or both parties to the contract have expressed either verbally or in writing and have agreed to include in the contract. Implied terms, on the other hand, are terms that the parties have not expressed verbally or in writing, and which therefore are not part of the verbal/written contract that has been agreed by the parties. The existence of implied terms depends upon legal rules, which determine in what circumstances the law will imply terms into a contract that have not been expressly stated by the parties. Some terms are implied by common law rules developed by judges and some are implied by statutes such as the Sale of Goods Act 1979. You will study specific examples of implied terms in study session 9 and specific examples of express terms in study sessions 10 – 13.

Although the classification of contract terms into express and implied terms will tell you how they became part of the contract, it will not help you decide what can be done by the courts where one of the parties to the contract has failed to carry out their obligations under the contract. If you want to know what the effect will be if a particular term is breached by a party to a contract, knowledge of a different classification will be useful to you – the classification of contract terms into conditions, warranties and innominate terms. Each term in a contract, whether it is an express term or an implied term, will fall into one of these categories. This classification of conditions, warranties and innominate terms is important, as contract terms are not all treated the same way in the event of breach as they are not all equally important. This is the classification that you will be studying in the rest of this session.

Self-assessment question 8.1

State which of the following statements are false.

1   Advertising 'puffs' are:
     (a) exaggerated statements found in advertisements
     (b) clearly not intended to be relied upon

(continued on next page)

Self-assessment question 8.1 (continued)

    (c)   have no legal effect and can be ignored for contractual purposes.

2   Representations:

    (a)   are factual statements that are made during the pre-contractual stages

    (b)   induce one party to enter into the contract

    (c)   if untrue, can give rise to a claim for breach of contract.

3   Contract terms:

    (a)   may have their origin in statements made during negotiations

    (b)   are not legally binding

    (c)   may be pre-contractual statements which are incorporated into the contract.

4   Contract terms can be classified as:

    (a)   conditions and express terms

    (b)   warranties and implied terms

    (c)   express and implied terms.

Feedback on page 97

8

8.2 Conditions and warranties

Learning activity 8.2

Complete table 8.1. For each column give an example of a decided case (name, brief summary of the relevant facts and an explanation of the legal principle involved) where the courts have held that the term was a condition/warranty.

You will be able to research cases in appendix 2, Case law.

Table 8.1

	Conditions	Warranties
Case name		
Summary of the facts		
Legal principle involved		

Feedback on page 98

A **condition** is an important term in a contract, one that goes to the very root of the contact. If such a term is breached the contract itself will be in jeopardy. Breaching a condition is a serious matter as it entitles the other party not only to sue for damages but also to terminate the contract. If they so wish, however, the injured party has the option of affirming the contract and simply claiming damages.

A **warranty** is regarded as a minor term, something that is ancillary to the main thrust of the contract. As a result of its lesser importance, breach of a warranty will not entitle the injured party to terminate the contract; they will only be entitled to damages.

There are two particular cases with similar facts which explain the difference between conditions and warranties. In *Poussard* v *Spiers and Pond* [1876] an actress was employed to play the leading role in an operetta for a season. She was unable to attend until a week after the season began and the producers, who had to engage a substitute, refused her services when she eventually appeared. They purported to terminate the contract and she sued for breach of contract. The court heard evidence that as the opening night was regarded as very important, the actress's absence amounted to a breach of condition and so the producers were entitled to terminate the contract.

In *Bettini* v *Gye* [1876] a singer was engaged to perform for a whole season. The contract required him to appear six days before the start of the season for rehearsals. He could not attend until three days before the start of the season. The producers treated this as breach of condition and thought they had the right to terminate the contract. The singer sued for breach of contract. The court held that the term relating to attending rehearsals was ancillary to the main part of the contract and so it was a warranty, which only gave the producers the right to receive damages, not to terminate the contract.

When parties are agreeing the terms of their contract they can decide whether those terms are conditions or warranties and the contract can state this. This will give certainty to the situation in the event of those terms being breached. However, there are also circumstances where terms are implied into contracts regardless of the parties' wishes. These are, for example, terms implied by sections 12–15 Sale of Goods Act 1979 (as amended) (SGA 1979), which the statute specifies as conditions and warranties. You will study these statutory implied terms further in study session 9.

It is important not to confuse the uses of the word 'warranty'. In this section it is used as a category in a classification, a label that can be used to identify a term in a contract, to tell you how important it is to the contract and to tell you what the effect will be if it is breached. You may also have come across the word 'warranty' when it is used in other ways, for example to describe a 'guarantee' given when goods are purchased. Do not confuse the two. With law, as with many other subjects, words can be used in different ways – beware!

Self-assessment question 8.2

Explain what conditions and warranties are.

Feedback on page 98

8.3 Innominate terms

Learning activity 8.3

Complete table 8.3. Give an example of a decided case (name, brief summary of the relevant facts and an explanation of the legal principle involved) where the courts have held that the term was innominate.

You will be able to research cases in appendix 2, Case law.

Table 8.3

Innominate terms
Case name
Summary of the facts
Legal principle involved

Feedback on page 98

As you saw in section 8.2 above, parties to a contract can specify whether terms are conditions or warranties depending on how important those terms are. In the same way, statutes can specify whether the terms being implied are conditions or warranties depending on their importance. If the parties or statute do not specify the category to which these terms belong, then the courts have taken to classifying the terms as innominate terms. Innominate terms can also be referred to as intermediate terms.

When an innominate term is breached, the effect of the breach does not depend upon the importance of the term when the contract is entered into as with conditions and warranties. The effect of breaching an innominate term depends on how serious the consequences of the breach are on the contract when the breach actually occurs.

The idea of innominate terms first arose in the case of *Hong Kong Fir Shipping Co. Ltd* v *Kawasaki Kisen Kaisha Ltd* [1962]. The defendants chartered a ship from the plaintiffs for two years. The charter stated the ship was 'in every way fitted for ordinary cargo service' but it was in a poor state of repair, the engine room crew were incompetent, the plaintiff openly admitted the ship was not seaworthy and consequently 20 weeks of the charter were lost. The term was not stated to be a condition or a warranty in the contract. The defendants treated the contract as terminated claiming it was breach of condition, but the plaintiffs disagreed claiming they were only entitled to damages. The court held that the termination was wrongful and the plaintiffs succeeded in their claim. As the parties had not specified that the term was a condition or warranty, the court treated it as an innominate term. To decide what the defendants' rights were, the judges considered whether they had been substantially deprived of the whole of the benefit they were intended to have from the contract. If they had, they would have been entitled to terminate the contract and claim damages, but as the judges held they had not, they could only claim damages.

The new approach used in the *Hong Kong* case was followed in *Cehave NV* v *Bremer Handelsgesellschaft mbH, the Hansa Nord* [1975] and *Reardon Smith Line Ltd* v *Yngar Hansen-Tangen* [1976] where the court said the terms were innominate and considered what the effect of the breach was to decide on the appropriate remedy. Both of these cases are dealt with more fully in appendix 2, Case law.

However, using the approach established in the *Hong Kong* case has its problems since it introduces uncertainty as, with innominate terms, the parties do not know what their rights are on breach of contract until one of them takes the matter to court. The simplest solution is for the parties to a contract to specify in the contract what the consequences would be if the term was breached.

As a result of the uncertainty that innominate terms can introduce, the courts have been reluctant to follow the *Hong Kong* decision and have instead followed the more traditional approach, declaring the term that has been breached to be a condition or a warranty. This approach has been adopted in *The Mihalis Angelos* [1971] and *Bunge Corporation* v *Tradax Export SA* [1981], both of which are explained more fully in appendix 2, Case law.

The rules relating to innominate terms are also relevant for certain terms implied by statute such as sections 13, 14 and 15 Supply of Goods and Services Act 1982. The Act sets out terms relating to skill and care, the time of performance and the right to payment that it implies into contracts as implied terms, that is, innominate terms. Unlike the Sale of Goods Act 1979 (as amended), they are not referred to as implied conditions or warranties. You will study these statutory implied terms further in study session 9.

Self-assessment question 8.3

When would it be possible for a court to find that a term was innominate, and once declared to be innominate, how would the court deal with breach of that term?

Feedback on page 99

Revision question

Now try the revision question for this session on page 239.

Summary

In this session you have discovered classifications of statements and contract terms. You have also studied some of those classifications:

- Advertising puff – no legal effect.
- Representations – if they are untrue factual statements which induce the claimant to enter the contract, they may give rise to legal liability in misrepresentation.
- Contract terms – they can be express (agreed by the parties) or implied (included in the contract by the court or statute).
- Conditions – fundamental to the contract breach or which entitle the innocent party to terminate the contract and/or claim damages.
- Warranties – an ancillary term the breach of which only entitles the innocent party to claim damages.
- Innominate terms – the effect of breach depends on the consequences of the breach, termination and/or damages may be awarded.

You will be considering specific express and implied terms in later sessions.

The important thing to remember about classifications in law is that they are there for a purpose. Usually things are classified in a certain way to make rules easier to understand and to help you apply those rules correctly in appropriate circumstances. If you know the classifications and understand the rules for the different categories, it will help you apply the law in given situations.

Suggested further reading

Griffiths and Griffiths (2002). You should read the sections on contract terms.

Feedback on learning activities and self-assessment questions

Feedback on learning activity 8.1

You will probably have found that many statements are made in advertisements and during negotiations; the longer and more complex the negotiations, the more statements will be made. You may also have experience of false statements being made. If they were made your organisation may have become involved in litigation or may have had to do some hard negotiating to resolve the situation. If it was felt that the supplier was not to be trusted then the transaction may not have proceeded.

In this section you will go on to consider the various types of statements that can be made and what actions can be taken if the suppliers with whom you are negotiating make false statements.

Feedback on self-assessment question 8.1

1   They are all true.
2   (c). Representations, if false, give rise to a claim for misrepresentation.

3   (b). They are legally binding.

4   (a) and (b). The classifications are express and implied terms or conditions, warranties and innominate terms. Some express terms are conditions just as some implied terms are warranties.

Feedback on learning activity 8.2

You may have found cases in appendix 2, Case law which deal with various aspects of contract terms, but the two most suitable cases for answering this question are shown in table 8.2.

Table 8.2

	Conditions	**Warranties**
Case name	*Poussard* v *Spiers and Pond* [1876]	*Bettini* v *Gye* [1876]
Summary of the facts	An actress who was employed to play the leading role in an operetta for a season did not attend until a week after the season began. The producers engaged a substitute, refused her services when she eventually appeared and purported to terminate the contract. She sued for breach of contract. As the opening night was regarded as very important, the actress's absence amounted to a breach of condition, the producers were entitled to terminate the contract and the actress's claim failed.	A singer who was employed to perform for a whole season was required in the contract to attend rehearsals six days before the start of the season. He only attended three days before the season started. The producers treated this as breach of condition and purported to terminate the contract. He sued for breach of contract. As the term relating to attending rehearsals was ancillary to the main part of the contract, it was a warranty which only gave the producers the right to receive damages. They had no right to terminate the contract so the singer's claim succeeded.
Legal principle involved	The term breached was fundamental to the contract so it was a breach of condition permitting the other party to terminate the contract.	The term breached was ancillary to the main part of the contract so breach of it was breach of warranty which permitted a claim for damages but not termination.

Feedback on self-assessment question 8.2

Your answer should include an explanation that they are contract terms and you should go on to explain the differences between them, including the consequences of their breach. Your answer should refer to law, namely relevant cases and statute as set out in this section, the *Poussard* and *Bettini* cases and the SGA 1979 (as amended).

Feedback on learning activity 8.3

You may have found cases in appendix 2, Case law which deal with various aspects of contract terms. Cases where the courts identified terms to be innominate terms could be used in this learning activity as in table 8.4.

Table 8.4

	Innominate terms
Case name	*Hong Kong Fir Shipping Co. Ltd* v *Kawasaki Kisen Kaisha Ltd* [1962]
Summary of the facts	The defendants chartered a ship from the plaintiffs for two years. The charter stated the ship was 'in every way fitted for ordinary cargo service' but it was in a poor state of repair, the engine room crew were incompetent, the plaintiff openly admitted the ship was not seaworthy, and consequently 20 weeks of the charter were lost. The term was not stated to be a condition or a warranty in the contract. The defendants treated the contract as terminated claiming it was breach of condition, but the plaintiffs disagreed claiming they were only entitled to damages.
Legal principle involved	As the parties had not specified that the term was a condition or warranty, the court treated it as an innominate term. To decide what the defendants' rights were, the judges considered whether they had been substantially deprived of the whole of the benefit they were intended to have from the contract. The court held that the termination was wrongful and the plaintiffs succeeded in their claim.

You could also have used *Cehave NV* v *Bremer Handelsgesellschaft mbH, the Hansa Nord* [1975] or *Reardon Smith Line Ltd* v *Yngar Hansen-Tangen* [1976].

Feedback on self-assessment question 8.3

You should have realised that it is only possible for a term to be innominate if the contract either states it to be innominate or if the contract is silent as to what classification the term falls into. If that is the case the courts, when considering how to deal with breach of the term, will have to decide what the term is. From the cases studied in this section, the traditional approach in such circumstances would be for the court to decide whether the term was a condition or warranty and treat it accordingly as stated in section 8.2. If the court decided to follow judicial opinion in the *Hong Kong* case and the cases which followed it, then the term would be found to be an innominate term and to decide how to deal with a breach of that term, the court would consider whether the claimant had been substantially deprived of the whole of the benefit they were intended to have from the contract. If they had, they would have been entitled to terminate the contract and claim damages. If they had not, they could only claim damages.

8

Implied terms

'Everyone lives by selling something.'
(Robert Louis Stevenson (1850–1894), novelist, poet and traveller)

Introduction

In this section you will examine the circumstances when terms are implied into contracts and then you will go on to examine statutory implied terms. You will begin by studying the terms implied by sections 12–15 Sale of Goods Act 1979 (SGA 1979) (as amended) and the effect of their breach as well as attempts to exclude them. You will then study the terms implied under sections 2–5 Supply of Goods and Services Act 1982 (SGSA 1982) (as amended) and examine the effect if they are breached and whether they can be excluded.

Session learning objectives

After completing this session you should be able to:

9.1 Explain the circumstances when terms may be implied into contracts.
9.2 Describe the terms implied into contracts by sections 12–15 SGA 1979 (as amended) and sections 2–5 SGSA 1982 (as amended).
9.3 Explain the effect of breach of the implied terms under sections 12–15 SGA 1979 (as amended) and sections 2–5 SGSA 1982 (as amended) and identify any possible remedies.
9.4 Identify whether terms implied into contracts under the SGA 1979 (as amended) and sections 2–5 SGSA 1982 (as amended) can be excluded.

Unit content coverage

Learning outcome

Explain the impact of both implied and express terms in contracts.

Learning objective

3.3 Discuss and apply implied terms.
   • Key legislation relating to contracts
      – Sale of Goods Act (as amended)
      – Supply of Goods and Services Act
      – Unfair Contract Terms Act

Prior knowledge

Study sessions 4 – 8

9

Resources

Appendix 3, Legislation

Timing

You should set aside about 6 hours to read and complete this session, including learning activities, self-assessment questions, the suggested further reading (if any) and the revision question.

9.1 Why are terms implied into contracts?

An **implied term** is a contract term that has not been expressly agreed, drafted and included in a contract by the parties; instead it is implied into a contract by law regardless of whether both parties agree to it or not.

Learning activity 9.1

Why do you think that the law should find it necessary to imply terms into contracts that have already been agreed by the parties?

Feedback on page 113

Section 3.3 mentions the classical legal principle of 'freedom to contract', that a contract is freely entered into and reflects the will of the parties who are able to include whatever terms they wish. You may be wondering how well this fits with terms being implied into contracts by law. As mentioned in learning activity 9.1 above, sometimes the law might be filling the gaps in a contract to give effect to the unexpressed wishes of the parties, but sometimes the law implies terms regardless of the parties' wishes.

However, there are two important things to bear in mind about implied terms:

- Firstly, the courts will not write the parties' contract for them. If the contract has too many gaps the courts will declare it void for uncertainty. The courts will only imply terms that are vital to the contract when filling gaps, so if something which is not vital to the contract is forgotten, it will not be implied.
- Secondly, if the contract is very detailed, the courts will be reluctant to imply terms into it, presuming that the contract reflects the parties' intentions and that if something is not included it is because the parties did not intend to include it. In such circumstances the only terms that would be implied are those terms the law implies as a result of public policy.

Types of implied terms

Terms can be implied into a contract by:

- The courts

The courts can use rules of local customs or customs in a particular industry or trade as in *Hutton* v *Warren* [1836].

The courts can also use common law rules:

- The business efficacy test is used to decide whether the contract would be workable without the term. This was applied in *The Moorcock* [1889].
- Another of the common law rules is that the courts will imply common terms into all contracts of a particular type to give effect to contractual obligations, often as a matter of policy, as is seen in *Liverpool City Council* v *Irwin* [1976].

- Statute

  Towards the end of the 19th century some of the old common law rules were included in a programme of law reform and codified by the Sale of Goods Act 1893, which was followed by other statutes including the Sale of Goods Act 1979 and the Supply of Goods and Services Act 1982. This legislation was created for policy reasons to protect the consumer.

  The present law relating to implied terms in contracts for the sale of goods is found in the SGA 1979 which was amended by Sale and Supply of Goods Act 1994 (SSGA 1994).

Contracts for the hire of goods and for the supply of goods (when it is not a contract for sale) and services, have terms implied into them by SGSA 1982.

As in this course you will concentrate on the statutory implied terms in various types of contracts, the rest of this session will be devoted to considering the relevant statutory provisions only.

9

Self-assessment question 9.1

Outline the circumstances when terms may be implied into contracts.

Answer the question as a short essay of around 150 words.

Feedback on page 114

9.2 The implied terms under the Sale of Goods Act 1979 (as amended) and the Supply of Goods and Services Act 1982

Learning activity 9.2

Use appendix 3, Legislation to research the Sale of Goods Act 1979 (as amended) and the Supply of Goods and Services Act 1982 which imply terms into contracts. Then answer the following questions:

- What type of contracts have terms implied into them by the SGA 1979 (as amended)?

(continued on next page)

Learning activity 9.2 *(continued)*

- What type of contracts have terms implied into them by the SGSA 1982?

Consider the various contracts to which your organisation is a party. Make a note of any which may be subject to the SGA 1979 (as amended) or the SGSA 1982.

Feedback on page 114

Sale of Goods Act 1979 (as amended)

The SGA 1979 (as amended) applies to contracts which are specifically for the sale of goods as defined in section 2(1). If the contract is for any other type of transaction, for example hire or hire purchase, or if the goods were exchanged by way of barter or given as a gift, this Act does not apply. Sections 12, 13 and 15 apply whether the goods are sold in the course of a business or privately, but section 14 only applies to sales in the course of a business.

In section 61 the Act also explains what 'goods' means. A computer disk was held to be within the definition of 'goods' in *St Albans City and District Council* v *International Computers Ltd* [1996], but a computer program is not, as was held in *Horace Holman Group Ltd* v *Sherwood International Group Ltd* [2001]. However, if a disk which contained a program to enable a computer to perform a particular function was sold with a defective program, it would be subject to the implied terms of the SGA 1979 (as amended).

Sections 12–15 SGA 1979 (as amended) imply several terms into contracts for the sale of goods.

Section 12: the right to sell the goods

Section 12(1) implies a condition into contracts for the sale of goods that the seller has the right to sell the goods, and it implies a term into agreements to sell in the future, that he will have the right to sell the goods by the time the transaction occurs.

Section 12(2) implies a warranty that the goods are free from any encumbrance (for example where the seller had used the goods as security for a loan) not disclosed to the purchaser before the contract is made.

Section 13: description

This implies a condition that where goods are sold by description then they will correspond to that description even if the purchaser selects the goods.

Where a purchaser relies on a description to select the goods, this section will apply. This could include situations where the goods have been bought from a catalogue, or even where the purchaser has seen and handled the goods or inspected them.

However, not everything included in a description will be treated as the description for the purposes of section 13; only the words which identify some essential characteristic of the product will be treated as such. With commercial contracts detailed descriptions must be scrutinised carefully, as if some technical aspects of a detailed specification are not met then the goods can be rejected as being in breach of section 13.

It is also important to show that the description influenced the choice of goods, and that the purchaser did rely on it to make the purchase.

Section 14: quality and fitness of the goods

The implied conditions under section 14 only apply to goods sold in the course of business.

Section 14(2): satisfactory quality

Under section 14(2A) goods are of satisfactory quality if they meet the standard that a reasonable person would expect taking account of any description, the price (if relevant) and any other relevant circumstances.

Under section 14(2C) the implied term as to quality will not apply to anything making the quality unsatisfactory if it has been brought to the purchaser's attention, or where an examination of the goods by the purchaser before the contract was made would have revealed it, or in a sale by sample if it would have been revealed by examination of the sample.

Section 14(3): fitness for purpose

Where the purchaser makes known to the seller any specific purpose for which the goods are purchased, there is an implied condition that the goods supplied will be reasonably fit for the purpose for which they were bought, provided the purchaser relied on the seller's skill and judgement and it was reasonable to do so.

Section 15: sale by sample

This implies three conditions into a sale by sample that the bulk shall correspond with the sample in quality, that the purchaser will have a reasonable opportunity to compare the bulk with the sample, and that the goods will be free from any defect not apparent on reasonable inspection of the sample which would make them unsatisfactory.

Supply of Goods and Services Act 1982

The SGSA 1982 applies to different types of contracts. In Part I of the Act, sections 2–5 apply to contracts which are for the supply of goods, for example if repairs are carried out to an organisation's fleet of company cars, the spare parts used in the repairs would be transferred to the purchaser and

9

would be subject to the implied terms under these sections. They would not be considered as goods that are sold, so SGA 1979 (as amended) would not apply. Sections 2–5 SGSA 1982 are similar to sections 12–15 SGA 1979 (as amended).

Section 2: title

This section implies a condition that the supplier has the right to transfer the goods.

Section 3: description

Under this section there is an implied condition that the goods will match their description.

Section 4(2A): satisfactory quality

This implies a condition that the goods are of satisfactory quality if a reasonable person would regard them as satisfactory taking into account any description, the price (if relevant) and all other relevant circumstances.

Section 4(3): fitness for purpose

Under this section there is an implied condition that the goods are fit for the particular purpose which was made known to the supplier.

Section 5: sample

This section implies a condition that the purchaser will have an opportunity of inspecting the goods to compare the bulk with the sample. This is important in connection with acceptance of the goods.

In Part I of the Act, sections 7–10 apply to contracts which are for the hire of goods; for example, if an organisation's company cars are leased under a hire agreement, those hire contracts would be subject to the implied terms under these sections. Contracts of hire do not involve ownership of the goods being transferred although the person hiring the goods is under a duty to take care of them during the hire period. This is an example of **bailment**; the organisation offering the goods for hire will be the bailor and the person hiring is the bailee. Sections 7–10 SGSA 1982 are similar to sections 12–15 SGA 1979 (as amended).

Section 7: title

This section implies a condition that the bailor of the goods has the right to transfer possession of them for the period of hire, or if the hire is in the future, they will have the right by that time.

Section 8: description

Under this section there is an implied condition that the goods will match their description.

Section 9(2A): satisfactory quality

This implies a condition that the goods are of satisfactory quality if a reasonable person would regard them as satisfactory taking into account any description, the price (if relevant) and all other relevant circumstances.

Section 9(3): fitness for purpose

Under this section there is an implied condition that the goods are fit for the particular purpose that was made known to the bailor.

Section 10: sample

This section implies a condition that the bailee will have an opportunity of inspecting the goods to compare the bulk with the sample. This is important in connection with acceptance of the goods.

In Part II of the Act, sections 13–15 apply to contracts which are for the supply of services; for example, a contract for a garage to service and repair an organisation's company cars would have these terms implied into it in respect of the labour element of the work. Sections 13 and 14 SGSA 1982 relate to contracts where the supplier is acting in the course of a business, but section 15 applies to all contracts whether the supplier is acting in the course of a business or not. Sections 13–15 SGSA 1982 are similar to sections 12–15 SGA 1979 (as amended). There is an important difference with sections 13–15 SGSA 1982 as the terms implied are innominate terms, not conditions or warranties.

Section 13

This implies a term that the supplier will carry out the service with reasonable skill and care.

Section 14

This provides that where the time for the service to be carried out is not fixed by the contract, the supplier should carry out the service within a reasonable time. Reasonableness here will depend on the facts and circumstances of the case.

Section 15

This implies that the purchaser will pay a reasonable price for the service if no price is determined by the contract.

Contracts for the hire purchase of goods are governed by Supply of Goods (Implied Terms) Act 1973, which implies similar terms to sections 12–15 SGA 1979 (as amended) into contracts for hire purchase. You are not required to know the details of that Act for this course.

9

Self-assessment question 9.2

1   Table 9.1 summarises the provisions of sections 12–15 SGA 1979 (as amended). Complete the missing information (denoted by '…').

Table 9.1 Summary table, Sale of Goods Act 1979 (as amended)

Section	Section applies to	Implied term
…	…	Title
		(1) The seller has/will have the right to sell the goods at time of sale
		(2) The goods are free from undisclosed encumbrances
s13	Business and private sellers	…
…	…	Satisfactory quality (SQ)
		Goods are of SQ if they meet the standard that a reasonable person regards as satisfactory taking account of description, price and all relevant factors
s14(3)	…	…
s15	Business and private sellers	Sale by sample
		Bulk is to correspond with sample and goods are to be free from inherent indiscernible defects

2
   (a) Listed below are sections of SGSA 1982. Describe the type of contract to which the sections apply and give an example:
   (i)   sections 2–5
   (ii) sections 7–10
   (iii) sections 13–15.
   (b) Table 9.2 and table 9.3 summarise the provisions of sections 2–5, sections 7–10 and sections 13–15 SGSA 1982 (as amended). Complete the missing information (denoted by '…').

Table 9.2 Supply of Goods and Services 1982 (as amended), sections 2–5 and sections 7–10

Implied term	Applies to	Sections 2–5	Sections 7–10
Title	…	s2	…
		Implies a condition that the supplier has the right to transfer the goods	
Description	Business and private sellers	…	…
	…	…	s9(2)

(continued on next page)

Self-assessment question 9.2 (continued)

Implied term	Applies to	Sections 2–5	Sections 7–10
Satisfactory quality			Implies a condition that the goods hired are of satisfactory quality if a reasonable person would regard them as satisfactory taking into account any description, the price (if relevant) and all other relevant circumstances
Fitness for purpose	...	s4(3) Implies a condition that the goods are fit for the particular purpose which was made known to the supplier	...
Sample	...	...	s10 Implies a condition that the bailee has opportunity to inspect the goods hired to compare bulk and sample

Table 9.3 Supply of Goods and Services 1982 (as amended), sections 13–15

Implied term	Applies to	Sections 13–15
...	...	s13 Implies a term that the supplier will carry out the service with reasonable skill and care
Time	Supplier acting in the course of a business	...
Consideration	...	...

Feedback on page 114

9.3 The effect of breach on the implied terms under the Sale of Goods Act 1979 (as amended) and the Supply of Goods and Services Act 1982

You need to have studied sections 8.2 and 8.3 before studying this section.

Learning activity 9.3

Explain why it is important to know the classification of implied terms.

Feedback on page 116

Sale of Goods Act 1979

Most of the implied terms under SGA 1979 (as amended) that you read about in section 9.2 above are conditions section 12(1) title, section 13 description, section 14(2) satisfactory quality, section 14(3) fitness for purpose and section 15 sale by sample. The implied term under section 12(2) that the goods are free from encumbrances (charges) that have not been disclosed, is a warranty. Consequently when they are breached the parties are aware of the remedies usually available.

Although usually breach of condition under SGA 1979 provides the remedies of termination and damages, in certain situations breach will only give rise to a claim for damages, termination will not be granted. These circumstances are where:

- the purchaser has accepted the goods. Once they are accepted the contract cannot be terminated although damages can be claimed; or
- the purchaser has chosen to treat the breach as a breach of warranty in accordance with section 11(2) SGA 1979 and does not wish to terminate the contract; or
- under sections 13–15 the purchaser is selling in the course of a business and the seller can prove the breach is so slight it would be unreasonable for the purchaser to have the right to terminate the contract by rejecting goods.

Supply of Goods and Services Act 1982

As you might expect the SGSA 1982 treats breach of the implied terms in a similar way to the SGA 1979. The implied terms under SGSA 1982 (as amended) which deal with goods (sections 2 and 7 title, sections 3 and 8 description, sections 4(2) and 9(2) satisfactory quality, sections 4(3) and 9(3) fitness for purpose, and sections 5 and 10 sale by sample) are conditions. If these terms are breached, the purchaser usually has the right to terminate the contract and/or claim damages.

However, there are some circumstances, as with SGA 1979, when breach of sections 3–5 and sections 8–10 will only give rise to a claim for damages, termination will not be available. These circumstances, which are set out in sections 5A and 10A, apply to contracts where:

- the purchaser/bailee is not a consumer; and
- the breach is so slight it would be unreasonable for the purchaser/bailee to terminate the contract.

The implied terms dealing with services (section 13 care and skill, section 14 time, and section 15 consideration) are different. The statute states that they are terms not conditions or warranties and so they are dealt with as innominate terms. As a result the appropriate remedy available in the event of breach cannot be known in advance, as with such terms it is left to the discretion of the court to decide what would be the appropriate remedy; whether this is termination or damages or both depends on how serious the effect of the breach is.

Self-assessment question 9.3

Read through the following questions, identify any statutory implied terms that are breached and explain what remedies are available.

- Jack bought a second-hand flat-screen TV for £400 from one of his neighbours who was emigrating. When he tried to watch it later, it was impossible to see the images on the screen properly and the sound did not work.
- Perfect Printers (PP) received an order to print specialised marketing materials. They contacted All Presses (AP) who sell and hire printing presses and explained their requirements. AP suggested a particular press that would be suitable for PP to hire. Soon after delivery PP commenced printing but realised that the press was not printing as expected. They then discovered that although the machine seemed to work for normal printing it was not capable of producing the type of material required.
- Cousins Ltd (CL) was having the boardroom decorated by Diablo Decorators (DD), a local firm. When the work was almost finished, Alison, the purchasing manager, was able to inspect the room but she immediately saw by the pattern on the wallpaper that it had not been put on straight and that the ceiling paint was starting to peel off after only a few days. DD had selected and used poor-quality paint.

Feedback on page 117

9.4 Excluding implied terms under the Sale of Goods Act 1979 (as amended) and the Supply of Goods and Services Act 1982

Under common law rules an express term could be included in a contract to exclude or limit the liability of a party to a contract, for example a seller of goods. This means that had this been the current law when the SGA 1979 and SGSA 1982 were enacted, sellers/suppliers/bailors could have avoided liability under the statutory implied terms simply by including an express term to exclude liability when forming contracts. In order to protect against express terms which were included in contracts to avoid liability, the Unfair Contract Terms Act 1977 was passed. This established the circumstances when a party can or cannot exclude or limit their liability by including an express term to that effect when they form contracts.

You will be studying exclusion or limitation clauses in study session 12.

Learning activity 9.4

Using appendix 3, Legislation, find out what criteria are applied to decide whether express terms to exclude or limit liability are permitted.

Feedback on page 117

Details of the statutory control of this area are found in the Unfair Contract Terms Act 1977 (UCTA 1977) and the Unfair Terms in Consumer Contracts Regulations 1999 (UTCCR 1999). UTCCR 1999 apply to consumer contracts made by individual consumers. They render invalid terms which are unfair, that is, terms which cause a significant imbalance in the parties' rights and obligations. In the examination you will not be required to demonstrate detailed knowledge of the UTCCR 1999.

Sale of Goods Act 1979 (as amended)

Under section 6(1) UCTA 1977, any express clause which purports to exclude liability in respect of the implied term as to title under section 12 will be void. As to the other implied terms (sections 13–15), to ascertain whether they can be excluded you must consider the position of the parties. If a purchaser deals as a consumer then any express term in the contract which purports to exclude liability will be void under section 6(2) UCTA 1977.

If the purchaser does not deal as a consumer then according to section 6(3) UCTA 1977, any such express term will be subject to the reasonableness test.

The concept of the 'consumer' is important. Under section 12 UCTA 1977 a person deals as a consumer if:

- they do not make the contract in the course of business; and
- the other party does make the contract in the course of business; and
- the goods being sold are of a type ordinarily supplied for private use or consumption.

The courts have applied this concept of the consumer and have found that sometimes a company can purchase goods as a consumer. In *R&B Customs Brokers Co Ltd* v *United Dominions Trust Ltd* [1988], a company, which only purchased cars occasionally, bought a car for a director which was defective. The court held that the purchaser (the company) was dealing as a consumer; the seller could not exclude liability.

The requirement that an exclusion clause should be reasonable is found in section 11(1) UCTA 1977, and section 11(2) specifies that Schedule 2 contains guidelines as to what should be considered when deciding if a clause is reasonable.

Supply of Goods and Services Act 1982 (as amended)

It is permissible under section 11(1) (for transfer of goods and hire) and under section 16(1) (for the supply of services) to exclude terms under SGSA 1982 only as far as allowed by UCTA 1977. Under section 7(1) UCTA 1977, any express clause which purports to exclude liability in respect of the implied term as to title under sections 2 and 7 will be void. As to the other implied terms (sections 3–5 and 8–10), to ascertain whether they can be excluded you must consider the position of the parties. If a purchaser deals as a consumer then any express term in the contract which purports to exclude liability will be void under section 7(2) UCTA 1977.

If the purchaser does not deal as a consumer then according to section 7(3) UCTA 1977, any such express term will be subject to the reasonableness test.

The concept of the consumer and the reasonableness test have already been considered above.

As to sections 13–15 SGSA 1982 which deal with the supply of services, it is possible to exclude them in so far as exclusion is permitted by UCTA 1977. Under section 2 UCTA 1977, if death or personal injury are caused by negligence, they cannot be excluded, but liability for other damage can be excluded provided that the exclusion passes the reasonableness test.

Self-assessment question 9.4

Read through the questions in self-assessment question 9.3 above and then explain whether, if an express exclusion clause had been included in the contract between the parties, it could have been relied upon to avoid liability under the relevant statutory implied term.

Feedback on page 118

Revision question

Now try the revision question for this session on page 239.

Summary

In this section you have studied implied terms. You have learned:

- To describe the terms implied into:
  - contracts for the sale of goods under SGA 1979 (as amended)
  - contracts for the supply of goods and services and the hire of goods under SGSA 1982 (as amended).
- To know and understand the rules relating to the effect of breach of the statutory implied terms and the remedies available.
- To know and understand the rules relating to the limitation or exclusion of liability under the statutory implied terms according to the provisions of UCTA 1977.
- To be able to apply the rules relating to breach of the statutory implied terms and exclusion/limitation of liability for them in given situations.

Suggested further reading

Griffiths and Griffiths (2002). You should read the sections on contract terms.

Wyborn (2000). You could read the section on implied terms.

Feedback on learning activities and self-assessment questions

Feedback on learning activity 9.1

If the parties forgot to state in the contract something that had already been agreed – something which is important – the law could imply a term to 'fill the gap' in order to ensure that the contract will still 'work'. Sometimes there are policy reasons why the law wants to ensure that certain matters should be included in contracts to protect consumers of goods and services.

Feedback on self-assessment question 9.1

Your answer should mention that the courts imply terms into contracts using custom or common law rules when it is necessary to fill gaps where the parties have not expressed their intention to include a certain term, where an implied term is necessary to make the contract work or where as policy the courts decide that contracts of a certain type should have common terms to state the contractual obligations of the parties. Apart from the terms that are implied due to custom and common law there are also the implied terms inserted into various types of contract, namely contracts for the sale and hire of goods and for the supply of goods and services, by statutes such as SGA 1979, SGSA 1982 and SSGA 1994 as a result of Parliament developing legislation to protect consumers as a matter of public policy.

Feedback on learning activity 9.2

- The SGA 1979 covers contracts for the purchase/sale of goods.
- The SGSA 1982 covers contracts for the purchase of services, for the hire of goods, and for the purchase of services where some goods are supplied in connection with the service.

Your lists should include examples which fit into the categories explained in section 9.1.

In the rest of this section you will study these Acts more closely, so if you were not sure which transactions are covered by the Acts, when you have finished the section you could come back to this part and reconsider the lists you have made.

Feedback on self-assessment question 9.2

1

Table 9.4 Summary table, Sale of Goods Act 1979 (as amended)

Section	Section applies to	Implied term
s12	Business and private sellers	Title
		(1) The seller has/will have the right to sell the goods at time of sale
		(2) The goods are free from undisclosed encumbrances
s13	Business and private sellers	Sale by description
		Where the purchaser relies on the description, the goods must match the description (even if you select them

(continued on next page)

Table 9.4 *(continued)*

Section	Section applies to	Implied term
		yourself). Not all words will be descriptive, the test is identification.
s14(2)	Goods sold in the course of business	Satisfactory quality (SQ) Goods are of SQ if they meet the standard that a reasonable person regards as satisfactory taking account of description, price and all relevant factors
s14(3)	Goods sold in the course of business	Fitness for a particular purpose Goods are fit for the particular purpose for which they were bought, whether or not it is the usual purpose provided, it was made known to the seller and the purchaser relied on the seller's skill and judgement in selecting the goods
s15	Business and private sellers	Sale by sample Bulk is to correspond with sample and goods are to be free from inherent indiscernible defects

2
   (a)
      (i) Sections 2–5 – contracts for the supply of goods, for example the paint provided by a firm of decorators engaged to redecorate your offices.
      (ii) Sections 7–10 – contracts for the hire of goods, for example a contract for the hire of the company cars.
      (iii) Sections 13–15 – contracts for the supply of services, for example the labour element provided by the firm of painters redecorating your office.
   (b)

Table 9.5 Summary table, Supply of Goods and Services Act 1982 (as amended), sections 2–5 and sections 7–10

Implied term	Applies to	Sections 2–5	Sections 7–10
Title	Business and private sellers	s2 Implies a condition that the supplier has the right to transfer the goods	s7 Implies a condition that the bailor has the right to hire out the goods
Description	Business and private sellers	s3 Implies a condition that the goods supplied will match their description	s8 Implies a condition that the goods hired will match their description
Satisfactory quality	Goods transferred/ hired in the	s4(2A) Implies a condition that the goods transferred are of	s9(2) Implies a condition that the goods hired are of satisfactory

(continued on next page)

Table 9.5 *(continued)*

Implied term	Applies to	Sections 2–5	Sections 7–10
	course of business	satisfactory quality if a reasonable person would regard them as satisfactory taking into account any description, the price (if relevant) and all other relevant circumstances	quality if a reasonable person would regard them as satisfactory taking into account any description, the price (if relevant) and all other relevant circumstances
Fitness for purpose	Goods supplied/hired in the course of business	s4(3) Implies a condition that the goods are fit for the particular purpose which was made known to the supplier	s9(5) Implies a condition that the goods hired are fit for the particular purpose made known to the bailor
Sample	Business and private sellers	s5 Implies a condition that the purchaser has an opportunity to inspect the goods supplied to compare bulk and sample	s10 Implies a condition that the bailee has an opportunity to inspect the goods hired to compare bulk and sample

Table 9.6 Supply of Goods and Services 1982 (as amended), sections 13–15

Implied term	Applies to	Sections 13–15
Care and skill	Supplier acting in the course of a business	s13 Implies a term that the supplier will carry out the service with reasonable skill and care
Time	Supplier acting in the course of a business	s14 Implies a term that where the time for the service to be carried out is not fixed by the contract, the supplier should carry out the service within a reasonable time. Reasonableness here will depend on the acts and circumstances of the case
Consideration	Supplier acting in the course of business and non-business suppliers	s15 Implies that the purchaser will pay a reasonable price for the service if no price is determined by the contract

Feedback on learning activity 9.3

It is important to know what type of term the implied term is as, if the term is breached (broken), you will be able to work out what the effect of breach will be, that is, what remedies are available. If conditions are breached, termination and/or damages are available. If a warranty is breached only damages are available. If the term is an innominate term, the court will decide whether the purchaser is entitled to termination and damages or just damages depending on how serious the effect of the breach is.

Feedback on self-assessment question 9.3

- This is a contract for the sale of goods which proved not to be of satisfactory quality. However, section 14(2) SGA 1979 would not apply as it appears the neighbour was not selling the TV in the course of business.
- This is a contract for the hire of goods to which SGSA 1982 would apply. It appears that there may be breach of section 9(5) fitness for purpose, which implies a condition into the contract that the goods hired are fit for the particular purpose made known to the bailor. Here, PP informed AP of their special requirements and AP advised which was the appropriate press for them to hire. However, the press seemed totally unsuitable as it could not produce the required material. It is likely that PP will be able to prove breach of the condition, which would enable it to terminate the contract and claim damages. Under section 10A, however, if the bailor is not a consumer and the breach is so slight that it would be unreasonable for it to terminate the contract, only damages are available as a remedy. Here, although PP is not a consumer, the breach appears to be a serious one so section 10A is unlikely to apply.
- This is a contract for the supply of goods and services to which SGSA 1982 would apply. It appears that there may be breaches of section 4(2A), which implies a condition that the goods be of satisfactory quality, and section 13, which implies an innominate term that the supplier will carry out the service with reasonable care and skill. If CL is able to prove its claim under section 4(2A), it will be entitled to terminate the contract and/or claim damages provided section 5A does not apply. Here, it appears that the paint may be of unsatisfactory quality. Under section 5A, if the purchaser is not a consumer (CL is not) and the breach is so slight that it would be unreasonable for it to terminate the contract, then it would only be able to claim damages. Here it is likely that the breach will be considered serious enough that CL will not lose the right to terminate.

  As to section 13, DD may not have carried out the work with reasonable skill and care as the wallpaper was not hung properly. This is likely to be breach of an innominate term and so the remedy, which CL could receive, would depend on how serious the effect of the breach was. If it were serious, CL would be entitled to terminate the contract and may also be able to claim damages. If it is not serious then only damages are available. As the breach here seems serious, CL may have the right to terminate the contract.

Feedback on learning activity 9.4

The criteria that must be considered are:

- The status of the purchaser/bailee, namely whether they are dealing as a consumer or not. This will determine whether the term can be relied upon or not where goods are involved.
- Whether the terms are reasonable. Those terms that are permitted must be reasonable to be effective.

9

Feedback on self-assessment question 9.4

- As none of the statutory implied terms applied, they would not need to be excluded.
- Section 9(5) SGSA 1982 is implied here. If the hire contract between PP and AP included a clause excluding AP's liability under section 9(5), the provisions of UCTA 1977 would need to be considered. PP is not dealing as a consumer within the definition in section 12 UCTA 1977, and so under section 7(3) UCTA 1977 the exclusion clause would only be valid if it was reasonable. Such a clause is unlikely to be found to be reasonable by the courts so the clause is unlikely to be valid.
- Section 4(2A) and section 13 SGSA 1982 apply here. If the contract for the supply of goods and services between CL and DD included a clause excluding AP's liability under section 4(2A) and section 13, the provisions of UCTA 1977 would need to be considered. CL is not dealing as a consumer within the definition in section 12 UCTA 1977, and so under section 7(3) UCTA 1977 the exclusion clause in relation to section 4(2A) would only be valid if it was reasonable. Such a clause is unlikely to be found to be reasonable by the courts, so the clause is unlikely to be valid. The same would be true of section 13 which would also have to pass the reasonableness test.

9

Express terms – key contract terms

Introduction

In this session you will be considering how the courts deal with the various terms that are found in contracts. You will then go on to examine some of the key contract terms in detail, consider what their purpose is, which party is likely to want to rely on particular terms and why this is so.

Session learning objectives

After completing this session you should be able to:

10.1 Explain how the courts will treat contract terms.
10.2 Identify suitable key terms to be used in different contract situations.

Unit content coverage

This study session covers the following topic from the official CIPS unit content document.

Learning outcome

Explain the impact of express terms in contracts.

Learning objective

3.5 Recognise and discuss the use of express contractual terms.
  • Liquidated damages
  • Guarantees
  • Passing of property
  • Subcontracting and assignment
  • Payment
  • Transfer of undertakings and protection of employment regulations
  • Confidentiality
  • Other terms

Prior knowledge

Study sessions 4 – 9 and especially study session 8.

Resources

Appendix 3, Legislation and appendix 4, Contract terms.

10

Timing

You should set aside about 6 hours to read and complete this session, including learning activities, self-assessment questions, the suggested further reading (if any) and the revision question.

10.1 How do courts treat contract terms?

Learning activity 10.1

Find out if your organisation has been involved in any court disputes involving contract terms. Search newspapers, professional journals and the internet to find out about any court actions based on contract terms. What contract terms were involved and what was the court's decision?

You could look at the law or business sections on the following news websites:

- http://timesonline.co.uk
- http://guardianunlimited.co.uk
- http://telegraph.co.uk
- http://news.bbc.co.uk/.

Feedback on page 127

Feedback on page 127

In study session 9 you studied terms that are implied into contracts either because of common law rules developed by judges or due to parliamentary intervention by statutes such as SGA 1979 and SGSA 1982. In this session, and indeed in the three sessions that follow it, you will be studying express contract terms. The parties normally engage in negotiations to reach agreement on the various aspects of the deal between them. That agreement is usually then expressed in the terms of the contract. Normally in negotiations both parties will be trying to get the best deal for themselves, but each side may have to compromise on some points during the negotiations. However, if one of the parties is in a much stronger position, they may be able to insist on the inclusion in the contract of terms more favourable to them.

During the course of the contract the parties will have the various agreed terms to remind them exactly what was decided between them. In most situations either the contract runs smoothly or, if any difficulties or potential disputes do arise, the parties are able to resolve them themselves and come to some arrangement that satisfies them both and so avoids having to take problems elsewhere to seek resolution. Sometimes, however, the parties may find themselves in dispute over the terms of the contract and they may become involved in litigation. When this occurs it is up to the court to examine the evidence and give judgment. In doing so in matters relating to contract terms there are certain matters that the court will always consider whatever the type of term.

10

Firstly the court will consider incorporation. Quite simply this means whether the term is actually included in the contract. When the contract is clearly all set out in one signed document this is a simple thing to check, but life is not always so simple and in some circumstances things may be a little more complicated. You will consider incorporation gain in a little more detail in study session 12 and it is worth remembering that the comments on incorporation, whether they are in this section or in later sessions, are relevant for all contract terms. The reason the court will begin by considering whether a term is incorporated is because if it is not it cannot be relied upon and so the claimant's claim will fail as the term is not part of the contract.

If the court finds that the term is incorporated then it will consider what the clause actually says – it will interpret the clause. Interpretation is relevant for all terms in contracts, but some clauses such as liquidated damages clauses (see section 10.2 below) and force majeure (see section 12.2) will be strictly interpreted by the courts and are by their nature more likely to have problems in this area than others. However, there are some general rules of interpretation that the courts will follow when interpreting contract terms. One of the most important is that if there is any ambiguity the term will be interpreted *contra proferentem*, which means that if there is any ambiguity, the clause will be strictly construed against the person who is seeking to rely on it. You will consider interpretation again in study session 12 and, as with incorporation, interpretation is relevant for all contract terms, as if a term is incorporated the courts must examine it and decide what it aims to do.

10

Self-assessment question 10.1

Answer the following questions by stating which of the answers is correct.

1 If a court finds that a term is incorporated it means that:
   (a) it is not part of the contract
   (b) it is included in the contract
   (c) it is only relevant in company contracts.
2 If a clause is interpreted *contra proferentem*, it means that:
   (a) it will be interpreted against the party who is seeking to rely upon it in the event of any ambiguity
   (b) it is not interpreted strictly
   (c) it will be invalid.

Feedback on page 127

10.2 Some key contract terms

Learning activity 10.2

Obtain copies of your organisation's standard terms and conditions and read them carefully. From your own knowledge and experience, and from

(continued on next page)

Learning activity 10.2 *(continued)*

speaking to your colleagues, find out the purpose of at least three of the clauses.

Feedback on page 127

In this section you should refer to appendix 4, Contract terms, which contains examples of some of the different clauses that can be found in contracts.

Liquidated damages clauses and penalty clauses

Liquidated damages clauses are often used in contracts. They state the amount payable in the event of the contract being breached. These clauses can benefit both parties as the party in breach has the certainty which comes from knowing in advance the sum they will have to pay if they breach the contract. It also benefits the party on the receiving end of the breach, as they do not need to pursue the matter through the courts to prove their case and obtain judgment for whatever sum the court thinks appropriate. Thus they will not waste time and money with litigation. Instead, a purchaser relying on a liquidated damages clause against a seller who is in breach can deduct the relevant sum specified in the clause from any monies payable by them to the seller.

However, liquidated damages clauses must be carefully drafted to ensure that they are interpreted as such. It is essential that the damages claimed are a genuine pre-estimate of the losses that are likely to occur in the event of breach. If they are not then the court may decide that the so-called liquidated damages clause is instead a penalty clause and it will be declared void. The courts have interpreted liquidated damages clauses in many cases including *Dunlop Pneumatic Tyre Co.* v *New Garage & Motor Co. Ltd* [1915], where Dunlop supplied tyres to garages under an agreement for a minimum price on resale. In the event of the agreement being breached by sales below the minimum price, the agreement stated that liquidated damages of £5 were payable per tyre sold in breach. This was held to be a valid liquidated damages clause. The court also indicated that a presumption would be made that a clause was a penalty clause if it referred to different breaches, some slight, some important, but gave rise to the same sum as liquidated damages as they could not then be genuine pre-estimates of loss.

Guarantees

If a contract includes a term under which a seller provides a guarantee for the goods supplied then the term would be legally enforceable. Usually, however, manufacturers are the ones to provide guarantees and as there is no consideration passing between a manufacturer and the ultimate purchaser there may be no contract between them, so manufacturers' guarantees may not be legally enforceable.

In accordance with the Consumer Transactions (Restrictions on Statements) Order 1976, in order for any guarantee which purports to certify goods in respect of defects, satisfactory quality and fitness for purpose to be valid, it must be accompanied by an indication that the purchaser's statutory rights are not affected. Usually this is a statement such as 'Your statutory rights are not affected'.

Passing of property and risk

Property

The phrase 'passing of property' can perhaps be better understood as being the passing of ownership or title to property from one party to another. It is vital for the parties to a contract to know when property passes in the transaction, as when property passes (that is, when title to property passes), the purchaser becomes the owner and can deal with the property as he or she wishes.

Under section 17 SGA 1979, the parties can state in the contract when property is to pass. If the contract is silent on this matter then section 18 SGA 1979 specifies five rules which are used to decide when property passes. You will not be examined on the content of the rules in this course.

The time at which you want property to pass will depend on whether you are the purchaser or the seller. Purchasers usually want property to pass sooner rather than later, perhaps as soon as possible after the contract has been made. Sellers prefer it to pass later, certainly after they have received payment.

Risk

Another reason why it is vital to know when property passes is because section 20(1) SGA 1979 states that when property passes, risk also passes, unless the parties agree otherwise. This means that when ownership passes to the purchaser the risk also passes. For example, should goods be destroyed or damaged in a fire prior to the passing of property, the seller would bear any losses and would still be expected to supply appropriate goods to the purchaser in accordance with the contract. If the goods were destroyed or damaged after the passing of property the purchaser would bear any losses and might be faced with a situation where although the goods were destroyed they would still be obliged to pay for them. Once the parties have established when property and therefore risk passes, they can ensure that appropriate insurance arrangements are made for the period when the risk lies with them.

It is likely that a purchaser would want to include a clause in the contract which would state that, on the making of the contract, property in the goods being purchased under the contract would pass to the purchaser, but that the risk would not. However, the seller is likely to require a different clause to postpone the passing of ownership of the goods; such clauses are known as retention of title clauses.

Retention of title

Under section 19 SGA 1979 the seller has a right to retain ownership of goods until certain specified conditions are fulfilled. The conditions usually concern payment in full being received by the seller. Reliance on retention of title clauses can protect sellers who sell goods to purchasers who then go

10

123

into receivership before payment has been made. In such circumstances, as ownership of the goods has not passed to the purchaser, the seller has the right to recover the goods. Without the clause to rely upon, ownership of the goods may pass to the purchaser and the goods will then be under the control of the receiver with the unpaid seller being treated the same as other unsecured creditors with little prospect of recovering a fraction of the purchase price.

In *Aluminium Industries Vassen BV* v *Romalpa Aluminium Ltd* [1976] the court considered a retention of title clause in a contract for the sale of aluminium foil where the purchaser went into receivership and the seller successfully sued the receiver for recovery of unused foil and also the proceeds of sale of some foil the purchasers had sold on, both of which could be easily traced.

However, difficulties can still arise if the goods are used by the purchaser in a process with other materials such that it becomes impossible to distinguish them. This was considered in the *Romalpa* case where the court held that the foil that had been used in a manufacturing product could not be traced, the seller's title was lost and so the seller could recover neither the foil nor monies for its value. Similar problems were faced in *Borden (UK) Ltd* v *Scottish Timber Products Ltd* [1981] where resin was supplied under a contract which included a retention of title clause. After delivery a receiver was appointed for the purchasers, but the resin supplied had been mixed with other materials to produce chipboard. In circumstances like these the courts only recognise that the retention of title clause will preserve the seller's right of ownership of the goods as long as they remain unused and can be traced.

Retention of title clauses are therefore of most use to sellers where easily identifiable goods are sold that can be traced and recovered and payment has not been made. The actual clause itself can also be used to specify that although property in the goods (ownership) will not pass until the seller has received payment in full, risk can pass. This then means that the purchaser bears the risk of the goods being destroyed or damaged – after all, the goods will be in the possession of the purchaser. The seller my stipulate in the contract that the purchaser must insure the goods as the risk is with them. Sellers may want to state in the retention of title clause that they also reserve the right to enter the purchaser's premises in order to repossess the goods.

Subcontracting and assignment

Subcontracting or assignment usually means that the seller has effectively handed the contract over to a third party. This may not be what the purchaser wants, especially if there are concerns as to whether quality requirements will be met.

With subcontracting, A may have contracted to provide goods/services to B but A will be performing its duties to supply those goods/services by employing C as a subcontractor. In this situation there is a contract between A and B and a contract between A and C, but there is no contract between C and B although C is the one actually performing the service or providing the goods. This means that usually the purchaser (B) is unable to sue the subcontractor (C) in contract. If the subcontractor has been negligent, B may be able to sue in negligence to recover damages for personal injury or damage to property, but B will be unable to sue for damages for pure economic loss where there is no injury or physical damage.

With assignment, the seller A is transferring to the third party C his rights under the contract with B the purchaser.

The purchaser should consider carefully the possible effects of the seller subcontracting or assigning. Generally, sellers can subcontract or assign unless the seller was obviously chosen because of some unique quality. If the purchaser wants to prevent the original seller subcontracting or assigning the work to another, a term could be included in the contract with the seller forbidding subcontracting or assignment. This might be relevant if for example the purchaser wanted to prevent the seller factoring any unpaid invoices, that is, assigning the right to collect monies due on unpaid invoices to a third party.

It may not always be practical to forbid subcontracting where, for example, the sellers rely on subcontractors to carry out some aspect of production of the goods. In such circumstances the purchaser may instead prefer to include a term in the contract with the seller to place restrictions on any subcontracting. Such a clause could identify the subcontractor involved; the purchaser would then know who it was at the contract negotiation stage. It could also specify, for example, that any subcontractor used must belong to the relevant trade organisation or have certification of its quality standards. The purchaser would therefore have some input in the choice of subcontractor.

Payment

Under the SGA 1979, once the price has been agreed, the purchaser is under a duty to pay it, and once property has passed, the seller can sue the purchaser for the price if it remains unpaid. If the purchaser is late in paying, however, the seller cannot simply terminate the contract as the SGA 1979 states that time is not 'of the essence' unless the contract says otherwise. This means that the time of payment is not fundamental to the contract and, as such, late payment will only give rise to a claim for damages not termination. If the seller wants time for payment to be treated as a condition giving rise to a right to terminate the contract then a clause should be included in the contract to that effect.

The seller has a right to claim interest at a rate of 8 per cent above the base rate on any late payments under Late Payment of Commercial Debts (Interest) Act 1998 (LPCDA 1998). The Act also states that if no time is specified for payment, the monies fall due 30 days from either the date of delivery of the goods/performance of the services or the day when the purchaser receives notice of the sum due, whichever is later. If any contract term tries to exclude or postpone the date from which interest runs, it will be subject to the reasonableness test under Unfair Contract Terms Act 1977. You will be examining this reasonableness test in more detail in study session 12. In addition to the interest claimed under LPCDA 1998, sellers also have the right to claim a fixed sum (between £40 and £1,000

10

depending on the amount outstanding), under the Late Payment of Commercial Debt Regulations 2002.

Transfer of undertakings and protection of employment regulations

Organisations may decide to outsource some of their functions to save costs. In the public sector, as a result of compulsory competitive tendering, if a public sector provider loses the tender then that service will effectively be outsourced. If the function is outsourced with some or all of the existing staff, the Transfer of Undertakings (Protection of Employment) Regulations 1981 will apply. Effectively the whole business or the department is being transferred from the seller's legal ownership to the purchaser's as a going concern. The regulations ensure that the purchaser of the business automatically takes on the contractual rights and obligations of the existing employees.

Confidentiality

There is usually a range of information that an organisation would like to keep confidential. Some of the information may be so vital to the organisation that it could be regarded as a bank of trade secrets. If this information unlawfully fell into the hands of a third party, the organisation may then be able to take steps against the third party should they try, for example, to use the knowledge or disclose it further whether or not there was any agreement in force about non-disclosure.

On the other hand, an organisation might have commercial information that others may not recognise as being valuable, but disclosure of it would give competitors an advantage. In this situation the confidential information could only receive protection if it was the subject of a confidentiality clause or a non-disclosure agreement. Sometimes they are used to prevent disclosure of information made available in the tendering procedures, or alternatively the tender documentation can include a proviso on the first page that the document contains information that the purchaser regards as a technically or commercially confidential and it must not therefore be disclosed or copied.

Self-assessment question 10.2

For each of the contract terms mentioned below explain the purpose of the term, state which of the parties is likely to rely on the term and explain why.

- Liquidated damages.
- Passing of property.
- Retention of title.

Feedback on page 128

Revision question

Now try the revision question for this session on page 239.

Summary

In this session you have:

- Considered how the courts will approach contract terms when they have to consider disputes between the parties to a contract and you have seen that the courts will:
  - firstly consider whether the term is incorporated into the contract
  - secondly interpret the term.
- You have also considered various key contract terms that are commonly found in contracts and can explain the purpose of the terms, state which party would usually rely upon the term and explain why. The terms that you have studied in this session are:
  - liquidated damages and penalty clauses
  - guarantees
  - passing of property and risk
  - retention of title
  - subcontracting and assignment
  - payment
  - transfer of undertakings and protection of employment regulations
  - confidentiality.

Suggested further reading

Griffiths and Griffiths (2002). You should read the sections on retention of title, passage of property and risk, liquidated damages, assignment, payment and confidentiality.

Singleton and Lawson (2002). This book has detailed information, set out in short sections, about all of the common terms found in contracts.

Feedback on learning activities and self-assessment questions

Feedback on learning activity 10.1

The news reports you may find will vary according to when you research this activity, but it is not unusual to find stories about disputes in the construction industry which usually involve large projects with several different parties involving contractors and many subcontractors. Disputes often revolve around contract terms relating to delay and faulty work.

Feedback on self-assessment question 10.1

The correct answers are 1(b) and 2(a). The other statements are all wrong.

Feedback on learning activity 10.2

You may find that you are able to work out the purpose of some of the clauses quite easily, but there may be others that are more difficult to understand. Depending on the size and type of organisation that you work

10

in, it is possible that there may be several different sets of standard terms and conditions for various situations. If this is the case you could compare them and see what differences and similarities you find.

In the rest of this section we will look at different kinds of terms and we will continue to do this in the next three sessions too, so by the time you have finished working through study sessions 11 – 13 you should be familiar with various terms commonly found in contracts.

Feedback on self-assessment question 10.2

- Liquidated damages clauses are used to allow a party to a contract to claim damages to compensate for losses suffered as a result of the other party to the contract being in breach of a particular term of the contract.

  Usually it would be the purchaser relying on the clause in situations where, for example, the seller delivered the goods late. A purchaser in these circumstances would want to rely on the clause as it would be a quick, simple, cheap way of receiving the benefit of the damages as they could be deducted from the invoice price without the need to take the matter to court.

  The seller would also be likely to want to rely on such a clause as there would be certainty in the amount that would have to be paid, whereas if a claim was made to court the amount payable in damages would be decided by the judge.
- Passing of property clauses deal with the transfer of ownership from one party to the contract to the other. SGA 1979 says that property passes when the parties want it to pass, so the parties can state in the contract when it is to pass.

  Usually the purchaser will want ownership to be transferred as soon as possible and will want a clause in the contract to that effect. The seller on the other hand will want it to pass later and may want a retention of title clause.
- Retention of title clauses are used to allow a seller to postpone the transfer of ownership of goods until some condition is met, usually payment of the price. Until this happens the seller retains ownership of the goods.

  Sellers use these clauses to avoid them losing the value of goods supplied where ownership of the goods has passed to the purchaser who has not paid for them and who then goes into receivership. If the seller ranks with other unsecured creditors, they are unlikely to receive anything but a fraction of the sum due.

10

Express terms – standard terms for indemnities

Introduction

In this session, first of all you will examine what an indemnity clause is, then you will go on to consider some of the contracts where you are likely to find standard indemnity clauses, namely in intellectual property contracts, in contracts for insurance, where there are accidents and damage and situations involving third parties.

'Make fair agreements and stick to them.'
(Confucius (551–479 BC), Chinese teacher, philosopher and political theorist)

Session learning objectives

After completing this session you should be able to:

11.1 Explain what an indemnity clause is.
11.2 Discuss standard indemnity clauses in contracts.

Unit content coverage

This study session covers the following topic from the official CIPS unit content document.

Learning outcome

Explain the impact of both implied and express terms in contracts.

Learning objective

3.4 Discuss standard contract terms for indemnities.
   • Intellectual property rights
   • Insurances
   • Accidents and damage
   • Third parties

Prior knowledge

Study sessions 4 – 10.

Resources

Appendix 4, Contract terms.

Timing

You should set aside about 4 hours to read and complete this session, including learning activities, self-assessment questions, the suggested further reading (if any) and the revision question.

11.1 What is an indemnity?

Learning activity 11.1

Make a note of what you think the word 'indemnity' means. If you are unfamiliar with the general meaning of the word 'indemnity' look it up in a dictionary. You might want to use online dictionaries such as [www.dictionary.cambridge.org, *Cambridge Dictionaries Online*] or [www.ldoceonline.com, *Longman Dictionary of Contemporary English Online*].

Feedback on page 134

In the learning activity 11.1 above you were able to check your understanding of what an indemnity is. Often indemnities and guarantees are confused. When manufacturers or suppliers give undertakings about the quality of the goods supplied, they are often called guarantees, which may or may not be contractual. However, indemnities compensate for the loss or liability which one person has incurred whether the duty for one of the parties to indemnify arises out of an agreement or not. The word 'indemnity' is also used in connection with insurance as certain kinds of insurance are referred to as contracts of indemnity.

However, there is a fundamental difference between contracts of guarantee and contracts for indemnity. Under a guarantee, the party compensating for the loss has a liability to the party who suffered the loss, which is secondary to and dependent on the liability in the principal contract, so they will 'stand in the shoes' of the original person liable if they cannot pay. Under a contract for indemnity, however, the party indemnifying takes on a liability to the person being indemnified which is separate to the original contract. This can be illustrated by the following examples.

- Situation 1: Company X agrees to supply goods to Company Y on the strength of Director A's promise that 'if Company Y does not pay you, I will'.

  Here, A is taking on a secondary liability for payment of the purchase price of the goods, which is dependent on the liability of Company Y. Is this a guarantee or an indemnity? You will find the answer at the end of this section.
- Situation 2: Company X agrees to supply goods to Company Y on the strength of Director A's promise that 'I will see you paid'.

  Here, A is giving a separate undertaking in that he will make payment in respect of the purchase price of the goods; he has assumed the debt in his own right. Is this a guarantee or an indemnity? You will find the answer at the end of this section.

In the case of *Mountstephen* v *Lakeman* [1874] the courts had to consider this very point and decided that an indemnity had been provided when the defendant had told the plaintiff builder to go ahead and carry out work for a local Board of Health, the defendant being Chairman of the Board, saying 'Do the work and I will see you get paid'.

As you saw when you were considering the formation of contracts in study sessions 4 and 5, although in most contractual situations it is not a legal requirement that contracts should be in writing, where the parties are entering into a contract in a commercial context, it is certainly advisable that they are written. As you saw when you considered the 'battle of the forms' situation in study session 6, often businesses will be dealing with very similar contracts time and time again where they are likely to want to have the same contract terms applying to the contracts they make. As a result of this, most organisations develop their own standard terms which, in negotiations, they try to persuade the other party to agree to use as the basis of the contract between them. Sometimes, however, where there are no negotiation procedures, battle of the forms situations may arise. Situations where indemnities are likely to be relevant arise in many contracts, and consequently organisations tend to include standard terms for indemnities in their contracts where appropriate. In section 11.2 below you will examine some of the types of contracts where standard terms for indemnities are often used. In study session 14 you will also consider situations where the use of standard terms and conditions is taken even further by organisations in particular areas of business who will not only be using standard terms and conditions, but will be using standard model form contracts which have been developed in particular areas of business.

Answers to the questions in the text:

- Situation 1 is a guarantee.
- Situation 2 is an indemnity.

11

Self-assessment question 11.1

State which of the following statements are true:

1
  - (a) An indemnity is an undertaking about the quality of goods supplied.
  - (b) An indemnity is compensation for loss or liability a person has incurred.
  - (c) The duty to indemnify can never arise out of a contract.

2
  - (a) Contracts of guarantee and contracts for indemnity are fundamentally the same.
  - (b) Under a guarantee, the person giving the guarantee takes a separate liability.

(continued on next page)

Self-assessment question 11.1 *(continued)*

   (c) Under an indemnity, the person indemnifying takes on a separate liability.

3   In the case of *Mountstephen* v *Lakeman* [1974]:

   (a) The court decided the defendant gave an indemnity.

   (b) The court decided the defendant gave a guarantee.

   (c) The court decided the defendant gave neither an indemnity nor a guarantee.

Feedback on page 134

11.2 When are indemnity clauses likely to be used?

Learning activity 11.2

Read through the terms of contracts that your organisation uses and the terms in appendix 4, Contract terms. Can you identify any indemnity clauses? What situations are they designed to cover?

Feedback on page 134

Indemnities in the supply chain

With regard to the supply chain, there is no contractual relationship between the parties at the ends of the supply chain. This means that due to the doctrine of privity that you studied in study session 5, the purchaser will not be able to sue the manufacturer directly in contract if, for example, defective goods were supplied. However, a solution to this is provided by the use of indemnities. A chain of indemnity clauses in the various contracts between the parties can link the purchaser and manufacturer so liability for any defective products, for example, can be passed back up the chain from the purchaser to the manufacturer.

However, the chain of indemnity does have its weaknesses.

*   When P purchases 'as a consumer' R is unable to exclude liability for certain matters as a result of the Unfair Contract Terms Act 1977 (UCTA 1977). As between R and D, however, that protection does not exist. R is not purchasing from D 'as a consumer' so under UCTA 1977, D is able to exclude liability provided the exclusion is reasonable. R could therefore be unable to claim an indemnity from D.
*   If one of the parties in the chain, for example D, cannot be traced, or if D becomes insolvent, the chain will break and liability will stay with the last party in the chain.

Different standard terms for indemnities

*   Intellectual property: intellectual property rights (IPR) refer to the rights which protect 'ideas' and can include things such as patents, designs, copyright and trade marks. In situations where IPR are involved in a contract it is not unusual for an indemnity (often limited) to be given in respect of infringement of IPR. Whoever provides the indemnity, it is usual that they would want to be notified as soon as any

11

claim is made against the other party and require the other party not to make any admission of liability. They are also likely to want to have control of any negotiations to settle claims or of any court action that is commenced.

- Insurance: there are two types of insurance contracts – contingency and indemnity. Contingency contracts are typically for things such as life insurance where the insurer promises to pay a fixed sum on the contingent even happening, for example on the death occurring. Indemnity insurance (also often known as indemnity contracts) on the other hand provides full financial compensation if a particular event arises which damages or destroys the thing which is insured, for example fire damage to a factory. The indemnity insurance will pay the full cost of the fire damage provided the factory was insured to its full value. If the factory is under-insured, perhaps only being insured for 75% of its value, then the equivalent percentage would be paid out in respect of the claim for the cost of the damage.

- Accidents and damage: apart from in insurance contracts, indemnity clauses can also be used when one of the parties to a contract is seeking to be indemnified or may be providing an indemnity in situations where accidents could occur or the goods being supplied under the contract could be damaged. Redress could then be obtained from the other party under the indemnity clause.

- Third party rights: claims involving third parties could also involve accidents and damage where, for example, the purchaser incurs costs in defending an action relating to the goods which may have caused damage to a third party or perhaps infringe a third party's trade mark or patent. In such situations the supplier would be liable for costs such as the legal fees of defending the claim.

Indemnity clauses and reasonableness

In study session 12 you will study the Unfair Contract Terms Act 1977 (UCTA 1977) in relation to limitation/exclusion clauses in contracts. In certain circumstances these contract terms are subject to the reasonableness test, that is, they are only valid if they are reasonable. Indemnity clauses too can be subject to this test. Under section 4 UCTA 1977, indemnity clauses in contracts can only be used to make consumers liable to indemnify another person (whether it is a party to the contract or a third party) in respect of liability in contract (or in negligence) if the term is a reasonable one. If it is not, then the term is not valid.

Self-assessment question 11.2

Identify different types of standard form contracts for indemnities and discuss when they would be used.

Write an essay to answer the above question. The word limit is 500 words. Remember – there is information in appendix 5, Advice on answering examination questions which will help you to write essays.

Feedback on page 135

Revision question

Now try the revision question for this session on page 240.

Summary

In this session you have:

- Examined what indemnity clauses are.
- Studied when indemnity clauses are likely to be used by considering:
  - the general position of the chain of indemnity within the supply chain
  - intellectual property rights
  - insurances
  - accidents and damage
  - third parties.

Suggested further reading

Griffiths and Griffiths (2002). You should read the section on indemnities.

Singleton and Lawson (2002). You could read the section on indemnities.

Feedback on learning activities and self-assessment questions

Feedback on learning activity 11.1

You should have found a definition which explained that an **indemnity** is protection against possible losses or damage which may occur. An indemnity will often be in the form of a promise to pay for such losses or damage. In this session you will be examining the circumstances when a party to a contract may wish to have the protection of an indemnity clause against loss or damage by ensuring that the other party to the contract will pay for the loss or damage.

Feedback on self-assessment question 11.1

1. (b) An indemnity is compensation for loss or liability a person has incurred.
2. (c) Under an indemnity, the person indemnifying takes on a separate liability.
3. (a) The court decided the defendant gave an indemnity.

Feedback on learning activity 11.2

There are some areas of business, which, in negotiation, will often be covered by indemnity clauses, and as a result you may have found indemnity clauses in your organisation's contracts in relation to intellectual property rights, insurance and third parties. In section 11.2 you will consider the standard clauses which are often found in contracts in these areas.

Feedback on self-assessment question 11.2

As you saw in section 11.2 it is common to have standard form indemnities in areas such as intellectual property rights, insurance, situations where accidents and damage can arise and also circumstances where there is third-party involvement. In your essay you should examine each of these areas in turn and then give examples of practical situations when they would be used. For example, with situations involving damage to goods which your organisation may be purchasing, your organisation may wish to be indemnified by the other party against that damage. As a result of your consideration of your organisation's contracts, the information in this session and from your discussions with other students or purchasing professionals you will hopefully be able to gather examples of transactions where indemnities are used.

11

11

Express terms – limitation of liability/exclusion clauses

Introduction

In this session you will be considering more of the express terms commonly found in contracts, namely clauses by which the parties attempt to limit or exclude their liability under the contract. You will examine the different problems which can arise with these clauses and understand how the courts will treat them. You will also consider the circumstances where they can and cannot be relied upon by the parties.

On contract clauses 'there's all this language where you can't jump out of a plane or ride motorcycles. You have to go home and just sit there.'
(Ben Affleck, American actor)

Session learning objectives

After completing this session you should be able to:

12.1 Identify clauses, which are limitation of liability or exclusion clauses and explain how the courts will treat such clauses.
12.2 Apply the tests of incorporation, interpretation and reasonableness to limitation/exclusion clauses.
12.3 Identify suitable limitation/exclusion clauses to be used in contracts.

Unit content coverage

This study session covers the following topics from the official CIPS unit content document.

Learning outcome

Explain the impact of both implied and express terms in contracts.

Learning objectives

3.3 Discuss and apply:
  • Key legislation relating to contracts
  • Unfair Contract Terms Act
3.5 Recognise and discuss the use of express contractual terms.

Prior knowledge

Study sessions 4 – 11 and especially study session 10.

Resources

Appendix 2, Case law, appendix 3, Legislation and appendix 4, Contract terms.

12

Timing

You should set aside about 6 hours to read and complete this session, including learning activities, self-assessment questions, the suggested further reading (if any) and the revision question.

12.1 What are limitation of liability/exclusion clauses?

Learning activity 12.1

Look at the terms used by your organisation and its suppliers, also use the internet to find other organisations' terms. Find examples of:

- clauses which try to avoid liability either by excluding it completely or by limiting it in some way
- clauses where one of the parties is trying to limit its liability if some event specified in the clause which is outside their control should occur.

Read through the clauses to familiarise yourself with them. You will be returning to them in the activities which follow in this session.

Feedback on page 145

In contractual situations, each party will often try to avoid or limit its liability to the other party when problems arise which means that they are unable to fulfil their obligations under the contract. The parties do this by including certain clauses in the contract.

If a party attempts to exclude or be exempt from all liability, the clauses are often referred to as exclusion or exemption clauses. If a party is trying to limit its liability, the clause will be referred to as a limitation clause. You may come across all of these names, but essentially these clauses are all treated the same way by the courts as far as deciding if they are enforceable or not.

There is also another common clause found in many contracts that is subjected to exactly the same rules as exclusion/limitation clauses and this is the force majeure clause which is a type of limitation clause. One of the ways a contract can end is by frustration. This means that when the parties entered into their contract it was quite feasible, but as a result of an unforeseen change of circumstances beyond the parties' control, the contract became impossible to perform, and so it is terminated because it is frustrated. If the parties do not want the contract to terminate for frustration, they can include a force majeure clause specifying certain events which could occur in the future and which may make the contract impossible to perform. As those events are now foreseen and included in the contract in a force majeure clause, this prevents the contract from being frustrated if any of those events occur and prevent the party from fulfilling its obligations under the contract. In study session 13 you will consider

12

frustration and force majeure clauses again when you study termination of contracts and related clauses.

When the parties to a contract are in dispute over the terms, one of the parties may decide to commence legal proceedings against the other. When hearing the case, before giving its judgment the court will examine the terms of the contract and any other relevant evidence presented by the parties. In coming to its decision, there are certain tests that the court must apply to exclusion clauses. Two of them – incorporation and interpretation – have already been mentioned in study session 10. Incorporation is important for all terms, and whilst interpretation is relevant for all terms too, it is more important for some rather than others, as, due to the nature of some contract clauses, they must be drafted extremely carefully. However, the third test – the 'reasonableness' test – is only applicable to exclusion/limitation clauses. You will examine these tests in more detail in section 12.2 below.

Self-assessment question 12.1

Use the clues below to identify the correct words and complete the quiz. When the word quiz is completed correctly you should be able to identify the mystery word in the column marked with the asterisk.

1 To be enforceable an exclusion clause must be ....
2 UCTA 1977 states that some exclusion clauses must be ....
3 A way that contracts can terminate.
4 The presence of this can avoid frustration.
5 What does the court apply to exclusion clauses?
6 The clause is scrutinised by the judge when this is done.

Figure 12.1

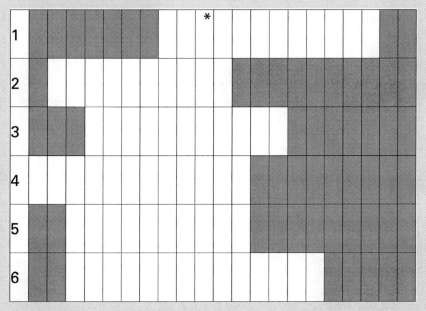

Feedback on page 145

12.2 Common law and statutory tests applicable to limitation/exclusion clauses

Learning activity 12.2

Consider the procedures followed when contracts are being entered into at your organisation. Could situations arise when terms that your organisation wanted to rely upon were not part of the contract? What steps could be taken to avoid such occurrences?

Feedback on page 146

In this section you will examine the three tests applied by the courts when considering contract terms. It is important that you know what the tests are and that you understand them well enough to apply them when faced with situations in problem questions and in real life.

The first two tests – incorporation and interpretation – are common law tests that have been developed by the courts over a period of time. The third test, the reasonableness test, is statutory.

Incorporation

It is worth remembering that the comments on incorporation, whether they are in this section or in later sections, are relevant for all contract terms.

Firstly the court will consider whether the clause is incorporated or included in the contract. You may think that this would be an obvious thing to check, but the issue of whether a term is included is not always as simple as it might seem.

A clause must be validly incorporated at the time the contract is made. This is illustrated by the case of *Olley* v *Marlborough Court Ltd* [1949] in which the plaintiffs booked into a hotel, the contract being made at the reception desk although in their room was a notice containing a clause excluding liability for theft, which they saw later. During their stay some of their belongings were stolen but as the exclusion clause was held not to be incorporated the hotel were liable.

In deciding whether the clause is incorporated, it is useful to consider whether the contract formation and the exclusion clause were connected by time and place, or whether, as in *Olley*, they were separated by them. The reason the court begins by considering incorporation is that if the clause is not incorporated there is no need to go any further as the clause is not valid and will provide no protection for the liable party.

- *Signed documents* There are, of course, situations where all the terms in the contract are clearly set out in one signed document and they are all clearly incorporated into the contract as the parties to the agreement are bound by their signatures whether they have read the document or not,

12

as the plaintiff found to her cost in *L'Estrange* v *Graucob* [1934], when she was bound by her signature on an agreement that she had not read which included an exclusion clause.

- *Notices* If there is no signed document, only an unsigned ticket or notice, an exclusion clause can still be incorporated provided the person receiving the unsigned ticket realised it was a contractual document and also the exclusion clause was brought to their attention. The more serious the exclusion clause, the more notice should be given of the clause. In *Interfoto Picture Library* v *Stiletto Visual Programmes Ltd* [1988], a very onerous clause in a standard form contract was held not to be incorporated due to a lack of appropriate notice being given.

- *Previous course of dealings* Where parties have a longstanding course of dealing, or where certain customs or trade practices apply, the courts may find that exclusion clauses are incorporated into contracts. This really applies to a business context. The courts are unlikely to find clauses incorporated in this way if one of the parties is a consumer, as can be seen in the cases of *Kendall (Henry) & Sons (a firm)* v *William Lillico & Sons Ltd* [1969]] and *Hollier* v *Rambler Motors (AMC) Ltd* [1972].

In other situations, however, in order to decide whether a term is incorporated, you may need to consider how the contract was formed. If, for example, with standard terms and conditions, a battle of the forms situation arose, you would need to decide who won the battle and consequently whose terms bind the contract. Having decided this it will be clear whether the term in question was incorporated or not.

Interpretation

If the court finds that the term is incorporated, then it will consider what the clause actually says – it will interpret the clause. Interpretation is relevant for all terms in contracts but it is particularly important for some. The courts interpret exclusion clauses, and especially force majeure clauses, strictly. If a party wishes to rely on an exclusion clause it should be carefully drafted, as if the wording of the clause does not specify the liability that has arisen, the clause will not apply to the situation that has occurred. The situation is the same with force majeure clauses which specify events outside the parties' control which may cause damage. If, for example, the clause includes inability to supply the goods due to a strike but the goods could not be supplied due to delay in receipt of materials, then the force majeure clause would not cover those circumstances.

In the event that there is any ambiguity, the term will be interpreted *contra proferentem*, which means it will be construed or interpreted against the person who is seeking to rely on it, and only if it clearly covers the exclusion in question will it be allowed.

The reasonableness test under the Unfair Contract Terms Act 1977 (UCTA 1977)

The Unfair Contract Terms Act 1977 applies to exclusion/limitation clauses. According to UCTA 1977, certain exclusion clauses will be void

12

whereas others will be valid if they are reasonable. UCTA 1977 applies the reasonableness test to business liability where contracts are on written standard terms or are made with a consumer.

The status of the party wishing to rely on the clause is therefore considered. The status of the other party is also examined to decide the level of protection the Act will provide. This depends on whether the other party is 'dealing as a consumer', which is defined in section 12 as being that:

- the person does not make the contract in the course of a business or hold himself out to do so; and
- the other party seeking to rely on the exclusion does make the contract in the course of business; and
- if the contract is for the sale or hire of goods, the goods are of a type which is normally supplied for private use.

The idea that someone is dealing as a consumer includes those normally considered to be consumers (non business) but a business can also be dealing as a consumer if it is purchasing goods which are merely incidental to the business. For example, if a foundry purchased a car for its managing director, the car would be incidental not integral to the foundry's business of smelting metal and consequently in that purchase the foundry is dealing as a consumer; but if it were to purchase raw materials for the foundry it would not be dealing as a consumer as they would be an integral part of its business, as was decided in the case of *Feldaroll Foundry plc* v *Hermes Leasing (London) Ltd* [2004].

UCTA 1977 applies to exclusion/limitation clauses (and remember – force majeure clauses also try to exclude liability) which seek to exclude liability under express or implied terms. In study session 9 you considered section 6 UCTA 1977 in relation to attempts to exclude the implied statutory terms under the Sale of Goods Act 1979 (SGA 1979) in relation to contracts for the sale of goods, and you considered section 7 UCTA 1977 in relation to attempts to exclude the implied statutory terms under Supply of Goods and Services Act 1982 (SGSA 1982) in relation to contracts for the supply of goods and services and the hire of goods. You may wish to return to study session 9 to refresh your memory about excluding statutory implied terms. Attempts to exclude liability relating to title and description will be void. As to the test of reasonableness, generally it applies to business sellers, although if the purchaser deals as a consumer the exclusion clause may be void. If the purchaser does not deal as a consumer, usually the clause will be valid if it is reasonable. Section 11 UCTA 1977 states that the burden of showing that the exclusion clause is reasonable lies with the person who is seeking to rely on it. In addition, Schedule 2 UCTA 1977 sets out criteria to be applied when the reasonableness test is being considered. The court's decision as to whether a clause is reasonable or not is a question of fact. In the case of *St Albans City and District Council* v *International Computers Ltd* [1996], a clause seeking to limit the defendant's liability to £100,000 was held to be unreasonable as the figure was too small in comparison to the potential and actual losses when an error in software sold by the defendant to the plaintiff local authority meant that it miscalculated the community charge. It was treated as a business-to-business transaction and when the reasonableness test was applied the clause was held not to be reasonable and was invalid. The defendants were not therefore able to rely upon it.

Apart from the control of exclusion clauses in UCTA 1977 the law also regulates this area of law by the Unfair Terms in Consumer Contracts Regulations 1999. However, these regulations only apply to contracts which have not been individually negotiated where the seller or supplier is a business and the other party is a consumer and regulate terms which are unfair. There is limited coverage of these regulations in your syllabus and you will not be required to know about them in detail.

Self-assessment question 12.2

Write an essay answering the following question. The word limit is 750 words.

What restrictions does the law place upon the right to exclude or limit liability for contractual breaches in a commercial contract?

Feedback on page 146

12.3 Contract terms to limit or exclude liability

Learning activity 12.3

Consider any experience you have but also talk to colleagues and other purchasing professionals to discover what their experiences are of exclusion clauses being successfully or unsuccessfully relied upon. Have any disputes gone to court?

Imagine that you are the judge hearing cases based on exclusion/limitation clauses and force majeure clauses. Take some time with this activity and think of the various matters you might need to consider in your judgment in order to decide if the clause in question can be relied upon. Make a list of these.

Now return to the exclusion and force majeure clauses which you used in learning activity 12.1 above. Decide whether it is likely that those clauses could be relied upon to exclude liability.

Feedback on page 146

It is common for organisations to take steps to protect themselves by using clauses to exclude liability, so such clauses are commonly found in contracts. Alternatively an organisation may wish to protect itself by limiting its liability rather than excluding it completely. This way the organisation is actually accepting some responsibility and therefore liability, but they may be capping that liability at the contract price or a percentage of it. However, whichever course the organisation decides to take with its clauses, they will all be subject to legal control in the form of the three tests examined in section 12.2 above.

Force majeure clauses deal with situations where the parties are trying to state what will happen if the contract cannot be performed due to events beyond their control. An example of frustration could be that a contract to hire a theatre for a performance on a specific night was frustrated (impossible to perform) when the theatre burned down, as happened in *Taylor* v *Caldwell* [1863]. The clause will specify the events that are foreseen by the parties, and if the event does occur and it prevents the performance of the contract, then the contract can specify what is to happen. This could be that additional time can be given for performance, or the supplier would be allowed to delay performance without being penalised in any way, or could perhaps even terminate the contract.

Whenever you are considering exclusion/limitation clauses and force majeure clauses in contracts with suppliers you should bear in mind the issues covered in this session. When you are considering given situations in problem questions you should remember the type of questions you asked yourself in learning activity 12.3 above when deciding whether those clauses could be relied upon or not. They should help you develop a systematic approach to analysing situations when applying the law.

12

Self-assessment question 12.3

Bikes 4 Hire Ltd (B4H) hires bicycles to members of the public for recreational purposes and it has outlets at most of the major UK holiday resorts. B4H negotiated the purchase of a large number of bikes from a major bicycle supplier in the UK, Wheels Galore Ltd (WG). These were to replace most of B4H's existing machines. Although it was agreed that the bikes would be delivered on specified dates ready for the beginning of the holiday season, they arrived six weeks late. During the Easter holidays, a busy time for B4H, most of the outlets had insufficient bikes to meet demand and B4H suffered loss of income in excess of £20,000 for the Easter holidays alone.

Jane, the newly appointed head of purchasing, has spoken to the suppliers who have referred her to clause 20 of the contract.

Jane checks the file for the contract that was negotiated by the former head of purchasing at B4H and discovers that the delivery dates were specified in the contract which also stated that time is of the essence. The contract also includes clause 20 which reads:

> We will do our best to meet your requirements however we will not be held liable for any loss of income in excess of £500 incurred as a result of missed or late delivery.

(continued on next page)

Self-assessment question 12.3 *(continued)*

Advise Jane as to what rights, if any, B4H may have against WG's failure to deliver in accordance with the dates stated in the contract.

Feedback on page 147

Revision question

Now try the revision question for this session on page 240.

Summary

In this session you have:

- examined what limitation/exclusion clauses are
- considered the common law tests of incorporation and interpretation and the statutory test under the Unfair Contract Terms Act 1977 of reasonableness that are applied to exclusion/limitation clauses
- examined practical problems to apply the legal principles relevant to limitation/exclusion clauses.

Suggested further reading

Griffiths and Griffiths (2002). You should read the sections on limitation and exclusion clauses.

Singleton and Lawson (2002). This book has detailed information set out in short sections on all of the common terms found in contracts.

Wyborn (2000). You could read the sections on force majeure, frustration of contract and unfair contract terms.

Feedback on learning activities and self-assessment questions

Feedback on learning activity 12.1

You should have been able to find appropriate clauses in the contract terms which you examined. If you have not been able to do so, look at appendix 4, Contract terms. Remember, when you read a contract if each clause has a title do not assume that the title is correct. Read the clause yourself and decide what type of clause it is by what the clause states, not what its label might say.

Feedback on self-assessment question 12.1

You should have completed the word quiz as shown; 'clause' is the mystery word.

12

Figure 12.2

1						I	N	C*	O	R	P	O	R	A	T	E	D
2		R	E	A	S	O	N	A	B	L	E						
3			F	R	U	S	T	R	A	T	I	O	N				
4	F	O	R	C	EM	A	J	E	U	R	E						
5		T	H	R	E	E	T	E	S	T	S						
6		I	N	T	E	R	P	R	E	T	A	T	I	O	N		

Feedback on learning activity 12.2

This could happen if your organisation's administrative procedures were disorganised when entering into contracts or if it lost the battle of the forms. To avoid such situations arising correct procedures should be adopted when entering contracts. To check whether you correctly identified ways to avoid the battle of the forms look at section 6.3.

Feedback on self-assessment question 12.2

This question requires you to explain the three ways that the law controls the use of exclusion clauses in contracts. You are expected to deal with the common law controls or tests of incorporation and interpretation and also the statutory control of the reasonableness test under UCTA 1977. Good answers will include relevant cases and will also refer to and explain relevant sections of the Act.

Feedback on learning activity 12.3

Your list should include matters such as:

* Is the clause part of the contract?
* Was the other party's attention drawn to the exclusion clause appropriately?
* How is the clause drafted – what does it say exactly?
* Is the clause clear?
* Is there any ambiguity?
* If the clause specifies certain events or situations, is what happened in the facts of the present case you are judging included in the specified events?
* How is UCTA 1977 relevant to the clause?
* What is being excluded?

12

146

- What is the status of the party relying on the clause?
- What is the status of the other party?
- Is the exclusion clause void?
- Should the reasonableness test be applied?
- What criteria are considered when considering if a clause is reasonable?
- What are the relevant sections of UCTA 1977 which deal with these issues?

You should also have considered any of the above matters which are relevant for transactions involving the clauses you considered.

Feedback on self-assessment question 12.3

You should refresh your memory about the correct technique for answering legal problem questions in appendix 5, Advice on answering examination questions.

This question concerns the application of an express term of the contract which seeks to limit liability. B4H have suffered loss of income due to late delivery of bikes and need to consider whether they have a valid claim for the losses they have incurred against WG, who will seek to rely on the limitation clause. To advise Jane you must consider the contract terms and, by applying the relevant tests, decide if the limitation clause is valid.

Firstly, you must consider whether the clause is incorporated or included in the contract. If it is, WG can rely on it; if it is not, they cannot. You could illustrate your answer by using a relevant case such as *Olley* v *Marlborough Court Ltd* [1949] which illustrates the principle. You should then apply it to the acts and advise Jane. Here it seems that the clause is validly incorporated into the contract agreed between B4H and WG.

As to interpretation of the clause, it appears to apply to the situation in question where there was late delivery which caused loss of income. The courts are likely to find that the clause is unambiguous and applicable to the events in question.

The third test is found in the Unfair Contract Terms Act 1977 under which consideration must be given to the status of the purchaser and supplier. The Act applies to business sellers like WG. Here B4H are not dealing as a consumer so the rule to be applied is that if it is reasonable it will be valid. Under section 11 UCTA 1977 the burden of proving that the clause is reasonable will fall upon WG as they are seeking to rely upon it. Schedule 2 UCTA 1977 sets out criteria which the court will apply to decide whether or not the clause is reasonable. You could also refer to the case of *St Albans City and District Council* v *International Computers Ltd* [1996] in which the court considered a clause which purported to limit liability for losses caused by defective software to £100,000. In that case the court found the clause was unreasonable in the circumstances taking into account the likely losses that could be incurred. Applying the law to the present case it would appear that the courts are likely to find that the limitation of £500 for losses is too small bearing in mind the possible losses that could occur, and so it is unlikely that WG will be able to rely upon it. B4H could therefore claim in full for the losses they have incurred.

12

Express terms to resolve disputes and vary, renew and terminate contracts

Introduction

In this session you will be studying various terms which are used to deal with issues such as changing, renewing and terminating the contract. Before that, however, you will study some of the issues relating to the use of alternative forms of dispute resolution and consider contract terms which are used in connection with dispute resolution.

'Litigation: A machine, which you go into as a pig and come out of as a sausage.'
(A Bierce (1842–1914), American writer, journalist and editor)

Session learning objectives

After completing this session you should be able to:

13.1 Compare and contrast litigation and alternative dispute resolution.
13.2 Identify suitable contract terms to deal with resolution of disputes, variation, renewal and termination of contracts.

Unit content coverage

This study session covers the following topic from the official CIPS unit content document.

Learning outcome

Identify a range of legal aspects in relation to the contracting process.

Recognise the remedies for breaches of contracts and draft terms to cover such risks.

Learning objective

3.6 Identify the provision in contracts for amendments, change, review and renewal.
  • Contract duration.
  • Dispute resolution.
  • Default and termination clauses.
  • Variation and change control.
  • Contract renewal.

Prior knowledge

Study sessions 4 – 12

Resources

Appendix 2, Case law and appendix 4, Contract terms.

13

Timing

You should set aside about 4 hours to read and complete this session, including learning activities, self-assessment questions, the suggested further reading (if any) and the revision question.

13.1 Litigation or alternative dispute resolution?

Learning activity 13.1

Find out from colleagues whether they have been involved in any litigation or alternative dispute resolution and what their experiences were. Consider your own experience of these things. What conclusions can you draw from your experiences and those of other business professionals?

Feedback on page 156

Types of alternative dispute resolution

When parties have contractual disputes they do not always turn to the courts to resolve them. There are alternative methods of dispute resolution. When problems arise, wise individuals try to find a solution by negotiation. Most disputes are resolved this way, often with the parties taking a commercial view of the situation and coming to a mutually satisfactory arrangement themselves. Sometimes matters are resolved with the assistance of a conciliator. Mediation is another method of dispute resolution available, whereby a neutral third party encourages all of the parties involved to consider not their legal rights, but their commercial interests, and aims to get them to agree to a compromise that will give both sides something of benefit. If the negotiations are successful and all parties agree to observe the outcome, they can sign an agreement to signify their acceptance to have a legally binding agreement to settle the dispute. Some professional or trade organisations have their own schemes for mediation or arbitration which businesses may use to resolve disputes, and there are also bodies such as ACAS which can become involved in contractual disputes between employers and employees. If negotiations are not successful or are only partially successful, however, the parties can still take the outstanding issues to arbitration or litigation if they wish.

With arbitration or litigation, all of the parties involved are bound by the decision reached after the arbitrator or judge has considered the submissions and the evidence. They are therefore different in that respect to negotiation, conciliation or mediation. If the parties must decide between going to arbitration or litigation in order to seek resolution of their dispute, there are various factors to consider.

Litigation or arbitration?

Advantages of arbitration over litigation include the following:

- Less formality – arbitration is less formal both in respect of the atmosphere at hearings and the procedures involved.

13

- More flexibility – as precedent does not apply to arbitration hearings, arbitrators do not have to follow previous decisions and so there is greater flexibility.
- Choice of arbitrator – parties can choose the arbitrator, who could be an expert in a specialist technical field and would therefore have greater specialist knowledge than a judge.
- No publicity – as proceedings are held in private, arbitration avoids publicity.
- Less expensive – the procedure is often cheaper, and as arbitration usually takes less time even though the arbitrator's costs are high, overall the costs are likely to be less than with litigation. Fees may be reduced further if there is no legal representation.
- Speed – it is usually quicker than litigation.
- Enforcement – the arbitrator's award can be enforced in the same way as a court judgment if the party at fault refuses to comply.

Disadvantages of arbitration in comparison with litigation include the following:

- Lack of legal expertise – arbitrators may be unskilled in interpreting and applying complex legal rules.
- Lack of formal rules – this may lead to unpredictable decisions which may be inconsistent.
- Parties may still be involved in litigation – whether for the proceedings or just to enforce the arbitrator's award.
- Restriction on appeals – appeals from arbitration can only be on a point of law not fact.

You will be considering alternative methods of dispute resolution again in study session 16 when international contracts are considered.

13

Self-assessment question 13.1

Explain why organisations might choose to include a dispute resolution clause in their contracts.

Feedback on page 156

13.2 Contract terms for dispute resolution and variation, renewal, and termination of contracts

Learning activity 13.2

Read through the terms of contracts that your organisation uses and try to identify any alternative dispute resolution, variation, renewal or termination clauses. Why do you think these terms were included in the contracts?

Feedback on page 156

Dispute resolution

Although a contract clause which seeks to prevent the parties having their rights determined by the courts would normally be void, a clause stating that any dispute arising will be dealt with by arbitration is valid, provided that it does not preclude any point of law which arises being dealt with by the courts. This principle was decided in the case of *Scott* v *Avery* [1855]; consequently such clauses are often known as *Scott* v *Avery* clauses. If they are included in a contract, before any dispute can be taken through the courts it must first be dealt with by arbitration.

Variation

Situations might arise where a party to a contract may wish to make changes to the contract. It would normally not be possible for this to occur without the other party agreeing to any change. However, if both parties wish to amend the contract, it would be possible to do so and consequently, once amended, the 'new' contract would, in some way, be different to the original contract. If the parties did amend the contract it would be necessary for each of them to assume a new duty under the contract as, if you think back to what you learned in study session 5, for a contract to be valid, consideration must be given. The same is true if a contract is amended.

The need for consideration could prove to be a stumbling block if an amendment means that one party will receive some sort of benefit perhaps by its obligations being reduced or relaxed, whereas the other party may receive no benefit at all, for example if organisation A agreed to purchase goods from organisation B for £10,000 but then A contacts B saying they now only wish to pay £9,500 for the goods. If the parties agree that the price should be reduced, then it appears that A is receiving benefit from the amendment as it is paying a lower price for the goods. B appears to be receiving no benefit from the amendment, no consideration is being given by A for the benefit of a reduction in price which B is agreeing to A having. This amendment then would not be a valid variation of the contract between A and B. However, if the parties were to also agree that instead of B delivering the goods to A's many depots all around the country, under the amendment they would only deliver to a central hub not far from their own premises, that could be consideration for them agreeing to the reduction in price, as the requirement for them to deliver the goods has been relaxed. You could read about the case of *Atlas Express Ltd* v *Kafco (Importers and Distributors) Ltd* [1989] in the case appendix which deals with this situation where one party imposed a change in the contract on the other party.

It is best for all concerned if any changes to the contract are agreed in writing. The parties may also wish to include in the contract a written procedure to deal with any suggested changes which will ensure that suggestions are recorded in writing usually in the form of a Change Control Note (CCN). The CCN can record all relevant details about the amendment such as

- the reason it is made
- the results of any impact analysis carried out to see what the impact of the amendment will be on the contract

13

- the details of the amendment including any changes to the specification
- the price of the variation
- the timetable for implementation.

If the seller is suggesting a change, it will issue a CCN; if the purchaser wishes to amend the contract, it will request the seller to issue the CCN. The other party will then have a specific time to consider the CCN and then reply with an acceptance, rejection or a request for further information. If the CNN is accepted it will be signed by both parties and it will be a valid variation of the contract.

Contract renewal

Should the parties include a renewal clause in the contract it would mean that, before the existing contract comes to an end, the parties will agree to enter into a new contract. Usually the new contract would begin immediately after the original ends. If the parties wish to have provision for renewal of contracts, as with variations, it would be advisable to set out in the contract a procedure to deal with the possibility of renewal. If one of the parties wanted to renew, a notice to this effect could be served on the other, who would then consider it and either accept or reject the proposal.

Contract duration

Contracts often contain provisions relating to the duration of a contract as well as the circumstances when a contract will come to an end. You will consider termination of contracts later in this section. As for duration, if the contract is for a fixed term this would usually be stated. At the end of the fixed period the contract would naturally come to an end through lapse of time. Alternatively, should the parties, when drafting the contract, wish to keep open the chance of continuing to trade under the same contract after the end of the initial term specified of perhaps 12 months for example, they could include provision in the contract for this to happen. After the initial period ends they could continue to supply/purchase the same goods or services under the same terms until such time as the contract is terminated by some means which the contract would specify, usually by notice. If, alternatively, the parties do not have a particular duration in mind for the contract, then it would be silent as to how long it would last and instead it could continue indefinitely until one of the parties terminated it or they both agreed that it would come to an end.

Default and termination clauses

There are several ways in which, under the law, contracts come to an end.

If the contract includes a clause specifying that it is for a specific duration, for example if a cleaning service is to be provided for 12 months, at the end of that period, provided the parties have each performed their part of the contract, it will quite simply end as you saw in the previous section on duration. If instead the contract is not for a specific duration but for a particular transaction, for example an organisation is purchasing new office furniture for the purchasing department, once both the parties have performed their part of the contract it will terminate 'by performance'.

13

However, there are situations where everything does not go according to plan and the contract may come to an end in other circumstances.

A contract can terminate as a result of frustration. This means that when the parties entered into their contract it was quite feasible, but as a result of an unforeseen change of circumstances beyond the parties' control, the contract became impossible to perform. An example of frustration could be that a contract to hire a theatre for a performance on a specific night was frustrated (impossible to perform) when the theatre burned down, as happened in *Taylor* v *Caldwell* [1863]. If this happens, the law states that the contract is terminated. If the parties do not want the contract to terminate for frustration, they can include a force majeure clause which specifies certain events which they can foresee may make the contract impossible to perform. As those events are now foreseen and included in a force majeure clause, this prevents the contract from terminating due to frustration. Study session 12 deals with force majeure clauses in a little more detail.

As you saw in study session 8, if one of the parties is in breach of their obligations under the contract, the other party may have the right to terminate. Default clauses can specify what will happen in the event of a party defaulting on its various obligations under the contract and can state what default will trigger the right to terminate.

It is also possible for the parties to specify in the contract if there are any other circumstances when they will have the right to terminate when there is no breach of contract, for example with termination for convenience. Such clauses are used where, for example, the purchaser decides to cancel the goods it ordered under the contract. Where such clauses are used they would usually allow cancellation before delivery provided the purchaser pays all costs incurred by the supplier up to the date of termination (the supplier would be expected to give a full account of the calculation of its costs and allow the purchaser to audit them), and provided the purchaser has delivery of all work in progress or alternatively the supplier disposes of those goods and deducts the proceeds from its claim.

If on the other hand the parties both wish to have a simple right to terminate the contract on giving the other party notice, then a clause could be included in the contract to that effect. This would be necessary in a contract which was not for a fixed term or a specified number of transactions and would often be considered along with the clause specifying the duration of the contract. This would be the mechanism to bring 'open-ended' contracts to an end in the absence of any failure on the part of either party.

From a practical point of view, whether the right to terminate depends on breach or not, it is usual for the contract to specify the procedure to be followed. Usually the clause will state that the party wishing to exercise its right to terminate the contract will give notice to the other party to that effect.

Finally, it is always possible that the parties may simply agree that the contract should come to an end. The position when this happens is similar to that of variation of the contract.

Self-assessment question 13.2

Read the following sample contract clauses, identify each clause and state its purpose.

- 1.1 The Purchaser shall have the right at any time by giving notice in writing to the Supplier to terminate the Contract forthwith without liability to the Supplier in any of the following events:
  - 1.1.1 if the Supplier commits a breach of any of the terms of the Contract;
  - 1.1.2 if the Supplier (being an individual) becomes bankrupt or (being a company) holds a meeting of creditors or enters into or proposes any arrangement or composition with or for the benefit of creditors or has a supervisor, receiver, administrator, administrative receiver appointed over the whole or a substantial part of its assets;
  - 1.1.3 if the Supplier ceases or threatens to cease to carry on its business or trade.
  - 1.2 Without prejudice to the rights of the Purchaser under this contract the Purchaser may for any other reason whatsoever terminate the Contract and/or Orders at any time by giving reasonable notice to the Supplier and specifying the date from which termination shall be effective.
- 2.1 The Supplier shall not vary any of the Conditions of the Contract, except as directed in writing by the Purchaser but the Purchaser shall have the right, from time to time during the execution of the Contract, by notice in writing to the Supplier to add to or omit, or otherwise vary, the terms of the Contract and the Supplier shall carry out such variations and be bound by the same Conditions, so far as applicable, as though the said variations were stated in the Contract.
  - 2.2 If the Purchaser notifies the Supplier of any variation to the Contract that would occasion an amendment to the Price, the Supplier shall, within 7 days of receipt of such notification, advise the Purchaser in writing of the proposed amount of any such amendment to the Price.

Feedback on page 156

13

Revision question

Now try the revision question for this session on page 240.

Summary

In this session you considered the different types of alternate dispute resolution and then outlined the advantages and disadvantages of arbitration as compared to litigation.

You considered various contract terms that are commonly found in contracts with a view to being able to identify them. The terms that you have studied in this session relate to:

- dispute resolution
- variation and change control
- contract renewal
- contract duration
- default and termination.

Suggested further reading

Griffiths and Griffiths (2002). You should read the sections on amendments and express terms.

Singleton and Lawson (2002). This book has detailed information, set out in short sections, about all of the common terms found in contracts.

Feedback on learning activities and self-assessment questions

Feedback on learning activity 13.1

The conclusions you draw from this activity will depend on what your research revealed about the personal experiences of the individuals you asked. You may find comments about the length of time involved or the formal nature of litigation, likewise you may have received comments about the more relaxed attitude in alternative dispute resolution such as arbitration or even mediation or conciliation.

Feedback on self-assessment question 13.1

They will usually do that as they wish to avoid litigation as a means of resolving disputes. If they want to obtain a binding agreement they would need to use arbitration, and the advantages set out in section 13.1 are likely to be relevant. If they prefer a more informal method they could use conciliation or mediation.

Feedback on learning activity 13.2

The general answer which could apply to all the clauses is that the parties wanted to regulate what would happen in the event that those situations arose, and what steps they could take. Specifically including an alternative dispute resolution clause would ensure that the parties did not go to court automatically in the event of dispute but instead would use an alternative method, probably arbitration if a binding decision was required. Variation, renewal and termination clauses would also indicate, when those situations arose, what steps the parties could take to either change, renew or end the contract.

In the rest of this section you will consider these clauses in more detail.

Feedback on self-assessment question 13.2

- Clause 1 is a termination clause. The purpose of this clause is to set out the circumstances when the purchaser can terminate the contract, these being that the supplier breaches a term of the contract, becomes bankrupt/enters into an arrangement with creditors and so on, or ceases or threatens to cease trading.
- Clause 2 is a variation clause. It allows the purchaser to vary the contract but the supplier can only vary it if directed to do so by the purchaser by informing the purchaser of any price change which results from the purchaser's amendments.

13

Standard model form contracts

Introduction

In this session you are going to learn about standard model form contracts – why and how they are used – and you will look at examples together with a description of some of their main provisions.

Plain-language model contracts are to ease the understanding of contractual terms and conditions. The intention is clear but proof of the pudding is in the eating!

Session learning objectives

After completing this session you should be able to:

14.1 Explain what is meant by a standard model form contract.
14.2 Discuss why and how standard model form contracts are used.
14.3 Identify examples of model form contracts and briefly describe some of their main provisions.

Unit content coverage

This study session covers the following topics from the official CIPS unit content document.

Learning objective

2.4 Discuss standard model form contracts and their uses and applications.
  • The use of model form contracts
  • Examples of model form contracts such as CIPS, the New Engineering Contract, Joint Contracts Tribunal

Prior knowledge

Study sessions 4 – 7

Timing

You should set aside about 4 hours to read and complete this session, including learning activities, self-assessment questions, the suggested further reading (if any) and the revision question.

14.1 Standard model form contracts

Definition

Standard model form contracts are contracts which contain standard terms and conditions the purpose of which is to make the process of contract

14

formation less time consuming and they are prepared in plain language for easier understanding by all parties to the contract.

Parties to a standard model form contract still need to examine the clauses and identify which clauses are applicable to their particular situation.

Learning activity 14.1

Look back at study sessions 4 – 6 inclusive and ensure you understand the contract formation process. Now look within your organisation at some contracts which are used which you would call standard model form contracts. Can you identify at least three clauses which appear in each of such standard models and on which your organisation wishes to rely?

Feedback on page 166

Standard model form contracts can and do provide a foundation for purchasing goods and services. However, purchasing professionals must carefully examine the clauses of the standard model contract and amend them to suit their particular requirements.

There are many types of standard model form contract and the Chartered Institute of Purchasing & Supply (CIPS) offer a range of documents which include, for example, a standard model form contract for the provision of warehousing services, such as the supply of storage space, services of packing and delivery to customers and confidentiality agreements.

Some standard model form contracts include:

- Standard Form of Agreement for the Appointment of an Architect (SFA/99)
- Conditions of Engagement for the Appointment of an Architect (CE/99)
- Standard Model Form Contract for Small Works (SW/99)
- Employer's Requirements (Design and Build) (DB1/99)
- Contractor's Proposals (Design and Build) (DB2/99)
- Form of Appointment as Planning Supervisor (PS/99)
- Terms and Conditions (T&Cs) of Engagement recommended by the Institute of Electrical Engineers (IEE) and the Institution of Mechanical Engineers
- Joint Contracts Tribunal (JCT) Contracts.

The above list is intended as a guide only and is not exhaustive.

The majority of building projects in the UK operate under contracts issued by the Joint Contracts Tribunal (JCT). The JCT has also published a 'consumer contract' which is a contract between a home owner and a builder.

14

14.2 The use of standard model form contracts

By carrying out learning activity 14.2 above you will be able to see how standard model form contracts can assist in increased efficiency of the procurement process. However, the procurement professional must not become lazy in their use of such documents. Each clause must still be examined and amended to suit the particular situation.

Purpose of a standard model form contract

The purpose of a standard model form contract is to have a contract which includes types of terms which you would expect to find in a contract. You should review study sessions 4 and 5 to refresh your memory on the requirements for formation of a contract. You should also look at study sessions 7 and 10 – 13 to ensure your understanding of express and implied terms and the classification of terms.

Having a document which contains standard terms and conditions does not mean that the procurement professional should accept all of the terms and conditions. It is vital to examine each clause to ensure that amendments are made to suit the particular situation. There are specific terms and conditions which either or both parties may wish to include in the contract, but these terms and conditions (clauses) must meet certain criteria if they are to be relied on. Some clauses include:

- Time of the essence clauses
- Exclusion and limitation clauses
- Force majeure clauses
- Dispute resolution clauses such as arbitration or adjudication clauses
- Liquidated damages clauses

14

159

- Indemnity clauses
- Retention of title clauses
- Penalty clauses.

Where a party to a contract wishes to rely on a specific clause then it must meet certain criteria. If the clause does not meet the criteria then the party wishing to rely on it may not be able to enforce it against the other party.

Criteria required for validity of a clause

There are three basic criteria which you may need to consider when examining the validity of clauses within a contract. This applies to standard model form contracts as well. The criteria are:

- **Incorporation** – this means that the clause is contained in the contract. The criteria for incorporation are based on common law. You must consider if the clause is incorporated into the contract. In most commercial contracts this is dealt with under the battle of the forms. You should revisit study session 6 to refresh your memory on this topic. Where a clause is in some other notice given after the contract is finalised, then it will not be incorporated. See the case of *Olley* v *Marlborough Court Ltd* [1949]. In this case a woman, Mrs Olley, entered a hotel and booked in. She went to her room and found a sign on the back of the door which stated that the hotel was not liable for any loss or damage to property left in the hotel. Mrs Olley's fur stole was stolen and she sued the hotel. The court held that the hotel could not rely upon the exclusion clause as it was not brought to Mrs Olley's attention before the contract was concluded. The contract was completed at the reception desk.
- **Interpretation** – it is important to examine the wording of a clause and ask yourself if it covers your specific circumstances. The criteria for interpretation are based on common law. For example, in the case of an exclusion clause or force majeure clause you should ask yourself if the wording will be interpreted in such a way as to enable you to avoid liability entirely for certain events or to limit the extent of your liability. Exclusion and limitation clauses are commonly used in standard model form contracts. Before such clauses can be enforced, the law requires that they fulfil the following criteria:
  - they must be incorporated into the contract
  - they must be fair and reasonable in all the circumstances (see the information on the Unfair Contract Terms Act 1977 below).
- **Reasonableness test** – this test applies only to exclusion and limitation clauses. This test was introduced by statute, that is, the Unfair Contract Terms Act 1977 (UCTA 1977). So when considering the standard model form contracts you must ask yourself if the exclusion or limitation clause is fair and reasonable in all the circumstances. UCTA 1977 was aimed at the control of exclusion clauses for consumer protection. However, the Act also applies to business dealings and introduced the 'reasonableness test' which is mentioned above. When looking at whether exclusion or limitation clauses are reasonable, you should have regard to all the circumstances which were or ought to have been known or in the contemplation of the parties at the time the contract was made. You must also consider the strength of the

14

bargaining power of the parties and any inducements received to agree to the terms.

Classification of terms

As you have already studied in previous sessions such as study sessions 10 – 12, all terms in a contract will usually be either conditions or warranties. Some information on these is repeated below for ease of reference. However, please revisit the appropriate sessions to refresh your memory.

- **Conditions** – these are fundamental terms which are deemed to be so essential to the existence of the contract that a breach of them, even a minor breach, gives the purchaser the right to terminate the contract and sue for a refund of the purchase price and claim damages for any consequential loss.
- **Warranties** – these are not vital to the contract and breach does not give a right to terminate the contract. However, the purchaser does have the right to claim damages in the event of a breach of warranty.

Remember that any clause in a contract may be made into a condition by expressly stating it as such within the contract. See the cases of *Bettini* v *Gye* [1876] and *Poussard* v *Spiers and Pond* [1876]. In the first case (*Bettini*) a singer was engaged to sing and attend rehearsals. The singer telegraphed the theatre owner to advise that he would be delayed and miss some rehearsals but that he would still be able to attend the performances. In the latter case (*Poussard*) the facts were similar, but in this latter case the singer became ill and was going to miss some rehearsals and performances. In both cases the theatre owner cancelled the contract and engaged another singer. In both cases the singer sued. In the case of *Bettini* the singer won, but in *Poussard* the singer lost. The difference between these cases was that in *Bettini* the breach was a breach of warranty to attend rehearsals, but in *Poussard* the breach was fundamental to the contract – a breach of condition as it covered the performances as well.

Self-assessment question 14.2

List three clauses which you might find in a standard model form contract and describe the three criteria which must be fulfilled for such clauses to be relied upon.

Feedback on page 167

14.3 Standard model form contract examples and main provisions

Learning activity 14.3

Describe at least two standard model form contracts and the kind of transactions they would be used for.

Feedback on page 168

In the above learning activity you have looked at some examples of standard model form contracts and hopefully those which are used within your organisation. You are now going to be looking at the main provisions of such documents. There will be certain similarities but some of the clauses will differ depending on the type of standard model form contract.

For example, some clauses in intellectual property contracts may be suitable for contracts for the supply of goods or services but you should take care when preparing any contract to ensure that the clauses contained within the contract are compatible with and suit the purpose of the contract you wish to enter into.

The information in this part of the session is not exhaustive as there are too many types of standard model form contract to cover in such a session. You are now going to look at some model clauses which can be considered as the main provisions of standard model form contracts.

Main provisions of standard model form contracts

The Chartered Institute of Purchasing & Supply (CIPS) provide a range of standard model form contracts with guidance notes. They also provide some model clauses. It is recommended that you look at some of these documents and the model clauses. Such documents include:

- Model Form of Agreement for IT Systems
- Model Form of Conditions of Contract for use of Computer Software Products
- Model Clauses – various clauses which may be suitable for different types of contract.

It is not possible in this session to provide information on all standard model form contracts or all model clauses. You have already looked at the main criteria required for model clauses to be valid. You have also looked at some of the model clauses which might be used in standard model form contracts, such as exclusion and limitation clauses. You are now going to consider some of the main provisions or main model clauses.

The crucial point of any contract is at the time of formation of the contract. You should revisit study sessions 4 and 5 inclusive to refresh your memory. Remember that a contract is based upon making a promise to do something. Breach of contract is therefore about breaking that promise.

Having read the above text, you also know that there are specific terms and conditions which either or both parties may wish to include in the contract. Some of the most common ones are listed earlier in this session. The model clauses published by CIPS can be obtained from CIPS and include:

- Supply and Installation (Purchase) of Computer Equipment – CIPS Model P
- Servicing (Maintenance) of Computer Equipment – CIPS Model M
- Licence Agreement for the Use of Computer Software Products – CIPS Model L
- Software Development – CIPS Model SD
- Support and Maintenance of Bespoke Software – CIPS Model S(M)

14

- Hire of Computer Staff – CIPS Model CS
- Facilities Management of Computer Operations – CIPS Model FM
- Procurement of IT Systems – CIPS Model IT.

Other standard form model contracts have been listed at the start of this session. Go back and look at this list. Your organisation may be involved in the construction industry and you will see from the earlier list that the majority of building projects in the UK operate under JCT contracts. By now you should be able to identify some of the common clauses included in standard model form contracts. You are now going to look at some of these, such as:

- definitions
- time of the essence
- terms of payment
- delivery
- acceptance
- dispute resolution alternatives
- health and safety
- force majeure
- law.

You are going to consider each of the above in turn. It is necessary for parties to the contract to understand the intention of the conditions and to apply them in their proper context. Model conditions aim to achieve a middle ground between buyer and seller. They are not biased in favour of one or the other. The buyer or the seller will prefer to have their own conditions drafted which are in their favour to a greater extent.

Model conditions can be added to or amended to suit the requirements of the particular contract, but only by agreement between the parties concerned. It must be remembered that the purpose of standard model form contracts is to have uniformity. In order to secure the advantages of uniformity it is recommended that alterations and amendments to clauses are kept to a minimum.

The following clauses are not exhaustive and are intended as a guide only.

Definitions

This clause is important because you can provide a certain definition to the terms used within the contract. This means that wherever the terms appear within the contract, they will be deemed to have the meanings applied to them as set out in the definitions clause.

Time of the essence

This clause is inserted into the contract to ensure that the buyer has the right to cancel the contract and claim compensation when and if the supplier is late in delivery or performance. If this clause is not inserted into the contract it normally means that the buyer will only have the right to compensation. When this clause is included in the contract then it is informing the parties to the contract that time is fundamental to the contract and is made a condition of the contract. It means that time for

14

delivery and/or completion of the work to be performed under the contract shall be of the essence of the contract. An example of such a clause is: 'delivery shall be made on the 20th of the month and time for delivery shall be of the essence of the contract'.

Terms of payment

This clause provides details of when and how payment is to be made. For example, the supplier shall be entitled to invoice the purchaser at the times and in the manner specified within the contract. The percentages to be paid and the events and circumstances against which payment is to be made must be specified elsewhere in the contract as these will clearly vary.

The 'terms of payment' clause allows the purchaser to deduct amounts for defects, work not properly performed and so on. Otherwise payment is to be made within 30 days. Purchasers may wish to extend this period but they must consider the Late Payment of Commercial Debts (Interest) Act 1998. If this Act applies then any significantly extended period may be void. Examples of this type of clause are published by CIPS and can be obtained in the Terms and Conditions of Contract – Model Clauses (1999).

Delivery

This clause lays down when and how delivery is to be made. The clause may state that delivery is to be made in a certain way to a particular location at a specific time and date. Delivery time and date will also be stated in the time of the essence clause.

Acceptance

You should revisit study session 4 to ensure that you understand the meaning of acceptance and when acceptance takes place. This clause is where you would state when you expect acceptance to take place. For example, if there is no detail of when acceptance is to take place you may wish to state that acceptance shall be deemed to take place on delivery or delivery and installation of the service in accordance with the other terms of the contract. It is worthwhile mentioning e-offers and e-acceptance here.

E-offers and e-acceptance

As a procurement professional you may or will use the internet or email to source goods. It is important to remember that the basic requirements for formation of a contract still apply. Revisit study sessions 4 and 5 to refresh your memory on invitation to treat/offer/counter-offer and acceptance. One highly publicised case which was widely reported in 1999 related to Argos. In September 1999 Argos faced legal action over its refusal to honour the sale of televisions they advertised on their website for £3. It was settled out of court, but it is worthwhile having a look at the facts of this case. Argos had advertised colour televisions on their website for £3 and it was not until it received orders valued at more than £1 million that Argos realised there was a mistake on the website. The advertised price should have been £299.99, but the software had incorrectly rounded the price down to £3 instead of rounding it up to £300. Argos put forward a defence based on long-established legal principles of contract formation. They successfully

14

argued that the price stated in the advertisement was a mistake and the website advertisement itself was an invitation to treat, not an offer open to acceptance by customers.

Dispute resolution alternatives

This type of clause is inserted into a model form contract to provide for the process which is to be undertaken in the event of a dispute or difference between the parties in connection with or arising out of the contract. In the event of a dispute or a difference then you may wish the matter to be referred to litigation, or adjudication or arbitration. Under the Arbitration Act 1996 arbitration is more flexible and retains the advantage of privacy as opposed to going to court. However, the first step in modern purchasing practice is Alternative Dispute Resolution (ADR) mediation.

Health and safety

This may be a useful clause to insert into the contract as it may strengthen the provision on environmental protection. However, it is important to avoid being too specific and therefore running the risk of omitting an important element. An example might be to provide that the supplier undertakes that he and his employees, agents and subcontractors will at all times comply with all health and safety requirements relating to the carrying out of the work under the contract.

Force majeure

This type of clause seeks to exclude or limit liability in the event of something untoward happening to prevent the contract from being performed or to make it significantly more difficult to perform. It provides for cancellation or suspension in certain circumstances, or even the extension of the performance time. It makes provision for the payment in such an event and specifies where any losses should lie. Obviously when such a clause is inserted into a contract a wise buyer or supplier will insure against the potential losses involved.

Force majeure clauses are strictly interpreted. This means that if there is any ambiguity then the clause is construed against the person seeking to rely on them. See the case of *Jackson* v *Union Marine Insurance Company Ltd* [1874] where a ship was chartered to proceed as quickly as possible, 'dangers and accidents of navigation excepted', from Liverpool to Newport where it was to load a cargo for carriage to San Francisco. On the way to Newport the ship ran aground and suffered damage. It was not repaired for eight months. The court held that the force majeure clause (dangers and accidents of navigation excepted) did not cover the situation which occurred and so the clause did not cover the accident and the contract could not be performed; that is, it was frustrated.

Law

This is known as the jurisdiction clause. Such a clause is inserted into a contract to provide for the law under which the contract is governed, for example English law. An example is 'the construction, performance and validity of the contract shall in all respects be governed by English law'.

14

Self-assessment question 14.3

Identify and describe three model clauses which might be contained within a standard model form contract.

Feedback on page 168

Revision question

Now try the revision question for this session on page 240.

Summary

In this session you have considered some standard model form contracts and why and how they are used. You looked at examples of these contracts, but the session did not exhaust all of these types of contract. The examples were intended as a guide only. The aim was to enable you to understand that although there may be a standard model form contract to suit particular situations, you still have to examine each clause and whether you wish to alter or amend it for the best advantage. You must also bear in mind that any alteration or amendment is with the agreement of the other party. You then considered different model clauses. Again the list was not exhaustive, but some of the more common clauses (main provisions) were described.

Suggested further reading

CIPS website for types of model form contract and clauses; see http://www.cips.org.

Sample model clauses, which can be obtained from CIPS branches or Chartered Institute of Purchasing & Supply, Easton House, Easton-on-the-Hill.

Feedback on learning activities and self-assessment questions

Feedback on learning activity 14.1

The learning activity is intended to make you aware of clauses within standard model contracts. You could have identified clauses such as exclusion clause, limitation clause, retention of title clause, time of the essence clause, penalty clause, arbitration clause, liquidated damages clause, indemnity clause.

Feedback on self-assessment question 14.1

Your answer should include the basic definition of standard model form contracts, such as that they are contracts which contain standard terms

14

and conditions the purpose of which is to make the process of contract formation less time consuming and they are prepared in plain language so that it is easier for all parties to the contract to understand them.

You should also mention that although such documents contain standard terms and conditions (clauses) the parties to a standard model form contract must still examine the clauses and identify which are applicable to their particular situation and fit their needs and requirements.

Feedback on learning activity 14.2

Hopefully you have been able to identify a standard model form contract which is used for the purchase of, say, storage space or for the purchase of services for packing and delivery, or perhaps a JCT contract. Even if your organisation does not use them, you should identify that the benefit is increased efficiency and ease within the procurement process. Such documents can ensure that there are sound contractual terms in place and help the parties to the contract develop mutual trust and continuous improvement.

Feedback on self-assessment question 14.2

Your list could include any three of the following:

- Time of the essence clauses
- Exclusion and limitation clauses
- Force majeure clauses
- Dispute resolution clauses such as arbitration or adjudication clauses
- Liquidated damages clauses
- Indemnity clauses
- Retention of title clauses
- Penalty clauses.

You should then go on to describe the three criteria of:

- **Incorporation** – this is based on common law and means that the clause is contained within the contract. You can also mention that in most commercial contracts this is dealt with under the battle of the forms. You can describe the case of *Olley* v *Marlborough Court Ltd* [1949] where a woman, Mrs Olley, entered a hotel and booked in. She went to her room and found a sign on the back of the door which stated that the hotel was not liable for any loss or damage to property left in the hotel. Mrs Olley's fur stole was stolen and she sued the hotel. The court held that the hotel could not rely upon the exclusion clause as it was not brought to Mrs Olley's attention before the contract was concluded. The contract was completed at the reception desk.
- **Interpretation** – this is also based on common law. You need to ask yourself if the clause covers the particular circumstances of the contract you wish to form. You can mention a clause such as exclusion, or limitation clauses where the wording will be important as to whether you are able to avoid liability entirely for certain events or to limit the extent of your liability. You should also mention that the law requires

14

exclusion and limitation clauses to fulfil two criteria, namely they must be incorporated into the contract and be fair and reasonable in all the circumstances as governed by Unfair Contract Terms Act 1977 (UCTA 1977). This leads neatly on to a discussion of the reasonableness test.

- **Reasonableness test** – this test applies only to exclusion and limitation clauses. You should describe how UCTA 1977 was aimed at the control of exclusion clauses for consumer protection. However, the Act also applies to business dealings and introduced the reasonableness test which is mentioned above. When looking at whether exclusion or limitation clauses are reasonable you must have regard to all the circumstances which were or ought to have been known or in the contemplation of the parties at the time the contract was made. You must also consider the strength of the bargaining power of the parties and any inducements received to agree to the terms.

Feedback on learning activity 14.3

In this learning activity you can describe any two of the following standard model form contracts:

- Standard Form of Agreement for the Appointment of an Architect (SFA/99)
- Conditions of Engagement for the Appointment of an Architect (CE/99)
- Standard Model Form Contract for Small Works (SW/99)
- Employer's Requirements (Design and Build) (DB1/99)
- Contractor's Proposals (Design and Build) (DB2/99)
- Form of Appointment as Planning Supervisor (PS/99)
- Terms and Conditions (T&Cs) of Engagement recommended by the Institute of Electrical Engineers (IEE) and the Institution of Mechanical Engineers
- Joint Contracts Tribunal (JCT) Contracts.

You might also have mentioned Confidentiality Agreements, Consultancy Agreements and even your organisation's standard model form contract for purchase of goods and/or services.

The type of transactions that standard model form contracts are used for will depend on your choice of standard model form contract. For example, if you have chosen JCT Contracts then you should describe that these are used for building projects for the purpose of having standard terms and conditions which apply to building projects.

It does not matter which type of standard model form contract you have chosen, you should describe that the purpose is to make the process of contract formation less time consuming and as they are prepared in plain language they are easier for all parties to understand.

Feedback on self-assessment question 14.3

For this answer you should describe three of the model clauses discussed in this session, or if you have found another clause within your organisation's

14

model form contract then you can describe it. Remember to advise what the clause is and what it provides for.

From the model clauses discussed within this session, you can choose from:

- definitions
- time of the essence
- terms of payment
- delivery
- acceptance
- dispute resolution alternatives
- health and safety
- force majeure
- law.

Go on to describe any three in a short paragraph.

Forming contracts for international trade

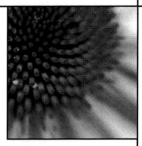

'Unless both sides win, no agreement can be permanent.'
(Jimmy Carter, 39th US President 1977–1981, Winner of the Nobel Peace Prize 2002)

Introduction

In this session you will be studying contracts in international trade. You have already studied the legal principles which apply to the formation of contracts in English law, now you will be considering contracts where there is an international element, the parties are based in different states with different legal systems and the goods are transported across national borders.

Session learning objectives

After completing this session you should be able to:

15.1 Outline the rules applicable to contracts for international trade.
15.2 Identify the main provisions of the Vienna Convention 1980.

Unit content coverage

This study session covers the following topics from the official CIPS unit content document.

Learning outcome

Identify a range of legal aspects related to the contracting process.

Learning objective

2.3 Identify and discuss the legal aspects relating to the formation of contracts in international trade.
   • International law
   • The Vienna Convention 1980, uniform law for international sale of goods

Prior knowledge

Study sessions 4 – 6.

Timing

You should set aside about 5 hours to read and complete this session, including learning activities, self-assessment questions, the suggested further reading (if any) and the revision question.

15

15.1 The law applicable to formation of contracts for international trade

When contracts are made between organisations in different countries whereby goods leave one country destined for a purchaser abroad, they are international contracts for the sale of goods. Contracts can also be made in this way for the international supply of services, for example where services are being supplied by an organisation in one country to an organisation in a different country to build dams, roads or large industrial sites or some other construction project.

Learning activity 15.1

Does your organisation enter into any international contracts? If not, consider whether there are any goods or services that your organisation could provide to or receive from non-UK organisations. What do you think would be the practical differences in developing a contract for international purchases and a contract to purchase inputs from an organisation in the UK?

Feedback on page 178

You have already studied the formation of contracts for the sale of goods and services and the rules that apply to them when they are made under English law. In this session you will study the formation of and rules that apply to contracts for international trade, and in study session 16 you will consider the terms in those contracts as well as how any disputes which might arise can be resolved. You may wish to reread appendix 1, The English legal system to remind yourself how international law and English law relate to each other.

The main difference between national and international contracts for the sale of goods is that international contracts are entwined with other contracts such as the contract for the carriage of goods, the contract for insurance and sometimes the contract with a bank to provide payment for the goods. Below you will consider the various documents used in international contracts and their importance.

The laws that govern contracts for international trade

In contracts for international trade the seller and purchaser are from different countries, it is also possible that the contract may be performed in a third country, the goods may travel through other countries to arrive at the destination, and the transport companies may be from different countries. In an international transaction what is certain is that there will be at least two legal systems which might be relevant for a particular contract. Therefore, purchasing professionals who are involved in international contracts should be aware of the rules relating to which laws will govern such contracts.

For many contracts the law that applies is determined by the Convention on the Law Applicable to Contractual Obligations (known as the Rome

15

Convention), which was brought into English law by the Contracts (Applicable Law) Act 1990 which came into force in 1991. The Convention appears as Appendix 1 to the Act. Some types of contract are excluded, for example matters relating to wills and family law, trusts and some agency contracts, but for other contracts it provides in Article 3(1) that the parties to the contract have freedom to choose either expressly or impliedly the law which applies to the contract. There may be an implied choice by the parties where they have not specified the law but they have indicated a particular standard form contract or a place of arbitration or where there is a previous course of dealings between the parties. Where the contract is silent and the law cannot be implied, the contract will be governed by the laws of the country with which it is most closely connected.

In contracts the parties could state that the laws of a particular state will apply, or they could agree to adopt uniform law as the law applicable to the contract.

Uniform law regime for international sales

As you have seen, in international trade the various countries involved all have their own laws and legal systems which often are very different. When a particular system of laws is not agreed to govern the contract, a conflict of laws may arise where it is not evident which country's law applies to the contract. To try to avoid or reduce the danger caused by conflict of laws, a uniform system of international laws for international trade has been developed. These international conventions have been adopted by various countries in order to avoid or reduce the danger of conflict of laws.

The Hague Conference of 1964 adopted two uniform laws known as the Hague Rules and these were introduced into English law by Parliament passing the Uniform Laws on International Sales Act 1967 which brought the uniform laws into force in the UK in 1972. Under this Act, the Hague rules would apply to a contract for international trade only if both parties chose them to apply, that is, the parties had to contract in to the uniform laws. In other countries which have adopted the uniform laws, they can apply automatically unless excluded, that is, the law applies unless the parties contract out. When the contract does not specify which law will apply to the contract and private international law must decide, it is very important to establish whether English or foreign law applies as that will govern whether the uniform laws apply. If foreign law applies, an English organisation may be subject to the uniform laws even when they have not adopted them into the contract. If English law applies, the uniform laws are only applicable if both parties have adopted them.

(You could reread appendix 1, The English legal system if you want to refresh your memory as to the creation of English law.)

The Hague Rules, which were not entirely satisfactory, were revised in 1968 and the revised rules, known as the Hague-Visby Rules, were implemented in the UK by the Carriage of Goods by Sea Act 1971 which came into force in 1977. Although these rules became applicable law in the UK in respect of carriage of goods by sea in international contracts, not all countries have ratified them.

15

Before leaving this section you should use the internet to familiarise yourself with the main provisions of the international conventions. You will find useful information at

http://www.uncitral.org/pdf/english/texts/sales/cisg/CISG.pdf.

In addition, if you look at

http://www.jus.uio.no/lm/un.conventions.membership.status

you can select different conventions and see which nations have ratified them.

The Hague-Visby Rules were criticised as being too much in favour of carriers, so they were fundamentally revised in Hamburg by the United Nations Convention on the Carriage of Goods by Sea 1978 which is known as the Hamburg Rules. Although a significant number of nations have ratified the Hamburg Rules, the UK has not.

The United Nations Convention on Contracts for the International Sale of Goods 1980 (the Vienna Convention 1980) came into operation in Vienna in 1988 and has been ratified by many countries. However, the UK is not amongst them. You will consider the Vienna Convention 1980 in section 15.2 below.

Documentation in contracts for international trade

Due to the nature of international trade with purchasers and sellers being in different countries, they are unlikely ever to meet and, as a result, the documentation for international contracts is more important than in national contracts between organisations within the UK.

Different types of documentation are commonly found in international contracts.

Bills of lading

These are the most common documents. The Hague-Visby Rules, which apply to the carriage of goods by sea, provide for the carrier's duty and liability for goods for which a bill of lading or other similar documentation has been issued. If the goods are shipped by air an airway bill is used. A bill of lading has three functions, it is:

- a document of title
- evidence of a contract of carriage
- a receipt.

Bills of lading include the following information:

- name of the exporter
- name of the shipping company
- names of the loading/unloading ports

- description of the goods being shipped
- weight and size of the load.

Documentary credits

As to the question of payment in international contracts, sellers will be reluctant to part with goods until payment is guaranteed, because if payment is not made it will be difficult to enforce the right to receive payment in a different country. In addition, purchasers will want to be able to receive and inspect the goods before they part with their money. In order to reduce the risks to both parties, irrevocable bankers' documentary credits were developed.

Once the contract is agreed:

- the purchaser instructs bank A in its country to prepare an irrevocable documentary credit in favour of the seller
- bank A does this and informs the seller who then ships the goods to the purchaser knowing he will be paid
- bank A then informs bank B in the seller's country about the irrevocable documentary credit and bank B confirms the arrangement
- the seller presents to bank B in its country, the bill of lading relating to the goods it has shipped; after bank B has checked and accepted the documents it pays the seller
- bank B then forwards the documents to bank A and receives payment
- bank A then sends the documents to the purchaser who authorises payment to bank A for the monies bank A provided in respect of the irrevocable documentary credit.

With this system both parties are protected.

Self-assessment question 15.1

Identify the use and content of bills of lading.

Feedback on page 178

15

15.2 United Nations Convention on Contracts for the International Sale of Goods 1980 (the Vienna Convention 1980)

As you saw in section 15.1 above there are some international conventions relating to international trade which have not been ratified by the UK.

The Vienna Convention 1980, the full title of which is the United Nations Convention on Contracts for the International Sale of Goods (otherwise known as CISG), came into operation in 1988 and has been ratified by many countries. However, the UK is not amongst them. The convention was an attempt to create a uniform set of rules to cover contracts formed for the international sale of goods. It was intended to be a centrepiece for the international harmonisation of international trade law.

Learning activity 15.2

Investigate which nations have adopted and ratified the Vienna Convention 1980 by using the internet. You could look at http://www.uncitral.org/uncitral/en/uncitral_texts/sale_goods.html and select the 1980 UN Convention for the International Sale of Goods to see which nations have already ratified the treaty.

Feedback on page 178

As you know, the UK has not ratified the treaty. This is because a state may not become party to the Vienna Convention 1980 if it wants to provide that the Convention shall only apply if parties to a contract have adopted it. This was possible for the Hague Convention and the UK availed itself of this exception, but it is not acceptable for the Vienna Convention 1980. If parties do not want the rules to apply they must contract out. With the Hague Convention, contracts would only be subject to it if they contracted in.

There are many differences between English law and foreign law for international sales. For example, the Unfair Contract Terms Act 1977 does not apply to international sales, and the Sale of Goods Act 1977 as amended by the Sale and Supply of Goods Act 1994 and the Sale of Goods (Amendment) Act 1995 only applies to contracts governed by English law. Contracts that are regarded as frustrated in English law will still be valid in foreign laws. There are also differences between English law and the uniform laws in the Vienna Convention 1980.

The main provisions of the Vienna Convention 1980 can be found on the UNCITRAL website. You should spend some time familiarising yourself with its main provisions which can be found at http://www.uncitral.org/pdf/english/texts/sales/cisg/CISG.pdf.

The Vienna Convention 1980 consists of four parts:

- Part I – sphere of application and general provisions. This sets out which contracts the Convention will apply to, namely contracts for the sale of goods between parties who have their place of business in different states when both states are contracting states (they are parties to the Vienna Convention 1980) or when the rules of private international law lead to the application of the law of a contracting state. It also identifies categories of goods to which the Convention does not apply and other limitations to its application. The general provisions deal with matters such as how the Convention is to be interpreted.
- Part II – formation of the contract. This sets out rules relating to offers and communication of offers as well as acceptance and formation of the contract.

15

- Part III – sale of goods. This sets out the obligations of the seller such as delivery of the goods and handing over the documents, conformity of the goods to the description and that they are fit for the purpose and are packaged appropriately, also that the goods delivered by the seller are free from any third-party claims.

  It also sets out the remedies for breach of contract by the seller, performance of the contract, substitute goods, avoiding the contract and seeking damages.

  It specifies the obligations of the purchaser, for example payment of the price and taking delivery.

  It also sets out the remedies for breach of contract by the purchaser, avoiding the contract, requiring the purchaser to pay the price and to take delivery etc.
- Part IV – passing of risk when risk passes and therefore which party is responsible if goods are lost or damaged.

  It is possible for countries to opt out of parts II and III.

Self-assessment question 15.2

Explain the purposes of the Vienna Convention 1980.

Feedback on page 178

Revision question

Now try the revision question for this session on page 240.

Summary

In this study session you have studied contracts for international sale of goods and services. In doing this you should have become familiar with:

- the Hague-Visby rules and their application in English law by the passing of the Carriage of Goods by Sea Act 1971
- the documentation used in international trade
  - bills of exchange which act as documents of title, evidence of a contract of carriage and receipts
  - documentary credits which are irrevocable instructions for payment
- the main provisions of the Vienna Convention 1980.

Suggested further reading

Griffiths and Griffiths (2002). You should read the sections on international trade.

15

Feedback on learning activities and self-assessment questions

Feedback on learning activity 15.1

You may have thought of various areas where differences would be apparent including the issues that might arise relating to the shipment of goods across borders and perhaps over long distances by different forms of transport, for example by road and sea. Payment might be made in different currencies and so fluctuating exchange rates could be important. Consideration would also need to be given to what would happen in the event of a dispute and decisions such as which country's legal system would govern the contract and which legal system would have jurisdiction to deal with any court action.

Feedback on self-assessment question 15.1

Bills of lading have three uses: as documents of title to the goods, as evidence of the contract of carriage for the goods and as a receipt for the goods.

They include the names of the exporter, shipping company and the loading/unloading ports. They also include a description of the goods being shipped as well as the weight and size of the load.

Feedback on learning activity 15.2

The website contains a list of the many nations who have ratified the treaty since 1988 (62 as of 2006). Nations are continuing to adopt the Vienna Convention 1980 and bring it into their national legal systems. The nations which have already done this cover a large part of the world including nations in Europe, Africa, North and South America, and some nations in the Middle and Far East. However, the UK has not done so.

Feedback on self-assessment question 15.2

The Convention was an attempt to create a uniform set of rules to cover contracts formed for the international sale of goods. It was intended to be a centrepiece for the international harmonisation of international trade law.

15

International considerations for express terms

'Litigation is the basic legal right that guarantees every corporation its decade in court.'
(David Porter (1813–1891), American Naval Officer)

Introduction

In this session you will study express terms that are found in international contracts for the sale of goods and services. Firstly you will consider clauses that specify which legal system and laws will apply to the contract and those which specify arbitration as the method of resolving any disputes that might arise. You will then go on to examine Incoterms, which are standard terms that are used in international contracts.

Session learning objectives

After completing this session you should be able to:

16.1 Discuss the inclusion of express terms specifying choice of legal system and dispute resolution method in contracts for international trade.
16.2 Compare and contrast different types of Incoterms.

Unit content coverage

This study session covers the following topic from the official CIPS unit content document.

Learning outcome

Identify a range of legal aspects related to the contracting process.

Learning objective

3.7 Appreciate and discuss international considerations in contract terms.
  • The choice of legal system
  • Arbitration
  • The use of Incoterms

Prior knowledge

Study sessions 4 – 6 and 8 – 15.

Timing

You should set aside about 5 hours to read and complete this session, including learning activities, self-assessment questions, the suggested further reading (if any) and the revision question.

16.1 Express terms in contracts for international trade

Learning activity 16.1

Give reasons why, as a purchasing professional, you might want to include a clause specifying which country's laws govern your organisation's international purchasing/sale contracts and why you might want to have disputes dealt with by arbitration.

Feedback on page 185

As you saw in study session 15, in contracts for international trade it is important to consider which country's laws will apply to the contract and which country's legal system will deal with any disputes which arise. During negotiation this will be agreed and the contract should include the appropriate clause to reflect the parties' agreement. As you saw above there are obvious reasons why an organisation would want to have disputes dealt with under the laws of its own country, namely, familiarity with those laws which ensures knowledge and experience in negotiating the legal aspects of the contract as well as knowledge as to the likely outcome of any dispute. As regards the venue, it is much simpler if the venue for any dispute resolution procedures takes place in the organisation's own country where there will be relative ease for attending any hearings that are required as well as no language barriers.

You considered the issues relating to the choice of dispute resolution method in study session 13 when you studied the choice of litigation or arbitration in national contracts. The issues that you considered about the reasons why organisations prefer to use arbitration in international contracts are also relevant in this session. You may therefore wish to reread the relevant sections of study session 13 to refresh your memory before proceeding further with this session.

In addition you must also be aware of the international aspect of dispute resolution by way of international arbitration. You should look at the website of the International Chamber of Commerce (ICC) which has ICC Model Clauses relating to dispute resolution in the International Court of Arbitration http://www.iccwbo.org. Not only do the parties specify in the contract that disputes arising under the contract are to be resolved by arbitration and possibly indicate a choice of arbitrator, they also must specify the venue for the arbitration. Organisations may wish to specify that the arbitration should take place at the London Court of International Arbitration (http://www.lcia-arbitration.com) as this would be a better venue for organisations in the UK. You should look at the websites of some of the international arbitration courts. You will find that they have the arbitration clauses for inclusion in contracts as well as the arbitration rules for their court and the procedures to be followed. Other websites that you could examine are the ICC in Paris (http://www.iccwbo.org) and the Hong Kong International Court of Arbitration (http://www.hkiac.org). There are many other websites that relate to other international arbitration courts.

16

Self-assessment question 16.1

What additional provisions would you need to consider for an arbitration clause in an international contract for the sale of goods or services that would not be required for a national contract?

Feedback on page 185

16.2 Standard terms in contracts for international trade

In study sessions 9 – 14 you studied terms that are found in national contracts for the sale and supply of goods and services. In study session 14 you also considered standard form contracts. These terms would be found in national contracts which are subject to English law. However, the types of contract that are used for national contracts are totally unsuitable for contracts for international trade where goods are usually transported over at least one national boundary. It is important in such contracts that the parties agree who bears the responsibility for making the arrangements for transport and insurance and for paying for them.

In study session 15 you began to study international laws relating to the sale and supply of goods and services. You should have seen from your examination of the conventions on the UNCITRAL website that international law has rules not only relating to formation of contracts but also concerning the duties of buyer and seller and the transfer of ownership and risk for the goods. In addition to the general legal rules, consideration must also be given to the specific clauses drafted into the contract between the parties.

As you saw in study session 14 it is not usual for organisations to draft each national contract on an individual basis. Organisations often have their own standard terms and conditions which they will try to use as the basis for the contracts into which they enter. Sometimes there are particular areas of business where model contracts contain standard clauses which could be commonly used in certain industries, for example in the construction industry JT forms of contract are common. International law also has its standard international trade terms which can be used by organisations as the basis for contracts for international trade. There is a range of standard terms for contracts for international trade to cover many different forms of freight and carriage contracts between countries which have been agreed by the International Chamber of Commerce (ICC). These contracts terms are known as Incoterms (International Rules for the Interpretation of Trade Terms) and the ICC publishes a guide to them. The most important aspects of the contract which Incoterms will specify is when ownership of the goods and the risk of damage to or loss of the goods passes from the seller to the purchaser.

There are many different types of Incoterms and you will study some of the more common ones in this course.

16

Learning activity 16.2

Use the ICC website (http://www.iccwbo.org) to familiarise yourself with the range of Incoterms available. Pay particular attention to the more common terms: CIF, FOB, EXW, DDP and FAS. You should pay particular attention to the seller's and purchaser's obligations under these Incoterms and summarise what they are for each of the Incoterms mentioned above.

Feedback on page 185

Cost insurance freight (CIF)

With CIF contracts, which are very common, the seller is responsible for arranging and paying for shipment and insurance. The price charged by the seller for the goods therefore includes this cost. If transport/insurance costs are rising, CIF contracts are beneficial to purchasers as it is the seller who will pay for any higher costs incurred.

The seller's duties include the duty to:

- provide goods which conform with the contract in respect of description, quantity and satisfactory quality and fitness for purpose
- deliver the goods to the correct port of loading during the time period specified in the contract
- arrange shipping to deliver the goods to the correct port of destination on a vessel with any special facilities required
- insure the goods against loss or damage on the voyage
- accept liability for payment of the freight and insurance charges
- ensure appropriate documentation is available and forwarded to the bank/purchaser to enable the purchaser to take delivery at the port of destination
- arrange for any necessary documentation, for example export licences.

The buyer's duties include the duty to:

- take delivery of the goods at the destination port (provided they comply with the contract)
- accept the bill of lading in its proper form and pay for the goods
- pay for any additional freight costs or costs caused by delays in loading at the departure port if the contract includes this
- arrange for transportation of the goods after their arrival at the destination port if the contract includes this
- inform the seller of the date/place of destination of the goods in sufficient time for the seller to make the shipping arrangements
- arrange and pay for any required import licences or customs duties.

Under CIF contracts, title (ownership) of the goods passes from the seller to the buyer when the shipping documents, which comprise the bill of lading, the insurance certificate/policy and the invoice, are delivered, at which time

16

the purchaser must pay even when, as is usually the case, the goods have not yet arrived and cannot therefore be inspected. Therefore, it is important for the goods to be insured. If there are any uninsurable risks and the goods fail to arrive or are damaged because of that risk, the purchaser will be obliged to pay the contract price for goods which might be damaged or lost at sea.

Free on board (FOB)

The main difference between CIF and FOB contracts is that with FOB contracts the purchaser is responsible for arranging and paying for shipment and insurance, whereas with CIF contracts this is the seller's responsibility. In FOB contracts once the goods are loaded on the ship the seller's responsibilities come to an end. As soon as the goods pass over the ship's rail during loading they become the purchaser's responsibility and the purchaser must have insurance cover in place.

The seller's duties include the duty to:

- provide goods which conform with the contract in respect of description, quantity and satisfactory quality and fitness for purpose
- arrange for the transportation of the goods to the port of departure
- deliver the goods to the correct vessel during the time period specified in the contract
- obtain a mate's receipt when the goods are loaded and give it to a forwarding agent to be sent to the purchaser.

The buyer's duties include the duty to:

- take delivery of the goods at the destination port (provided they comply with the contract)
- accept the bill of lading in its proper form and pay for the goods
- book appropriate shipping space on a suitable vessel and arrange insurance cover for the voyage
- inform the seller of the port, date of departure and name of the vessel in sufficient time for the seller to make the transport arrangements so that the goods are loaded on time.

Free alongside ship (FAS)

FAS is very similar to FOB except title and risk can pass before the goods are loaded.

Ex works (EXW)

In EXW contracts the purchaser arranges for the collection of the goods from the supplier's place of business and is responsible for everything. The seller is only responsible for providing goods which conform with the contract in respect of description, quantity and satisfactory quality and fitness for purpose.

Delivered duty paid (DDP)

This is the opposite of EXW. In DDP the seller must obtain all licences and pay all charges and customs duties and is responsible for everything until the

16

goods arrive at the purchaser's place of business or the place that has been designated in the contract for delivery.

Facilitating international trade

The UK has an agency to facilitate international trade, the Simpler Trade Procedures Board (SITPRO) which is sponsored by the Department of Trade and Industry. It works with commercial bodies, government departments and business to facilitate and standardise law and procedures in international trade. Standardised documents such as invoices, bills of lading, customs and insurance documents which are part of an aligned system of export documentation are available to exporters for electronic transmission and this makes e-commerce much easier in international trade. It also has a range of free fact sheets available on various aspects of international trade. SITPRO has a website which you could examine to familiarise yourself with this area of procurement practice ([http://www.sitpro.org.uk: http://www.sitpro.org.uk/]).

Self-assessment question 16.2

Elgar Ltd agrees to purchase wine from a French supplier, Clavier et Fils. The contract is subject to English law and is FOB. The goods are ready to transport to St Lazaire for shipment to Southampton as per the contract, but they are still at Clavier et Fils' warehouse in Angers. A ship, the *Constanza*, has been nominated to the contract but it does not arrive.

Which party will be responsible for any additional expenses incurred as a result of this?

Feedback on page 185

Revision question

Now try the revision question for this session on page 241.

Summary

In this session you have considered some specialist express terms found in international contracts.

You considered the issues involved in arbitration and the additional aspects involved when the contract is for the international sale of goods, for example:

- the choice of venue, which arbitration court is to deal with the dispute
- which international arbitration court's rules will apply
- examples of arbitration clauses which could be used in contracts for international trade.

You considered standard terms for contracts for international trade – Incoterms – and their application, namely CIF, FOB, FAS, EXW, DDP.

Suggested further reading

Griffiths and Griffiths (2002). You should read the chapter on international trade.

Feedback on learning activities and self-assessment questions

Feedback on learning activity 16.1

You may want to ensure that English law governs the contract. You might have knowledge of English law yourself and it may be easy to obtain advice from your organisation's legal department. That would be preferable to being party to a contract which is governed by the laws of a foreign legal system about which you and your legal department have no knowledge.

As to an arbitration clause, you may wish to have any disputes dealt with by arbitration instead of litigation, but you will need to consider the venue.

Feedback on self-assessment question 16.1

In addition to the usual provisions in a national contract, an arbitration clause in an international contract would usually require consideration of matters such as which country's law is applicable to the contract, which venue will deal with the arbitration in the event of dispute, and which arbitration rules will apply (these would usually be the rules of the international court of arbitration used as the venue).

Feedback on learning activity 16.2

This activity should give you ample opportunity to familiarise yourself with the range of Incoterms and their characteristics. You should also have listed the main obligations that sellers and purchasers have.

Feedback on self-assessment question 16.2

Under FOB contracts the purchaser is responsible for nominating a ship at a named port which is ready and able to take the cargo. As the *Constanza* is not ready, the purchaser Elgar Ltd has defaulted and so the goods will not be shipped when they should be. This may well add expense in terms of storage and redelivering them to the appropriate area of the docks for loading when the ship does appear.

Elgar Ltd will be responsible for this and liable for any additional costs incurred. Clavier et Fils could enforce this against Elgar Ltd through the courts or arbitration if appropriate.

16

The tendering process

Introduction

In this session you will study the tendering process. You will consider when tendering is used, types of tendering, the different stages in the process and the legal principles of tendering. You will then examine supplier pre-qualification and evaluation before post-tender negotiation and contract award.

'It is a very sobering feeling to be up in space and realise that one's safety factor was determined by the lowest bidder on a government contract.'

(Alan Shepherd (1923–1998), Rear Admiral US Navy, test pilot and astronaut)

Session learning objectives

After completing this session you should be able to:

17.1 Describe the stages in the tendering process.
17.2 Explain why pre-qualification and evaluation criteria are used.
17.3 Discuss the use of post-tender negotiations.

Unit content coverage

This study session covers the following topics from the official CIPS unit content document.

Learning outcome

Appreciate and discuss the legal and relationship issues arising through the use of tendering.

Learning objective

4.1 Discuss the stages of the procurement process underlining the tendering process.
- The stages of the procurement process
- The principles of tendering
- The use of pre-qualification and evaluation criteria
- Post-tender negotiation
- Contract award
- Contract transition arrangements

Prior knowledge

Study sessions 4 – 9, and especially study session 4.

Timing

You should set aside about 5 hours to read and complete this session, including learning activities, self-assessment questions, the suggested further reading (if any) and the revision question.

17

17.1 Tendering – process and principles

Tendering is used in both the private and the public sectors in the UK, but whereas in the private sector organisations can choose whether to use tendering as a method of supplier selection and contract formation, public sector bodies are subject to the European Union (EU) directives on public procurement and in certain circumstances they must use the tendering process to award contracts. These EU directives are legal rules, which only apply to public sector bodies in the European Union. They specify additional rules which stipulate how bodies in the public sector should go about awarding high-value contracts for the supply of goods and services. You will study the EU procurement directives in detail in study session 18.

In the public sector, therefore, in some circumstances organisations have no choice as the law requires them to use the tendering process. Otherwise, and certainly in the private sector, organisations can choose whether to use a tendering process to seek interested suppliers and award contracts in order to obtain the goods and services they require. However, the use of the tendering process is not always the most appropriate method of obtaining requirements and so the purchasing professional must recognise when tendering should and should not be used. Dobler and Burt (1996), two well-known American writers on purchasing, have identified five conditions for successful competitive tendering:

- The value of the purchase must justify the tendering expense of time and effort.
- Specifications must be clear to all parties, and suppliers must know their costs of production.
- There must be an adequate number of sellers.
- The sellers must be technically competent and must actually want the contract.
- There must be sufficient time for tendering to be used.

Additional conditions to consider are:

- The purchaser has a good idea of the price as otherwise they could be exploited by suppliers. It could be difficult for the purchaser to have an idea of the price, for example in the case of a first-time purchase of computer software, a building extension or even a contract for the

17

construction of an overseas facility. In these circumstances the lowest bid might still be inflated and the purchaser would not realise this.

- The purchaser has a good reputation for actually awarding contracts. Some purchasers have no intention of awarding the contract and instead they use the tendering process merely as a way to test the market. Suppliers are likely to quote high prices and put minimal effort into their bids in such circumstances or even not to put in a bid.
- The buyer's procedures are trusted by suppliers: if suppliers do not trust the system and suspect that certain suppliers will receive favourable treatment, they may refuse to tender or put little effort into their bids.

Types of tendering

There are two major types of tendering process:

- Open procedure. Here, any supplier is allowed to submit a bid for a contract. A disadvantage with completely open tendering is that a lot of work is then subsequently required to identify which of the suppliers will actually be able to carry out the work.
- Restricted or selective tendering. Here, only those suppliers who are considered capable of carrying out the work are invited to tender. These suppliers may have been pre-qualified through an earlier supplier appraisal exercise. You will consider supplier appraisal again later in this session.

The tendering process

In the tendering process the purchaser issues an invitation to tender either in an advertisement or directly to selected vendors in which potential suppliers are invited to make an offer to supply goods or services. In the invitation to tender the purchaser lists details of their requirements, which usually include an appropriate specification, a statement of the terms and conditions which will form the basis of any contract which is made, and the date by which the supplier's bid should be returned to the purchaser.

The supplier includes in their bid all of the relevant details of prices, specifications or deliveries in response to the purchaser's requirements and once the bid is submitted in accordance with the invitation to tender the supplier becomes the tenderer. The bid or tender submitted is an offer open to acceptance within a certain time period. You will consider the legal principles upon which tendering is based later in this section.

Stages in the tendering process

Generally, organisations broadly follow the stages outlined in this section when they are using the tendering process.

The purchasing function liaises with other departments according to the nature of the goods or services sought to prepare the tender documents, which can vary in relation to detail, structure and length from one organisation to another. The purpose of the tender documents is to obtain information from potential suppliers to enable an informed decision to be made as to which bid best meets the purchasing organisation's need for that tender. Tender documents usually include:

- the specification of the materials, services or equipment required
- the nature of the relationship expected with the supplier

17

- the proposed terms and conditions of the contract
- the criteria upon which the winning bidder(s) suppliers will be selected
- details of deadlines, timescales, contact points and procedures, for example post-tender negotiation
- space to allow the supplier to propose amendments to terms and conditions.

The tender is advertised and expressions of interest are requested from the supply market, so that tender documents may be sent out to interested parties.

The tender documents are sent out to the parties who have expressed an interest in open tendering and to those suppliers on a pre-qualified list in restricted tendering. You will study the pre-qualification criteria for potential suppliers in section 17.2 below. In their bids the parties must follow the precise terms requested in the tender document as otherwise they will be rejected. No variation in terms should be given to any one tenderer unless they are given to all.

Tenderers may request further information or clarification, but if so it should be provided to all so as to ensure fair competition.

Tenderers must send in all tender documents/bids so that they arrive by the closing date in the required format.

When the dosing date and time has been reached only the bids submitted in time will be considered to ensure fairness to all suppliers and to reduce the possibility of supplier collusion or sharp practice. They are opened at the specified date and time, before a panel of independent employees normally from outside the purchasing department, and the details of each bid are recorded and a bidding profile is produced.

The tenders are analysed with reference to the stated requirements and a recommendation is made as to which, if any, is the most attractive. You will consider the evaluation criteria used to analyse bids in section 17.2 below. (If there is evidence of collusion or if the buyer is not satisfied with any bid and has clearly stated at the outset that they are not obliged to accept any tender, all the bids can be rejected.) The analysis may then be passed to a tender board to formally decide which is the best tender. The contract is often awarded to the supplier who has offered the lowest price or is 'economically most advantageous'.

Once the decision is made, the purchasing department usually leads negotiations to clarify or improve the offer with the successful supplier. You will study these post-tender negotiations in section 17.3 below.

The purchasing department may be required to write and file a report for future reference.

If the tenders received back are not considered to be good value for money, then there is the possibility of re-tendering the contract by re-advertising the requirements and repeating the tendering process.

Legal principles of tendering

Having examined the stages in the tendering process you will now consider the legal principles which underpin the process. You first studied the legal principles applicable to the formation of contracts in study session 4. Later, in study session 6, you examined their application in situations where contracts are formed as a result of battle of the forms between parties each seeking to use their own standard terms and conditions. Usually it is the supplier who wins the battle of the forms and contracts are formed based on their standard terms and conditions. Now you will apply the basic legal principles developed in the case law you studied in study session 4 in relation to formation of contracts as a result of the tendering process.

The invitation to treat when tendering is used is the buyer's invitation to potential suppliers to submit tenders. This is true whether the process is one of open tendering or restricted tendering. In the invitation to tender the buyer will specify what the requirement is and can include in this whatever contractual terms it wishes the contract to be based upon; in other words, the buyer can specify that the contract be formed on its standard terms and conditions.

The bid or tender received from the supplier in response to an advertised requirement can be interpreted as an offer which is open for acceptance for a specific period or until it is withdrawn. The supplier is aware that to have any chance of success it should ensure its tender meets the requirements of the invitation, and if accepted the supplier will usually be contracting on the purchaser's standard terms and conditions.

In addition to the legal principles applicable to contract formation under the tendering process, there are other legal principles to consider. There is a contractual obligation to consider all compliant tenders received by the deadline; the standard legal case on this is *Blackpool Fylde Aero Club Ltd* v *Blackpool BC* [1990]. Unless explicitly stated otherwise, there is no obligation to accept the lowest bid; the precedent here is *Spencer* v *Harding* [1870].

Depending upon the wording of the tender, there is no obligation to actually award business to the successful bidder on their 'standing offer'. If, for instance, a local authority buyer went out to tender for the provision of up to 10,000 tonnes of salt to grit icy roads in winter, there would be no guarantee to the supplier of any order simply by virtue of winning the tender.

Notwithstanding the above, as always, what is acceptable legally may not be seen as fair or appropriate commercially. Tenders take a lot of time and effort to prepare and cost, and suppliers take a dim view of buyers who tender for contracts and never award, or who do not keep to agreed timescales. Abusing the tendering process for opportunistic advantage is likely to make the buyer an unattractive customer to the supply market in the longer term.

17

Self-assessment question 17.1

What would you say are the stages in the tendering process? Draw a flow chart to show the stages.

Feedback on page 198

17.2 Supplier pre-qualification and tender evaluation

Learning activity 17.2

From your own experience and from discussions with other purchasing professionals in your organisation, make a note of any instances of supplier pre-qualification being used in your organisation. What products or services were being sought and why do you think pre-qualification was used?

Feedback on page 199

Supplier pre-qualification

Supplier appraisal is an important part of the purchasing professional's task. In relation to tendering, suppliers can be appraised prior to the tendering process where the purchaser wishes to restrict supplier entry into the process. By using pre-selection the purchasing professional is able to assess whether possible suppliers will be suitable, that is, whether they are consistently able to supply the right goods or services (in accordance with the specification) which are the right quality, delivered to the right place at the right time and for the right price. These should sound familiar to you from study session 2 where you studied the rights of purchasing.

As pre-qualification of suppliers can be a costly exercise it would not be undertaken in all situations. By considering the factors of risk and spend which you studied in study session 7 the various requirements an organisation seeks can be analysed to decide how important it is to pre-qualify suppliers for that requirement. Pre-qualification is not usually necessary for low-risk/low-spend items, it can be useful for low-risk/high-spend items, it is important for low-spend/high-risk items and it is essential for high-risk/high-spend items.

Figure 17.2: Influence of risk and spend on whether to use pre-qualification procedure for suppliers

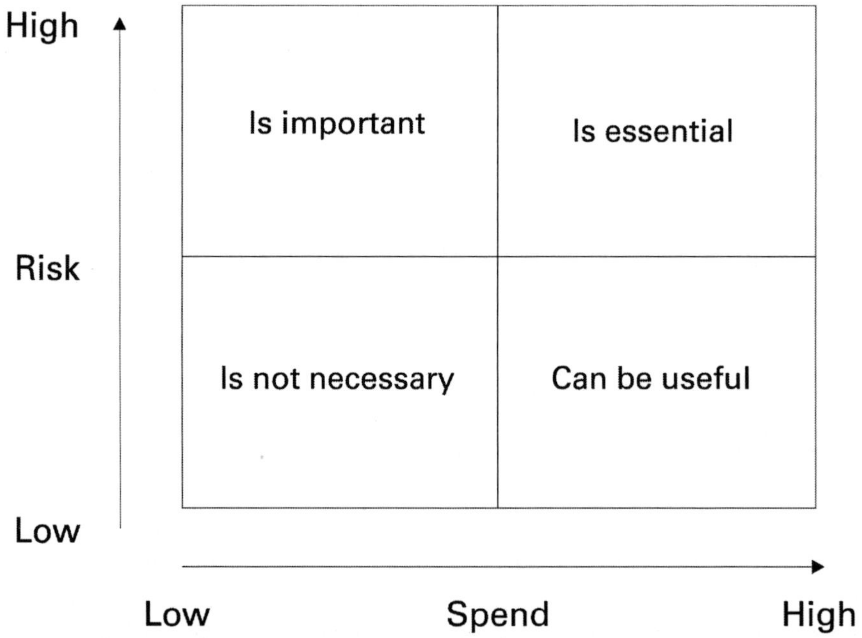

Once it has been decided to carry out pre-qualification, the various criteria which will be used to assess whether suppliers might be suitable should be listed. The criteria used may vary from one pre-qualification to another depending on what attributes the purchasing organisation is looking for in prospective suppliers for this particular requirement, but generally technical/quality, financial, commercial and environmental criteria such as the following may be relevant for high-risk/high-spend requirements:

- Financial. Is the organisation financially stable?
- Technical. Does the organisation have the technical capability to supply the requirement?
- Quality. Does the organisation have the capability to supply the requirement of the right quality? Does it have third-party certification for quality such as ISO 9000:2000?
- Capacity. Does the organisation have the available capacity to supply the requirement and can it respond to urgent demands for it when necessary?
- Delivery. Is the organisation able to deliver to the right place at the right time?
- Customer satisfaction. Are the organisation's current customers satisfied with them? Do they have good customer references?
- Culture. What is the organisation's culture and is it compatible with your own?
- Management. Is the organisation well managed?
- Health and safety. Does the organisation have a good health and safety record?
- Industrial relations. Does the organisation have a good record for industrial relations, that is, has it had strikes or other industrial action by its workforce?
- Research. What are the organisation's research facilities?
- IT. What is the organisation's IT capability?
- E-procurement. Is the organisation capable of trading electronically?
- Environment. What is the organisation's position on environmental issues? Does it have or is it working towards achieving ISO 14000, the certification for environmental management?
- Fair trade. What is the organisation's position on fair trade issues?

Once a supplier is pre-qualified it can be placed upon the approved supplier list (APL). If an organisation wishes to use tendering to source a requirement or even just to test the market, it may decide to invite suppliers on the APL to submit tenders and thus the process would be one of restricted tendering. If the invitation to tender was addressed to the world at large, any supplier could submit a tender and so it would be an open tendering process.

Tender evaluation

Once the suppliers submit tenders in accordance with the specified procedures they must be analysed. During the analysis the purchasing organisation will consider the tenders in relation to its evaluation criteria for that particular requirement. The risk and spend factors can be used to help analyse which criteria should be used for different categories of requirements.

17

Figure 17.3: Influence of risk and spend on the approach for evaluating tenders for different categories of requirements

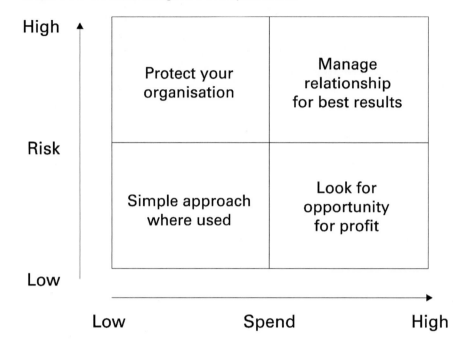

* High risk/high spend. Requirements in this category are very important to the purchasing organisation with the emphasis on value. Evaluation criteria are likely to reflect the whole-life cost approach studied in study session 1. The components of value, for example quality, must be given a particular weighting and then scored. When this is done, the whole-life cost is divided by the total weighted score; this then gives the monetary value per point scored for each bid. This value for each tender is then compared to find the lowest which is the one that gives the best value.
* High spend/low risk. A similar process can be used as for high risk/high spend, but as there is little risk with aggressive tendering requirements in this category it can be regarded as a source of profit for the purchasing organisation. Consequently value here usually means lowest price or lowest total life cost so other value components are often not important and so they are sometimes disregarded when bids are analysed.
* High risk/low spend. In purchasing requirements which fall into this category the most important thing for the purchasing professional is to protect their organisation by making security of supply a high priority. A high-threshold score can be allocated to security of supply and any supplier unable to meet it will not be considered. The more important security of supply is the more important this factor becomes. In some situations it may even be the only criterion to consider with some requirements.
* Low spend/low risk. With requirements falling into this category, price is usually the main criterion, although delivery, quality or other factors may be considered. Due to the cost involved in carrying out pre-qualification, however, the evaluation process is unlikely to be as thorough as in the previous categories.

Self-assessment question 17.2

Write a memo for the other members of your department explaining the criteria that could be used in a supplier pre-qualification process.

Feedback on page 199

17.3 Post-tender negotiations and awarding the contract

Learning activity 17.3

In what circumstances do you think post-tender negotiations would take place?

Feedback on page 199

Post-tender negotiations

A purchasing professional may enter into negotiations with a supplier at different points during the process of contract development. Negotiations may take place, for example, in situations where the contract is negotiated when the purchaser is not using the tendering process. In the event that during the course of the contract there is some dispute between the parties, then as you saw in study session 13 when you considered ways to resolve contractual disputes, negotiation is the first thing to attempt when seeking resolution. In this section, however, you will consider negotiations which can occur after the purchaser has received tenders from the various suppliers who are taking part in the tendering process. These are known as post-tender negotiations (PTN) and the purchaser may wish to enter into such negotiations with the tenderers (potential suppliers) in order to improve the offers (the tenders/bids) that have been made.

When PTN are used, the purchaser should have informed the tenderers of this possibility prior to the tendering exercise. In PTN, suggestions are made to the tenderer about ways of offering better value for money to the purchaser should the tenderer be awarded the contract. The tenderers are at liberty to accept or reject such advice and, if they consider it appropriate, to make changes to incorporate the suggestions. When PTN is used it is advisable that they take place with at least three tenderers as otherwise there is a risk that the element of competition will be lost from the process.

As to the negotiations themselves, there are certain guidelines which purchasing professionals should follow when conducting PTN.

- Negotiation meetings should be conducted by at least two officers from the purchasing organisation.
- They should have the authority to negotiate, but they should make it clear at the outset that during the negotiations they do not have authority to commit their organisation.
- They should ensure that any negotiating strategy they use has been authorised by the relevant person in their organisation before the negotiations commence.

17

- Notes should be taken of the meeting and sent to the supplier and their approval that they are an accurate record of the meeting should be obtained.
- They should have criteria already established which they will use to evaluate any offers made in negotiations so they know what is desirable and what is the minimum that is acceptable.
- They should not lie or mislead the supplier organisation during the negotiations.

Awarding the contract

Once the individual in the purchasing organisation who has the authority to approve the award of the contract to a particular supplier has given that approval, the contract can be awarded or 'let'. The way that the award of contract occurs depends upon how the tendering process has taken place.

Where the original tender was not amended after negotiation, it can be accepted by the purchasing organisation sending a letter to the successful supplier.

Where the original bid has been amended or where amendment has occurred after PTN, a contract is usually drafted (based on the notes of the negotiation meeting which were circulated and agreed) and sent to the successful tenderer for them to confirm it does set out exactly what was agreed. Two dated and signed copies of the contract are sent to the successful tenderer for their signature. One copy is then returned to the purchasers. Otherwise, if preferred the parties can meet and the documents are then dated and signed.

Once the contract has been signed, the unsuccessful tenderers should be informed that their tenders were not accepted, with information as to why the bid was unsuccessful. This information should be prepared after consultation with relevant departments in the purchasing organisation such as finance and legal, and approval of the information to be released should be sought from the head of procurement or some other suitable person in the purchasing organisation. It is also usual that the information be given in a telephone conversation or a meeting with the unsuccessful tenderer and that a note be retained of any comments from them together with any further responses made by the purchasing professionals involved.

Self-assessment question 17.3

Which of the following answers is true?

1   Purchasing organisations enter into post-tender negotiations with tenderers to:
    (a) accept the offer made
    (b) try to improve the offer made
    (c) to improve the commercial relationship with the tenderer.
2   During PTN the purchasing professionals should:
    (a) state at the outset that they have the authority to commit the purchasing organisation during the negotiations

(continued on next page)

Self-assessment question 17.3 *(continued)*

  (b) prior to the meeting ensure they have obtained approval from an appropriate person in their organisation of the negotiation strategy they intend to use

  (c) make brief notes of the negotiation meeting for their own purposes.

3

  (a) Where the original tender was not amended, a contract is usually drafted.

  (b) When the decision has been made to choose the successful tender, letters are sent out to the unsuccessful and successful tenderers to inform them of the decision.

  (c) Where the original tender has been amended, a contract is drafted, agreed and signed by representatives of the purchasing and supplying organisations.

Feedback on page 199

Revision question

Now try the revision question for this session on page 241.

Summary

In this session you have studied

  • The tendering process and the types of tendering, namely open and restricted.

  • The various stages in the tendering process from the preparation of the invitation to tender up to the final stage where, after the contract is awarded, a report is prepared.

  • The legal principles which underpin the tendering process in terms of formation of contracts and also in respect of the tendering procedures which must be followed.

  • The use of pre-qualification of suppliers and the criteria used for this.

  • The evaluation of the tenders submitted.

  • The post-tender negotiations which can take place once the tenders are submitted where the purchasing organisation wishes to try to improve the bids made.

  • The tendering process as it applies to the stage of contract award and the contractual arrangements which are usually necessary.

Suggested further reading

Carter and Kirby (2006). You could read the sections on tendering, supplier pre-qualification, evaluating bids, post-tender negotiations and letting the contract.

Griffiths and Griffiths (2002). You should read the sections on tenders.

Feedback on learning activities and self-assessment questions

Feedback on learning activity 17.1

In this activity you should have developed some appreciation of the types of requirements sourced using the tendering process as well as becoming more familiar with invitations to tender. In comparing other invitations to those of your own organisation you may also have found where improvements could be made.

Feedback on self-assessment question 17.1

Figure 17.1: Stages in the tendering process

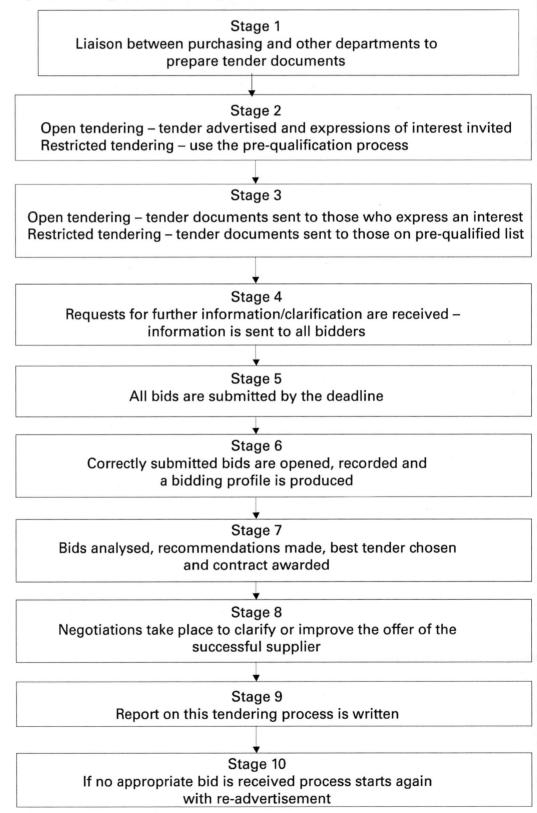

Stage 1
Liaison between purchasing and other departments to prepare tender documents

Stage 2
Open tendering – tender advertised and expressions of interest invited
Restricted tendering – use the pre-qualification process

Stage 3
Open tendering – tender documents sent to those who express an interest
Restricted tendering – tender documents sent to those on pre-qualified list

Stage 4
Requests for further information/clarification are received – information is sent to all bidders

Stage 5
All bids are submitted by the deadline

Stage 6
Correctly submitted bids are opened, recorded and a bidding profile is produced

Stage 7
Bids analysed, recommendations made, best tender chosen and contract awarded

Stage 8
Negotiations take place to clarify or improve the offer of the successful supplier

Stage 9
Report on this tendering process is written

Stage 10
If no appropriate bid is received process starts again with re-advertisement

17

Feedback on learning activity 17.2

Supplier pre-qualification is used so that purchasing organisations can filter out suppliers who are unlikely to be able to supply the required goods or services. If only suppliers from a pre-qualified list tender, then the purchasing organisation can hope to receive tenders which will have some possibility of meeting the requirement.

Feedback on self-assessment question 17.2

Your memo should be written clearly and it should explain the various supplier pre-qualification criteria set out in section 17.2.

As a general tip you should also consider whether you have any examples from your own professional experience which are relevant and to which you could refer in the examination. Relevant examples used well can enhance the quality of your answer and so improve your mark.

Feedback on learning activity 17.3

Essentially they would take place when a purchasing professional was trying to improve upon the offer which has been made during the tendering process. You will consider this further in section 17.3.

Feedback on self-assessment question 17.3

The correct answers are

1   (b).
2   (b).
3   (c).

17

EU procurement directives

Introduction

In this session you will be studying the objectives of the EU procurement directives. You will be finding out how these directives can be enforced to ensure compliance as well as the relevance of the threshold values. You will learn how to identify and describe the different procurement procedures, namely open, restricted, negotiated and competitive dialogue. You will find out what criteria needs to be used when awarding contracts under these procedures and finally, be able to explain the debriefing process under the EU procedures.

The aim of the EU directives was to introduce fair and non-discriminatory international competition while ensuring value for money.

Session learning objectives

After completing this session you should be able to:

18.1 State the objectives of the EU procurement directives.
18.2 Explain how the EU directives can be enforced to ensure compliance.
18.3 Explain the relevance of threshold values.
18.4 Identify and describe the different procurement procedures under the EU directives.
18.5 Describe the criteria used when awarding contracts under EU procedures.
18.6 Explain the debriefing process under the EU procedures relating to procurement.

Unit content coverage

This study session covers the following topic from the official CIPS unit content document.

Learning objective

4.2 Outline and discuss the EU procurement directives.
   • The objectives of the EU procurement directives
   • Supplies, services, works and compliance
   • Coverage of the directives – the thresholds
   • The consolidated procurement directive
   • Open, restricted, negotiated and competitive dialogue
   • Award criteria
   • Debriefing

18

Timing

You should set aside about 5 hours to read and complete this session, including learning activities, self-assessment questions, the suggested further reading (if any) and the revision question.

18.1 EU procurement directives objectives

Single, free, competitive market for EU public sector contracts

You have already studied the tendering process in study session 17 and you should revisit that session to refresh your memory. The reason for this is that tendering procedures can apply to both private and public sectors, but the major difference is that public sector bodies are subject to the European Union (EU) directives on public procurement. You are going to look at these directives in this session.

Learning activity 18.1

Use the EU website to examine the objectives of the EU procurement directives.

Feedback on page 214

History behind the EU public procurement directives

The Treaty of Rome (Article 86) established the European Community. This aimed at freedom of movement of goods, persons, services and capital by introducing a single market in which there are no internal borders which could be barriers to free trade and competition within external boundaries of the EU. Several directives were introduced to implement the provisions of the Treaty of Rome.

Main objectives

Given that the key objective of the EU was and still is to establish a free market without trade barriers between member states, it follows that the main objective of the directives is to ensure that public sector contracts are opened up to companies in all member states so that they can participate in the tendering process and submit a bid. Under the EU procurement directives all member states are obliged to incorporate the directives into their own national laws. This allows EU companies access to government contracts without any discrimination and in a transparent environment.

There are six directives which constitute the public procurement directives. These are applicable to contracting authorities. These include the state, regional authorities, local authorities, bodies governed by public law and associations formed by one or more such bodies.

18

Common features

The features which are common to all procurement directives are as follows:

- thresholds – discussed in section 18.3 below of this session
- advertisements and prior indicative notices (PINs) – discussed below
- specifications and technical standards – discussed below
- timescales – discussed briefly below
- framework arrangements – definition provided below
- procedures –discussed in section 18.4 below of this session
- evaluation criteria – discussed in section 18.5 below of this session.

Some of the above features are discussed in more detail later on in this session. Those which are not are discussed briefly below.

Advertisements and prior indicative notices (PINs)

There are rules regulating the minimum notice periods required for tenderers to submit bids. There are also rules regarding the announcement and detail of contract award notices. One of the main provisions of the directives is that contracts are published EU-wide. This gives organisations across the EU community an opportunity to participate in the tendering process and submit a tender. Where PINs are used then the open and restricted tendering procedures may be shortened.

Specifications and technical standards

Contracts which are subject to the Directives must refer to a British Standard that implements a European Standard where possible. Specifications should not refer to proprietary brands. However, if this is not possible then the words 'or equal' should be inserted after a brand name.

Timescales

The Directives lay down minimum timescales to give prospective suppliers sufficient time to respond to notices. The timescales can be reduced for urgent requirements under restricted and negotiated tendering procedures, but the reason must be stated within the Notice.

Framework arrangements

Framework arrangements have already been discussed in study session 4 and you should revisit that session to refresh your memory. You are now provided with some brief information again on framework arrangements.

Such arrangements are designed to provide better value for money. A framework agreement is defined under Article 1(5). The definition can be summarised as an agreement between one or more contracting authorities for the purpose of establishing the terms governing contracts to be awarded during a given period, particularly the price and, where appropriate, the quantity envisaged. Frameworks can cover supplies, works and services and can be used in conjunction with open, restricted, negotiated and competitive dialogue procedures.

18

You will look at the other common features in more depth later in this session. Now attempt self-assessment question 18.1 below.

18.2 Ensuring compliance with EU directives

You are now going to consider the remedies available to suppliers when they can prove that there has been a breach of the EU public procurement rules.

In section 18.1 above you considered the main objectives of the EU directives and learned some of the common features. You looked at some of the rules introduced by the EU directives such as those regulating the advertising of contracts and the use of technical standards and specifications, that is, non-discriminatory language in tender documents.

In later parts of this session you will look at certain procedures that must be followed as well as what is meant by **relevant contracts**, that is, those which are above a certain threshold value.

You will also look at the Compliance Directive which governs compliance with public procurement procedures for public works and supply contracts.

As you can see section 18.1 above and learning activity 18.2 above, rules enable organisations to know what is required for the tendering process governed by the EU directives. Further features are discussed below so that you will be aware of all of the criteria of the EU directives.

Remedies directives

To ensure that legal and administrative remedies are available to suppliers in the event of non-compliance with the directives and the fundamental rules laid down in the EC Treaty, two remedies directives were adopted, namely Remedy Directive 92/50 relating to traditional procurement and Remedy Directive 92/13 covering the utilities sector.

18

Any potential contractor who considers that they have been harmed by an unlawful decision on the part of a contracting authority can go to appeal. These Directives also introduced review procedures.

Remedies for breach of EU public procurement rules

There are High Court remedies available to suppliers who can prove that there has been a breach of the EU public procurement rules by public sector buyers. The remedies can be any of the following:

- declaring the contract void
- varying the contract
- awarding damages to the injured party.

As from 31 January 2006, the new Directive 2004/17/EC came into force. This is the Utilities Directive and Utilities Regulations 2006. This is a vast subject area and the full text of the Directive can be found at http://europa.eu.int. You can also consider the case of *Alcatel Austria* v *Bundesministerium fuer Wissenhaft und Verkehr* [C-81/98], known as the *Alcatel* case [1998]. The ECJ ruled in this case that for procurements caught by the EU procurement directives, a contract award decision must be open to review before the contract conclusion. This enables the award decision to be set aside by a court where an aggrieved bidder has been prejudiced by a breach of the rules, notwithstanding the possibility of damages being awarded after conclusion of the contract.

The new Directive also clarified, simplified and modernised existing legislation. By doing this it was anticipated that the savings from increased competition and structured procurement would outweigh the costs of compliance.

Compliance

There is a Compliance Directive which governs compliance with public procurement procedures for public works and supply contracts. This Directive set up a national appeals procedure for infringements and provided for damages for victims.

EU directives summary

The EU directives are a vast subject area and it is not possible to cover the topic in depth within this session. It is also an area which is continually evolving and developing. It is recommended that as a procurement professional you always seek up-to-date information from the appropriate government websites. The internet is a useful tool in this process. Learn to use it to your advantage and become familiar with the relevant websites.

The effect of the EU procurement directives varies across sectors, but there is no doubt that they have opened up supply markets in areas where there had only been indigenous competition previously.

The UK government is the strictest in the application of the Directives and, as you have already learned, the High Court introduced remedies for breach of the rules.

18

Feedback on page 215

Self-assessment question 18.2

Describe how the English legal system will deal with possible breaches of the EU procurement directives.

18.3 Threshold values

You will recall that these were at the top of the list of common features of all procurement directives in section 18.1 above. You are now going to look at them in more depth here.

The EU directives are only applicable to contracts which fall above certain threshold levels which are reviewed every two years. The directives do allow certain exceptions and you can find the EU Services Exceptions Table on the internet.

It is important to know what the threshold levels are and this information can also be found on the internet. The current levels as at 31 January 2006 are as detailed in table 18.1.

Table 18.1

	Supplies	Services	Works
Central government bodies subject to the World Trade Organization (WTO) and Agreement on Government Procurement (GPA)	£93,738 or €137,000	£93,738[1] or €137,000	£93,738[2] or €137,000
Other public sector contracting authorities	£144,371 or €211,000	£144,371 or €211,000	£144,371[2] or €211,000
Indicative notices	£513,166 or €750,000	£513,166 or €750,000	£513,166[2] or €750,000
Small lots	£54,738 or €80,000	£54,738 or €80,000	£54,738[2] or €80,000

[1]With the exception of the following services which have a threshold of £144,371 (€211,000): Part B (residual) services; research and development services – category 8; telecommunications services – category 5, that is, TV and radio, interconnection, integrated telecommunications; subsidised services contracts under regulation 34.

[2]Includes subsidised services contracts under regulation 34.

Utilities is not included in this session but information on thresholds is available on the government website http://www.ogc.gov.uk.

Remember, it is important to access up-to-date information on the threshold values.

Learning activity 18.3

Complete table 18.2 with the relevant threshold value (missing values or text denoted by '...').

Table 18.2

	Supplies	Services	Works
Central government bodies subject to the WTO and GPA	...	...	...
Other public sector contracting authorities	...	...	...
Indicative notices	...	...	...
...	£54,738 or	£54,738 or	£54,738 or
	€80,000	€80,000	€80,000

Feedback on page 216

As you are now aware, this is a vast subject area and it is worthwhile knowing about good practice information.

In order to improve the procurement process, development of suppliers and future competitiveness, the purchasing organisation should debrief all suppliers so that the unsuccessful bidders will understand why they were unsuccessful. Debriefing is discussed in section 18.6 below.

Self-assessment question 18.3

Advise what the following contracts are and whether they are above or below the threshold values:

* Contract for the building of offices for a central government body valued at £250,000.
* Contract for the supply of stationery for a local authority body valued at €150,000.
* Contract for cleaning services for all local schools within the local authority area under a framework agreement valued at €350,000.

Feedback on page 216

18

18.4 Different procurement procedures

The tendering process has already been discussed in study session 17. You should revisit that session to refresh your memory. In this session you are going to look again at the different types of procedure and particularly the competitive tendering procedure. The procedures include open, restricted, negotiated and competitive dialogue. Now do learning activity 18.4 below.

Learning activity 18.4

Prepare a table to summarise what you know about the different procurement procedures.

Feedback on page 216

We are going to look again at the different tendering procedures.

Open procedure

This is where any prospective supplier is allowed to submit a bid for a contract. This is also known as open tendering. The problem with this is that much work has to be undertaken after the prospective suppliers have submitted their bids to find out which supplier is able to carry out the work. Open procedure is competitive.

Restricted procedure

This procedure is limited to suppliers who are invited to submit a tender by the prospective purchaser.

In the open and restricted procedures the tendering process is competitive. In competitive tendering the prospective suppliers are invited to submit their prices for a particular contract. The procedure starts with the buyer issuing an invitation to tender either through an advertisement (in the open procedure) or directly to selected suppliers in the restricted procedure. The buyer lists his particular requirements and provides specifications and their statement of terms and conditions of the contract. They will also include the date by which the offers must be submitted to the buyer.

Although the tendering process can apply to both private and public sectors, it is the public sector with which we are concerned in this session as the EU directives only apply to public sector tendering.

Negotiated procedure

This is allowed in certain circumstances only. This can be in a genuine emergency or in the case of a forced repurchase from a supplier who retained some design or intellectual property and therefore must be used again.

Where tendering and competitive bidding is not appropriate and not legally required, an alternative is to consider direct negotiation with suppliers. This is where the buyer negotiates directly with the suppliers. In direct negotiations, the buyer approaches one or more suppliers with a view to discussing the buying organisation's requirements. Negotiated procedure can be used when it is impossible to estimate costs with certainty or where the price is not the only important variable. It can also be used when the purchasing organisation anticipates a need to make changes in the specification, or where set-up costs are a major issue, or where there is a need for close supplier collaboration.

Negotiated price level for an item purchased can be affected by many factors, including the quantity ordered, time of requirements, length of the contract, delivery requirements, discounts for prompt payment and of course the skill of the negotiator.

Competitive procedure

Before you consider whether to use the competitive tendering procedure you need to ask yourself some questions, such as whether the value of the purchase justifies the time and effort of the tendering process, whether there are enough suppliers and do those suppliers have sufficient technical competency and expertise, or even whether they actually want the contract. You must also ask yourself whether there is sufficient time to carry out the tendering process. The buyer must have knowledge of the prices of the goods and services.

Compulsory competitive tendering (CCT)

This was introduced in the UK in the 1980s to bring greater efficiency to local government and health services through the use of competition. The key aim is to ensure that value for money is achieved for the services which are used directly by the public sector organisation. The matter of 'best value authorities' was introduced by the Local Government Act 1992. Best value authorities include local authorities, the police, fire service and so on. Such authorities have a duty to ensure continuous improvement of all their functions by taking notice of efficiency, effectiveness and economy.

In order to fulfil their duty of continuous improvement they must consult with groups such as taxpayers, rate payers, those using the services and all interested parties. They must review their performance and prepare a performance plan every financial year. The public can view these plans prior to voting which takes place in May in local authority elections. The subject of best value authorities is vast and you should look at the government website http://www.ogc.gov.uk for more information.

Tendering procedures are discussed again in study session 19, but in this session you have been learning about the different types of tendering procedure which can be used. Before you use the competitive tendering process you need to know the questions to ask, as the method of tendering will depend on certain conditions.

Now try the self-assessment question 18.4 below.

18

18.5 Award criteria under EU directives

Now that you have learned about the tendering process in study session 17 and looked again at the different types of tendering procedure under the EU directives, you are going to consider the criteria used when awarding contracts under EU procedures.

As you have learned from the previous parts of this session the purchasing entities that carry out public procurement, whatever procedure is used, have to send a notice on the results of the procedure to the Office of Official Publications of the European Communities. This notice should be sent within two days following the conclusion of the contract. All notices are published in the Official Journal of the EC (OJEC) in all official languages of the EC .

However, from the perspective of the European Commission, the selection criteria and the award criteria are different and form two distinct stages in any public procurement procedure.

Selection criteria

In the open procedure the purchasing authority first of all checks that all bidders comply with the selection criteria and then the contract is awarded.

In the restricted or negotiated procedure, even if the candidates comply with the selection criteria, the purchasing authority is allowed to limit the number of prospective suppliers. Those invited to submit a bid or negotiate can only be chosen according to objective transparent criteria of qualitative selection. The qualitative selection is set at the beginning of the procedure and the purchaser must state in the contract notice how many prospective suppliers are to be admitted.

The selection criteria which the purchaser can take into account include the personal situation of the supplier; the economic, financial and technical capacity of the supplier; and the professional qualifications of the supplier. We will now look at these in turn.

18

Personal situation of the supplier

A supplier must be excluded if they are bankrupt or in liquidation or any similar situation under the national laws. They must be excluded if they have been convicted of any offence relating to their professional morality or committed a serious professional error. Where the supplier did not fulfil his fiscal obligations according to the relevant national legal provisions then they must be excluded. If they have made a false declaration as to their professional qualifications during the tender process then they must be excluded.

Economic, financial and technical capacity

The directives provide a limited list of requests which the purchaser can ask of the prospective supplier. These relate to the nature, quantity and use of the works or services or products to be provided and include:

- information on professional qualifications held by the supplier or senior employees
- list of principal services or products or works carried out in the last three years
- declaration relating to material and technical equipment that the supplier uses to carry out their tasks
- declaration as to how they assess the quality of the project
- controls for checking the technical capacity of the supplier
- information on how much of the work will be subcontracted.

The above information should be included in the tender documents.

Purchasing entities are also authorised to fix the level of financial and economical capacity required and to determine the nature of evidence to justify this capacity, for example appropriate declarations by banks, or submission of balance sheets or turnover during the last three months.

Professional qualifications

The purchaser can ask the prospective suppliers to evidence that their professional qualifications are registered with the appropriate professional body according to the national rules set up in their country.

Finally, although the selection and contract award criteria are considered separate stages by the European Commission and are not to be confused, in practice many contracting authorities, when awarding the contract, continue to take account of factors that are covered by the selection criteria.

Award criteria

This is also known as the evaluation criteria. Award or evaluation criteria has to be on the basis of either:

- **The lowest bid**: this leaves little room for interpretation problems. It means that only the prices suggested by the bidders are to be taken into account and the contract is awarded to the lowest offer; or
- **The most economically advantageous tender or most economical bid**: this refers to a quality/price relationship that needs to be further

specified and therefore must be stated as award criteria in the call for tenders. It is not sufficient to refer in general to the provisions of national legislation. Some examples of specifications include:

- technical value
- functional character
- after-sales service
- technical assistance
- date of delivery
- time of delivery or execution of work time
- price.

The above list is not exhaustive and is intended as a guide only. Remember, however, that criteria must be objective and strictly limited to the object of the contract. Bidders must be informed of the criteria by which their bids will be evaluated. The award criteria should be listed in decreasing order of importance with the most important stated first.

Unsuccessful tenderers are entitled to a debrief which is discussed in section 18.6 below.

Self-assessment question 18.5

Identify and describe the different types of selection criteria and award criteria.

Feedback on page 217

18.6 Debriefing process

You already know that debriefing of unsuccessful candidates in the tendering process must take place. This has been mentioned briefly before. We are now going to look at this in more depth.

It is good practice to debrief unsuccessful tenderers. They are entitled to be told the name of the successful tenderer but not the contract price. Where three or more bids have been received the range of prices should be disclosed.

Debriefing enables improvement of competitiveness of suppliers. It enhances the reputation of the purchaser who is deemed as a best practice purchaser and it promotes better value for money in the long term.

All unsuccessful tenderers should be offered the opportunity of a debriefing.

Although full debriefing might be more difficult to justify in minor contracts, it is beneficial and often of most value to newer and smaller supplier organisations.

Debriefing helps establish the purchaser's reputation as a fair, honest and ethical client and it helps suppliers to improve performance.

18

It requires skill and it should be carried out by a senior person with the appropriate level of skill and ability. It is often the same person who was responsible for the specification and evaluation of the tender process.

Debriefing should be tailored to the needs of each tenderer. Now try learning activity 18.6 below.

Learning activity 18.6

Describe the benefits of the debriefing process and who should carry it out.

Feedback on page 218

We will now consider the debriefing process and some of the techniques which can be used.

Debriefing process

There are some basic ground rules for carrying out the debriefing process. Debriefing must not be held before the contract is signed or concluded and all unsuccessful tenderers informed.

The debriefing process is informal and is for the purpose of building mutual, long-term, beneficial relationships. The unsuccessful supplier will be told honestly and diplomatically of perceived weaknesses. The unsuccessful candidate must also understand that this is not the perception of one person but of the whole evaluation team. It is important to remember that the debriefing is not the place for arguments or to change the decision on the choice of supplier. It should be made clear to each unsuccessful candidate that only their tender will be discussed at the debriefing and no comparison will be made with other tenders. No commercial information from one candidate should be disclosed to any other. No formal minutes should be taken as the debriefing takes the form of an information interview. However, the tenderers may and can take notes. At the end of the debriefing the purchasing authority can ask the unsuccessful candidate to comment on the invitation to tender documentation. This can be helpful for future contracts. Finally, the results of the debriefing interview should be recorded along with the conclusions for future reference.

Rejection reasons

It is worthwhile at this point to mention reasons for rejection. A tender may be rejected during the evaluation process where a mandatory requirement of the invitation to tender is not met or a tender passes the evaluation but is not offering the best value for money, that is, it is not ranked first.

Some parts of a bid may be favourable but not all, and these points can be covered at a debriefing session. Some points include:

- producing schedules that are too long
- unacceptable delivery periods

- inadequate experience
- equipment out of date
- poor control of subcontractors
- poor cost control
- inadequate quality management
- uncertain financial standing.

This list is not exhaustive and is intended as a guide only.

Self-assessment question 18.6

Describe when and how purchasing professionals should debrief unsuccessful candidates in tendering.

Feedback on page 218

Revision question

Now try the revision question for this session on page 241.

Summary

In this session you studied the objectives of the EU procurement directives. You will now be aware of how these directives can be enforced to ensure compliance. You know the relevance and level of the threshold values. You studied how to identify and describe the different procurement procedures, namely open, restricted, negotiated and competitive dialogue. You know the required criteria when selecting suppliers and awarding contracts under the EU procedures. Finally, you looked at why it is important to have a debriefing process and how it is conducted.

Suggested further reading

Websites on the EU procurement directives: http://www.ogc.gov.uk and http://europa.eu.int.

Dobler and Burt (1996).

Griffiths and Griffiths (2002).

Feedback on learning activities and self-assessment questions

Feedback on learning activity 18.1

This learning activity is designed to help you become familiar with finding information via the internet. You may have found several websites by typing the words 'EU procurement directives' into one of the search engines such as Google or Yahoo!. By doing this you may have found websites such as http://www.ogc.gov.uk, the Office of Government Commerce and http://europa.eu.int, Europa. These websites will provide you with information on the Directives and their objectives. One way of starting this activity is to understand the key objective of the EU which was and is to establish a free market without trade barriers between member states. Following on from this you will be able to identify that the objective of the Directives is to guarantee fair and non-discriminatory international competition in bidding for goods, services and works above certain thresholds (which are discussed later on in this session).

Feedback on self-assessment question 18.1

You should provide a short sentence describing each of the common features such as:

- thresholds
- advertisements and prior indicative notices (PINs)
- specifications and technical standards
- timescales
- framework arrangements
- procedures
- evaluation criteria.

Feedback on learning activity 18.2

For this learning activity you must remember that the key aim of the EU was to establish a free market without trade barriers. So you should describe how the regulating advertisement is important because it enables tenderers from all member states to submit bids as they are made aware of prospective contracts. The rule also provides for the award of contracts to be announced. This enables those who were unsuccessful to know who the contract was awarded to. Prior to the EU directives, suppliers outside the jurisdiction were not aware of government contracts, and even if they were aware they were disadvantaged when putting in bids.

Prior to the directives the use of local standards acted as a barrier. The rule relating to use of technical standards and specifications removed this barrier. You can mention that brand names should not be used, but if this is not possible then the words 'or equal' should be added.

These rules provide for fairness, openness, non-discrimination and transparency.

18

Feedback on self-assessment question 18.2

Your answer should include the remedies made available by the High Court and include any one of declaring the contract void; varying the contract; and/or awarding damages to the injured party. These remedies are available when the supplier can prove that there has been a breach of the EU public procurement rules by public sector buyers.

Feedback on learning activity 18.3

Table 18.3

	Supplies	Services	Works
Central government bodies subject to the WTO and GPA	£93,738 or €137,000	£93,738 or €137,000	£93,738 or €137,000
Other public sector contracting authorities	£144,371 or €211,000	£144,371 or €211,000	£144,371 or €211,000
Indicative notices	£513,166 or €750,000	£513,166 or €750,000	£513,166 or €750,000
Small lots	£54,738 or €80,000	£54,738 or €80,000	£54,738 or €80,000

Feedback on self-assessment question 18.3

You should identify that:

- This is a works contract and is above the threshold. The EU directives will apply.
- This is a supplies contract and is below the threshold. The EU directives will not apply.
- This is a services contract and is above the threshold. The EU directives will apply.

Feedback on learning activity 18.4

For this learning activity you can draw a table like table 18.4.

Table 18.4

Type of procedure	Description of the process
Open	Allows all interested suppliers to tender for the contract
Restricted	Limited to suppliers who are invited to submit a tender by the prospective purchaser
Negotiated	Even more limited as the prospective purchaser identifies the prospective supplier and negotiates the terms of the contract directly with them
Compulsory competitive tendering (CCT)	Introduced in the UK in the 1980s, it provides greater efficiency to local government and health services by using competition. The aim was to ensure value for money, and best value authorities were introduced by the Local Government Act 1992

Feedback on self-assessment question 18.4

Your answer should include questions such as:

- Is there enough time to carry out the tendering process?
- Does the value of the purchase justify the time and effort?

- Are there enough suppliers?
- Do the suppliers have the required competency and expertise?
- Are the specifications clear to all parties?
- Do the suppliers actually want the contract?

Feedback on learning activity 18.5

Although there are variations on the timetable of events for the different types of procedures (open, restricted and negotiated) the following list illustrates the step-by-step process:

- initial preparation of tender documents
- sending notice to Official Journal (OJ)
- notice issued in OJ
- suppliers respond to the notice
- send contract documentation to the supplier
- further information may be requested
- suppliers return the tenders
- recommendations made
- supplier appraisal/tender evaluation
- send contract award notice to OJ.

Feedback on self-assessment question 18.5

In your answer you should refer to the fact that the European Commission considers these two criteria to be two separate stages, but often purchasing authorities use the selection criteria when awarding the contract. You should then proceed to describe the selection criteria, namely:

- Describe that in certain personal circumstances the supplier must be excluded, such as where they are bankrupt or in liquidation or any similar situation under the national laws; convicted of any offence relating to their professional morality or have committed a serious professional error; where they did not fulfil their fiscal obligations according to the relevant national legal provisions; or they made a false declaration as to their professional qualifications during the tender process.
- Then describe the requests that can be made by the purchaser relating to economic, financial and technical capacity of the supplier with some examples:
  - information on professional qualifications held by the supplier or senior employees
  - list of principal services or products or works carried out in the last three years
  - declaration relating to material and technical equipment that the supplier uses to carry out their tasks
  - declaration as to how they assess the quality of the project
  - controls for checking the technical capacity of the supplier
  - information on how much of the work will be subcontracted.
- Finally, you should state that the purchaser can ask the prospective suppliers to evidence that their professional qualifications are registered with the appropriate professional body according to the national rules set up in their country.

18

On the award criteria you should describe the two main criteria for awarding bids. The first is the lowest bid, which leaves little room for interpretation problems. It means that only the prices suggested by the bidders are to be taken into account and the contract is awarded to the lowest offer.

The second criteria is the most economically advantageous tender or most economical bid, which refers to a quality/price relationship that needs to be further specified and therefore must be stated as award criteria in the call for tenders. It is not sufficient to refer in general to the provisions of national legislation. You should provide some examples and state that the list is not exhaustive and is a guide only. The list can include:

- technical value
- functional character
- after-sales service
- technical assistance
- date of delivery
- time of delivery or execution of work time
- price.

Feedback on learning activity 18.6

In this exercise you can think of your organisation and any tender processes undertaken. Can you describe the benefits and who carried it out?

Hopefully you will have been able to identify what happened within your organisation. If not, then you should describe the benefits which you have read about above. These can include the fact that it raises the reputation of the purchasing organisation in the eyes of the supplier. The suppliers will also try to improve their performance for the future.

You must then state that the debriefing requires skill and should therefore be carried out by someone within the purchasing authority who has the relevant skills and abilities. You can mention that it is often the same person who was responsible for the specification and evaluation of the contract.

Feedback on self-assessment question 18.6

In this question you should mention the basic ground rules for carrying out the process, particularly that it must not be held before the contract is signed or concluded and all unsuccessful tenderers informed.

You can also describe how the process is informal and aims to build mutual, long-term, beneficial relationships. The unsuccessful supplier will be told honestly and diplomatically of perceived weaknesses. The unsuccessful candidate must also understand that this is not the perception of one person but of the whole evaluation team. It is important to remember that the debriefing is not the place for arguments or to change the decision on the choice of supplier. It should be made clear to each unsuccessful candidate that only their tender will be discussed at the debriefing and no comparison will be made with other tenders. No commercial information from one candidate should be disclosed to any other. No formal minutes should be taken as the debriefing takes the form of an information interview. However, the tenderers may and can take notes. At the end of the debriefing the purchasing authority can ask the unsuccessful candidate to comment on the invitation to tender documentation. This can be helpful for future contracts. Finally, the results of the debriefing interview should be recorded along with the conclusions for future reference.

18

E-tendering

Introduction

In this session you will look at the uses of e-tendering and the legal issues relating to it.

Widening the web has opened up worldwide opportunities in the procurement process.

Session learning objectives

After completing this session you should be able to:

19.1 Identify the uses of e-tendering.
19.2 Outline the legal issues relating to e-tendering.

Unit content coverage

This study session covers the following topic from the official CIPS unit content document.

Learning outcome

Appreciate and discuss the legal and relationship issues arising through the use of tendering procedures, including e-tendering and the application of EU procurement.

Learning objective

4.3 Discuss the use of e-tendering and outline the legal issues.
  • Supplier databases
  • Electronic tender systems
  • Electronic notice systems

Prior knowledge

Study sessions 17 – 18.

Timing

You should set aside about 4 hours to read and complete this session, including learning activities, self-assessment questions, the suggested further reading (if any) and the revision question.

19.1 E-tendering

More and more organisations are turning to e-commerce and e-procurement. Some elements of the use of electronics by organisations in the procurement process include the following:

* e-sourcing
* e-transactions
* e-contents
* e-payments
* online contract management systems.

In view of the use of electronics in procurement we are going to look at e-tendering in this session.

Learning activity 19.1

Describe the advantages and benefits of using e-tendering.

Feedback on page 224

E-tendering

Learning activity 19.1 above will have helped you to think of some of the advantages and benefits of e-tendering. You should also have searched the internet for more information and assistance on e-procurement and e-tendering.

The internet is a useful tool for finding out how organisations use e-procurement. Some of the lessons learned by those organisations include the necessity of having a plan for communicating the process across the whole organisation.

When considering e-tendering it is essential to set out clear aims and objectives. You need to be disciplined in contract management. You should also remember that when anything new is introduced into an organisation it takes time for people to accept the change and the new system both mentally and emotionally as well as physically.

The National e-Procurement Project has case studies on the internet which represent real-life experiences of a range of authorities who use e-tendering. These authorities have provided details of the barriers which they faced and the decisions that they had to make to implement e-procurement solutions.

In any e-tendering exercise you must remember that all the steps which are taken in the traditional tendering process still exist. You should revisit study session 17 on tendering to refresh your memory.

Self-assessment question 19.1

Why would an organisation choose to use e-tendering?

Feedback on page 225

19

19.2 Legal issues of e-tendering

You considered the advantages of e-tendering in section 19.1 above as well as the essentials for making it work. You are now going to look at the legal issues relating to e-tendering such as confidentiality of information and the Data Protection Act 1998.

Learning activity 19.2

Use the internet to investigate the legal issues relating to e-procurement and especially to e-tendering. You could start by looking at the websites http://www.ogc.gov.uk and http://europa.eu.int.

Feedback on page 225

After completing learning activity 19.2 above you should be aware of some of the issues of carrying out a tendering process electronically. We will now look at some of those issues in more depth.

Security

Security is important with regard to e-tendering because in the process information is being made available outside the purchasing organisation to prospective suppliers. Ensuring sufficient security will necessarily involve IT and computer personnel. You must be aware of the differences between intranets and internets. Intranets are used by many organisations where employees have their own computers or access to computers. The computers can be and often are networked across the organisation but no information is passed outside the organisation, with the exception of some emails. There is often control over the sending and receiving of emails not recognised by the organisation intranets.

However, e-tendering is sending information outside the organisation and requires the necessary clearance from within the organisation. The necessary clearance can be achieved by having suppliers on a trusted supplier database or similar.

It is good practice to have a privacy code which can be made available to suppliers and customers outside your organisation. The code can provide an overview of how the organisation complies with data protection legislation to protect the rights of individuals and organisations that the purchaser deals with. This code can set out details of the purchasing authority. It should set out how personal information is collected and why, as well as how the information is safeguarded. The purchasing authority must also provide details on how, why and with whom any information is shared.

Data Protection Act 1998

When any information is requested by the purchasing authority they must comply with the Data Protection Act 1998. In the e-tendering process information may and often will be transferred across the UK and Europe. There are laws within the European Community that protect personal information. European data protection legislation prohibits the transfer of personal information to any country outside Europe unless that country provides adequate protection.

Under the Data Protection Act 1998, individuals have a right to see a copy of the information held about them. The individual must pay a statutory fee for this service which is currently £10. Individuals must provide sufficient evidence of their identity and adequate details of the information they wish to see to enable the organisation to locate it. The Act provides for correction of any errors in information held and the right to change information provided. The purchasing authority must register under the Data Protection Act 1998 if information is being collected and stored.

Confidentiality

You are already aware that the purchasing authority in the tendering process must not divulge information about one supplier who is involved in the tendering process to another. Even in the debriefing process information must not be disclosed to one supplier about another. You should revisit study session 18 and refresh your memory on the debriefing process.

Self-assessment question 19.2

Draft a memo to the other members of your department outlining the legal issues relating to e-tendering

Feedback on page 225

Revision question

Now try the revision question for this session on page 241.

Summary

In this session you looked at the uses of e-tendering and the legal issues relating to it. Although this session is short it must be read in conjunction with study sessions 17 and 18. You should revisit these sessions to refresh your memory.

Suggested further reading

Search websites such as http://www.ogc.gov.uk and http://europa.eu.int.

Feedback on learning activities and self-assessment questions

Feedback on learning activity 19.1

For this learning activity you may be able to look to your organisation if it uses e-tendering in the procurement process. If not, you should search the internet for assistance on e-tendering and e-procurement. There are websites which provide details of some case studies on public bodies using e-procurement. You can search by typing 'e-tendering' into the search engine.

Some of the advantages that you may have identified are business efficiency, improved supplier communication and relationships, consistency, savings, improved expenditure control, best value.

The benefits you can mention include some improved information on purchasing matters, improved purchasing practices, timely payments of supplier bills, reduction in paperwork, central management of contracts and so on.

Feedback on self-assessment question 19.1

Your answer should include the advantages and benefits which you learned about when doing learning activity 19.1. However, you should also mention that it is necessary to have a plan for communicating the process across the whole organisation. You must also have clear aims and objectives and have discipline in managing the contracts. You should mention that e-tendering is still a fairly innovative approach and that anything new can cause emotional strain on employees until they get used to the idea.

Feedback on learning activity 19.2

This is a practical learning activity and you should have found information on the internet which will assist in e-tendering within your organisation or when your organisation decides to start using e-tendering.

You are already aware that the e-tendering process follows the same steps as the traditional tendering process. However, as the e-tendering process is electronic you must consider security issues such as how information is provided electronically, to whom the information is available, what information is retained and how you get round confidentiality. Using the e-tendering process will necessarily involve your IT department and those with computer skills and technology. You might mention that your organisation, like many, uses computers and that they may and usually will be networked across employees. Also, usually many employees of various levels have open access to the organisation's intranet. This is different from access to the internet. This difference is an important one because an intranet is a form of limited access to employees whereas the e-tendering process makes use of the internet or emails which takes information outside your organisation.

Feedback on self-assessment question 19.2

Your memo should be written clearly and it should explain the various steps in the tendering process as the same steps apply to e-tendering. It is important that the memo is distributed across the whole organisation. You will recall that this was one of the lessons learned by organisations already using e-tendering.

19

Your memo should include clear aims and objectives. It will include the stages of the tendering process as well as the legal issues described in table 19.1.

Table 19.1

Steps in the process	Legal issues
List of people or organisations who are to be invited to bid	Data Protection Act 1998 – includes those from the trusted suppliers list
Information on type of contract, including value	EU directives, threshold values
Outline of tender documentation and type of procedure	Legal issues relating to open, restricted, negotiated, competitive dialogue
	Security of information
	Terms and conditions and related legislation UCTA 1977
Letter of intent or letter of comfort	Issues around being legally bound and the impact on the contract period as work can commence on issue of letter of intent
Awarding the contract; collateral obligations	Awarding to lowest bidder; not withdrawing within a specified time period; considering all tenders that comply with requirements; all tenders treated equally
Formal agreement	Concluding the contract; legal requirements of contract law
Debriefing	Confidentiality; Data Protection Act 1998

19

Contract review, management and improvement

Introduction

In this session you will be considering the management of contracts including the process of reviewing them and the need to improve the contract process.

Management by objective works if you know the objectives. Ninety per cent of the time you don't.
(P Drucker (1909–2005), American educator and writer)

Session learning objectives

After completing this session you should be able to:

20.1 Explain how contracts can be managed successfully.
20.2 Identify what is meant by contract review.
20.3 Identify how the contracting process can be improved.

Unit content coverage

This study session covers the following topic from the official CIPS unit content document.

Learning objective

4.4 Recognise the importance of reviewing the outcomes of contracts and identify problems that require immediate action.
 • Contract management
 • Contract review
 • Improving the contracting process

Prior knowledge

Study sessions 1 – 19.

Timing

You should set aside about 4 hours to read and complete this session, including learning activities, self-assessment questions, the suggested further reading (if any) and the revision question.

20.1 Contract management

Learning activity 20.1

State what steps are taken to manage contracts in your organisation.

Feedback on page 235

20

In this session, where you are referred to earlier parts of this course book, you might find it helpful to glance through the relevant sections once again to refresh your memory, as it will help your understanding of the ongoing process of contract management.

By managing contracts, an organisation can ensure that the parties to a contract meet their respective obligations efficiently and effectively, and by doing so it is able to ensure that its general business objectives and its specific objectives as regards the contract are met. In order to fully understand contract management, you must consider not only how it is done but also why it is used. Even before the contract is negotiated and agreed, consideration of issues in contract management arise, as it is in the early stages of consideration and preparation that the foundations are laid for the contract itself.

Not all contracts will require the same level of management however, as the degree of contract management depends upon various factors including the type of procurement. In study session 1 you studied the different categories of procurements, namely capital equipment, production materials, consumables and maintenance, repair and operating (MRO) items, resale goods and services. You also studied expenditure on capital/non-capital goods and considered such matters as total cost approach and life-cycle costing as well as financial appraisal methods. In addition you considered how the differences in the categories of procurements and the expenditure on them affect the role of the purchasing professional. Just as these factors affect the purchasing role so do they affect the level of contract management required. By their very nature some categories of procurements will require greater levels of contract management than others. For example, there will be a higher level of contract management for a capital purchase of high-value specialist machinery with an associated long-term maintenance contract than there would be for supplies of minor generic office supplies.

In study session 2 you studied procurement objectives. The procurement department will usually have objectives derived from the strategic corporate objectives of its organisation. The purchasing department's objectives usually reflect the classic definition of the purchasing professional's 'task', which is to obtain materials and services which meet the 'rights' of purchasing, namely inputs of the right quality in the right quantity, from the right source delivered to the right place at the right time for the right price. These rights define purchasing from a point of view of objectives, which the purchasing professional must balance against each other, as sometimes these rights are irreconcilable.

Once it is clear what the objectives of the organisation, the department and the future contract are, consideration should be given to how those objectives can be achieved. You considered these issues in study session 3 where you studied the important role that the purchasing professional can play in the preparation of specifications, the setting of measurable targets to assess performance and managing that assessment, for example with the key performance indicators used in the example of Fun 4 U and Speedy Service Couriers used in section 3.2. The measurement of supplier performance is the key to contract management. Procedures should ensure that the measurement process is applied and mechanisms should ideally be built into the contract to deal with failure to perform.

Enforcement of the targets studied in study session 3 can then be dealt with by including appropriate terms in the contract, and in the event of breach for failure to meet obligations under the contract, these will give rise to perhaps damages or the right to terminate the contract. The various terms that can be found in contracts, whether they are implied terms which you studied in study session 9 or express terms which you studied in study sessions 10 – 13, should be considered carefully at the negotiating and drafting stages of contract development, as it is by including the appropriate terms in your contract that you are in a position to have the tools you need to manage it properly and enforce your organisation's rights if the other party defaults on its obligations.

As to formation of contracts, you studied this in study sessions 4 and 5, and you considered the special circumstances of contract formation in the event of battle of the forms in study session 6 and tendering in study session 17. These two ways of forming contracts are especially important as they can determine whose terms bind the contract. If you find yourself on the losing side of the battle of the forms you are going to have difficulty managing the contract, as you will not be able to rely on your organisation's standard terms and conditions. Contract formation is clearly relevant in how you are able to manage your contract.

Therefore, good contract management is a process which begins long before the contract is awarded, it starts at the beginning of the process of contract development. With regard to what is done to manage the contract, before the contract is agreed or awarded the contract management team should already have identified where problems could occur and highlighted procedures which need to be monitored carefully. These could be:

- poor risk assessment
- poorly drafted specifications
- poor selection of suppliers
- poor negotiation
- poor contract drafting
- confusion about roles
- poor commercial relationships.

The list above emphasises the importance of preparation before contract award.

Not all contracts will require the same level of management, as you saw in study session 7 when different categories of procurements were considered. As well as the category of procurement affecting the degree of contract management required, the type of contract can also be a factor in determining the appropriate level of management. When examining the different types of contract which an organisation can enter into, the Kraljic matrix which balances the factors of risk to an organisation, and the amount spent by an organisation on that purchase, are compared.

20

Figure 20.1: Influence of risk and spend on the level of management required for contracts

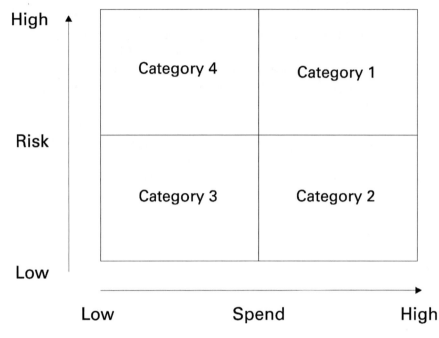

- Category 1 – This category of contracts are high risk/high spend. Contract management should be extensive. Requirements in this category are very important to the purchasing organisation and, as you saw in study session 17, the emphasis is on value, and often evaluation criteria for such purchases are likely to reflect the whole-life cost approach studied in study session 1 (life-cycle costing) to find the product or service which gives the best value.
- Category 2 – This category of contracts is high spend/low risk. Those contracts which fall within the area of high spend/medium risk will be the same as category 1 with regard to contract management. Those contracts which are truly high spend/low risk will not require high levels of contract management but will be treated in a similar way to categories 3 and 4.
- Category 3 – This category of contracts is low risk/low spend. Contracts in this category do not require high levels of contract management. The main focus of contract management with these contracts is to ensure that goods are received in an undamaged state and to ensure that services are delivered on time and at an acceptable quality level.
- Category 4 – This category of contracts is high risk/low spend. Contracts in this category are probably unlikely to require high levels of contract management and are likely to be treated in the same way as those in Category 3.

There are many roles in contract management that are played by different departments and individuals in the organisation. The purchasing department has a role to play but so too do other departments. Cannon (2005: 179) lists various responsibilities of the different departments such as:

- the legal and finance departments providing specialist advice

- the finance department clearing invoices and managing budgets
- internal customers liaising with the supplier about delivery and making decisions about whether the goods are of acceptable quality, and
- the purchasing department making commercial decisions, negotiating, and interpreting the contract.

He also emphasises the need for the contract management procedures to specify clearly what those roles are.

In addition, it is vital that good commercial relationships are maintained as poor ones can cause poor contract management to take place. Where poor commercial relationships exist it may be due to a simple clash of personalities between the individuals involved. However, it could be due to the organisations having different objectives or even due to the use of sharp practices by one of the parties.

It is possible that even when you have a contract that is being managed well and has been since the early planning stages, changes in circumstances might mean that the contract must be altered. Although foresight and good planning can avoid the need for some changes, it is possible that others are unavoidable. When changes must be made to the contract they must be managed properly and so it is necessary to include good change management procedures so that any change required will be considered, costed and documented before agreement. It is also important that if changes are necessary after the contract has been agreed, there should be provision in the contract clauses for amendment, as dealt with in study session 13.

Self-assessment question 20.1

How would you ensure a contract is managed successfully?

You should limit your essay to around 600 words. Remember that appendix 5, Advice on answering examination questions contains examination tips about how to approach essay questions.

Feedback on page 235

20.2 Contract review

Learning activity 20.2

Think about how your organisation deals with contract reviews and list the steps that it takes.

Feedback on page 235

It is vital that reviews take place in order that lessons can be learned to enable the implementation of improvements to the process of developing contracts. Reviews may take place at different times.

- Project evaluation review. This type of review should be carried out on all projects to focus on the management and processes of the

20

project and to see if any improvements could be made that could be implemented in future projects.

- Post-implementation review. This type of review should always be carried out for major projects. Here the focus is on whether the organisation has achieved what it intended to from the point of view of the business generally. Such reviews are used to assess whether the project supports the business objectives and whether it is in keeping with the strategy of the organisation.

- Contract review. This is primarily a review of contract performance, which should take place at regular intervals during the course of the contract especially if it is a contract of long duration as contract reviews can be used to detect problems at an early stage. If the contract is of a long duration you may need to have fairly regular short-term reviews to monitor performance at perhaps monthly intervals, with a larger review taking place at a longer term, maybe every six months. These reviews are vital with service contracts. The matters which you might consider at these two reviews are:

  - Monthly reviews – matters such as the following could be reviewed:
    ◦ any current areas of concern
    ◦ the level of information that is being made available to the review team – is it adequate?
    ◦ are there any trends developing?
    ◦ are the end users requesting any changes?
    ◦ are there any events which are likely to occur which may affect the contract?

  - Six-monthly reviews – these could review matters such as:
    ◦ are objectives being achieved?
    ◦ are quality standards being met?
    ◦ how satisfied are the end users?
    ◦ how effective are the relationships?
    ◦ how quickly and efficiently is the need for change being dealt with and is there forward planning to cope with possible changing needs?

If any matters are not reaching the standards expected, then consideration must be given to the problem to ascertain why so that appropriate steps can be planned and implemented. The reviews, whether they take place during or at the end of the contract, are an important part of the process of evaluation and implementation of improvement. You will now go on to consider the cycle of improvement in section 20.3 below.

Self-assessment question 20.2

State which of the following are true and which are false.

1   Project evaluation reviews should be carried out:
    (a) On an organisation's large projects
    (b) To focus on the management and processes of the project
    (c) To see if any improvements could be implemented in future projects.

2   Post-implementation reviews should be carried out:

(continued on next page)

Self-assessment question 20.2 *(continued)*

(a) For major projects

(b) To assess whether the project supports the business objectives

(c) To assess whether it is in keeping with the organisation's strategy.

Feedback on page 236

20.3 Improving the contracting process

Learning activity 20.3

Think about what could be done to improve the contracting process in your organisation and make a list of the changes you would implement to improve it.

Feedback on page 236

Contract management is a process of little value if nothing is learned from it. It is important therefore that any knowledge gained during the process of managing the contract is duly considered and then, where relevant, incorporated in future contract development. Although the management of each contract can be looked at individually, the process of contract development in an organisation is a continuous one as can be seen by figure 20.2.

Figure 20.2: Cycle of continuous improvement in contract management

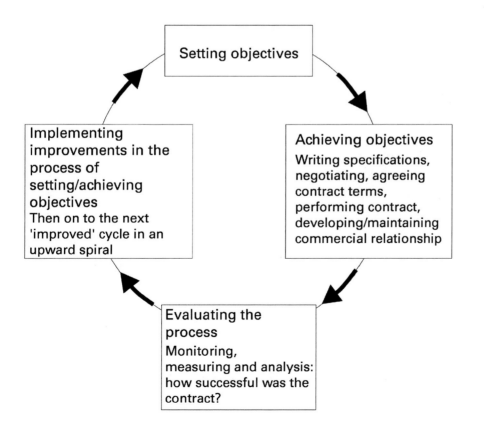

20

233

The process of contract management is an integral part of developing contracts and it should ideally ensure that an organisation follows an upward spiral of continuous improvement with each contract that travels around the cycle. Not all contracts will be the same and so with each contract there may be different problems which arise, but wherever possible the things learned from good contract management in one contract should be carried forward for consideration and implementation where appropriate in future contracts in order to continue the cycle of continuous improvement.

Self-assessment question 20.3

Answer the following questions to complete the horizontal words. Once the quiz is completed you should discover the mystery vertical word.

1 You decide what these are in the early stages.
2 This is what you do to a contract.
3 First word of the phrase describing what you use to achieve the aim of the cycle.
4 Second word of the phrase describing what you use to achieve the aim of the cycle.
5 This word is an adjective which describes the aim of the cycle.
6 This is the aim of the cycle.
7 This is what you do to changes.

Figure 20.3

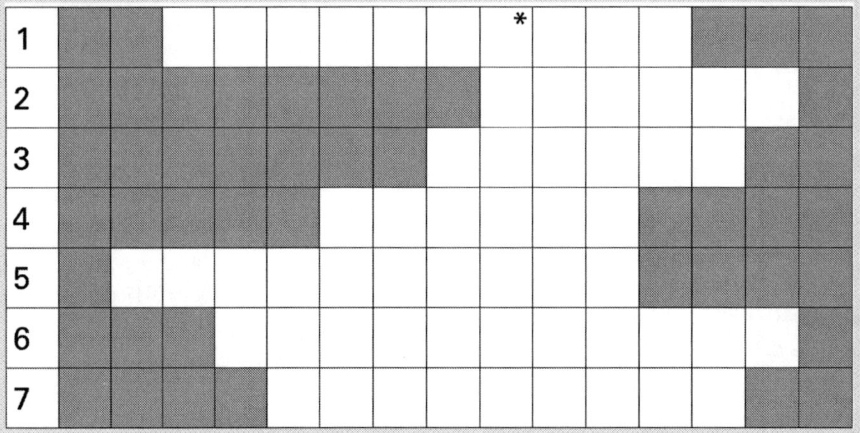

Feedback on page 236

Revision question

Now try the revision question for this session on page 241.

Summary

In this session you have studied:

- contract reviews – different types of reviews, when they occur and what can be considered

- the management of contracts – the various steps in the process of contract management which cover the whole process from the initial stages to the completion of the contract
- the aim of improving the contracting process and the cycle of continuous improvement.

Suggested further reading

CIPS website http://www.cips.org – professional resources area. CIPS Positions on Practice Contract Management.

Feedback on learning activities and self-assessment questions

Feedback on learning activity 20.1

If you consider contract management in your organisation you may find that little is done once the contract is awarded, or you may have some contracts where they are closely monitored and actively managed. As you work through this section you will begin to understand the broader picture of contract management and why not all contracts will be managed in the same way.

Feedback on self-assessment question 20.1

In order to answer this question you should consider the various stages in the development of a contract.

They commence with setting the contract objectives, and achieving those objectives by preparing specifications, choosing the appropriate supplier, setting measurable targets including mechanisms for dealing with failure to perform, and measuring supplier performance. Thorough preparation, including drafting specifications, choosing the right supplier and performance monitoring are some of the hallmarks of good contract management.

In negotiations, appropriate contract terms must be agreed to enable the organisation to enforce the contract if the other party fail to perform, and when the contract is formed, for example, purchasers should avoid the 'wrong' terms being included by inappropriate procedures such as battle of the forms. If the contract has been well negotiated and appropriate contract terms have been incorporated, you will also have the necessary tools available to take legal steps in the event of breach or to take steps to enforce compliance where necessary.

Finally, once formed, an appropriate commercial relationship should be developed and maintained to ensure that the process of correct contract management continues throughout the term of the contract.

Feedback on learning activity 20.2

In your organisation you may have procedures in place for procedures to be reviewed regularly; alternatively your organisation may take a more relaxed approach to reviews and to contract management generally. If this is the case, you could consider at what stages in the procedures you think reviews could be done in your organisation and upon which issues you should focus.

Feedback on self-assessment question 20.2

1
   (a) This is false; project evaluation reviews should be carried out on all projects.

2   They are all true.

Feedback on learning activity 20.3

Depending on the level of contract management that already exists in your organisation, you may be able to see possibilities for large-scale improvements or perhaps just minor ones. Do reviews take place when you think they are necessary? Are the issues considered always the ones that are important? Are the right people in your organisation the ones carrying out the reviews? Do they have all the information they need? These are just some of the questions you may have asked yourself and whatever conclusions you came to would indicate the level of improvement to the review stage of contract management in your organisation.

Feedback on self-assessment question 20.3

Figure 20.4

1			O	B	J	E	C	T	I*	V	E	S		
2									M	A	N	A	G	E
3								U	P	W	A	R	D	
4					S	P	I	R	A	L				
5		C	O	N	T	I	N	U	O	U	S			
6				I	M	P	R	O	V	E	M	E	N	T
7					I	M	P	L	E	M	E	N	T	

The mystery word is improve.

Revision questions

Revision question for study session 1

1   Explain what type of production materials are used in manufacturing processes. Provide TWO examples.
2   Explain the meaning of MRO and provide TWO examples.
3   Your company, Pet Foods (PF), is a small chain of pet-food stores located in the Midlands in the UK. It is part of a large pet food group, Multi Foods & Veterinary Services (MFVS), which owns more than 200 stores and veterinary services in the UK. MVFS has centralised administration in Manchester and all requirements are ordered from there and then delivered to the sites throughout the UK. Individual local managers are responsible for the maintenance and equipment purchasing. PF requires a 'grain/seed mixer machine' for birds in order to deliver a quality product to its growing number of customers.
    (a)   Describe what type of equipment the grain/seed mixer machine is.
    (b)   Describe the life cycle approach to the purchase of capital goods.
4   Describe the MRO purchaser's role in an organisation.

Feedback on page 243

Revision question for study session 2

1   Describe the classic definition of the purchasing task.
2   Explain why difficulties arise within a procurement department's objectives.
3   AB Company needs to purchase stationery and cleaning services for the organisation. Describe the steps the procurement manager should take to ensure the products and/or services meet the needs of the organisation.
4   Explain the difference between quality control and quality assurance and identify the disadvantages of relying upon a separate inspection to ensure supplier quality.

Feedback on page 244

Revision question for study session 3

1   Describe ONE category of specification.
2   Describe the basic functions of specification.
3   You are a procurement professional in a medium-sized construction company. You need to organise specifications for a new-build development in your local town. Describe various methods you will use to specify requirements for the project.

4   Describe the common agreement for specification for services. Draw a table which will enable purchasers to state their own service level needs clearly and unambiguously.

5   Considering that there are differences between whether you are the purchaser or the supplier, describe some of the important issues for each of these activities.

Feedback on page 244

Revision question for study session 4

1   Describe the difference between acceptance and counter-offer.

2   State what type of acceptance was decided in the case of *Brogden* v *Metropolitan Railway Company* [1877].

3   You own a small shop selling doll's houses which are priced from £200. You display a doll's house in the window with a price tag of £20. Mrs S enters the shop and asks for the doll's house in the window for £20. Explain if and why you can refuse to sell the doll's house to Mrs S. Refer to relevant case law in your answer.

4   An offer ends when it is unconditionally accepted or rejected. Describe TWO other ways of terminating an offer.

Feedback on page 245

Revision question for study session 5

1   Explain what is meant by consideration.

2   Describe the legal reasons why an agreement to meet a friend for dinner cannot be viewed as a contract.

3   CD Construction (CD) contract with New Town Developers (NTD) to build 20 units at a retail park. CD engaged Heat Serve (HS) to install a central-heating system in the units. The central-heating system in all but one of the units is defective. Explain who and why NTD can sue for the defective workmanship.

4   You are a procurement professional of a large organisation. You are concerned about who has authority to act in contractual matters. Describe what practical steps you can take to avoid problems relating to capacity and associated matters.

Feedback on page 246

Revision question for study session 6

1   Describe TWO methods that will avoid the battle of the forms.

2   Use the CIPS definition to define e-procurement.

3   Your organisation wants to increase sales and has decided that the future lies in using electronic communication. Explain what steps you need to consider in understanding how e-contracts are formed.

4   BR deliver cartons of vodka to XY for storage. BR's driver gave a delivery note to XY. The delivery note contains BR's terms and conditions (t&c). XY accept the cartons. Explain whether a valid contract exists referring in your answer to relevant case law.

Feedback on page 247

Revision question for study session 7

1 Define the meaning of effectiveness in relation to supply agreements.
2 Describe the styles of commercial relationship appropriate in procurement of different items under a supply agreement.
3 Describe how you would evaluate the effectiveness of a supply agreement.

Feedback on page 247

Revision question for study session 8

1 Explain how 'time of delivery' can be either a condition or a warranty in a contract.
2 Describe what kind of statement 'just like mother bakes' is.
3 Robinson Cruises Ltd charter a ship from Seaworthy Ltd for one year. Seaworthy stated that the ship was fitted out for the purposes of carrying ordinary cargo. Robinson commenced the charter but lost 32 weeks of the charter due to the ship being in a poor state of repair and the crew being incompetent. Robinson treated the contract as terminated. Explain, using relevant case law, whether Robinson were entitled to treat the contract as terminated.

Feedback on page 248

Revision question for study session 9

1 Explain the meaning of an 'implied term' in a contract.
2 Describe what terms are implied under section 14 of the Sale of Goods Act 1979 (as amended).
3 State terms implied under section 4 of the Supply of Goods and Services Act 1982.
4 John purchases a washing machine from his friend Anne for £100. When he tries to wash his clothes the machine overheats and shreds his clothes. Identify any implied term and explain whether it has been breached and whether John has any remedies.
5 Explain how statutory legislation controls exclusion and limitation of liability in a contract.

Feedback on page 249

Revision question for study session 10

1 Explain the difference between express and implied terms in a contract.
2 Describe what the court decides in the case of *Poussard* v *Spiers and Pond* [1876].
3 You are a professional opera singer and have been chosen to sing at the Singer of the Year festival in August. You must attend at least four rehearsals with the orchestra and supporting choir. You suffer a throat infection in July and are told by your doctor that you must not sing for at least six weeks, which means that you will miss all but one rehearsal. When you do not turn up for the first three rehearsals you are told by the organisers of the festival that they have engaged another singer.

Explain whether the organisers were entitled to terminate your contract and if not, why not. Refer to appropriate case law in your answer.

Feedback on page 249

Revision question for study session 11

Explain the difference between a contract of guarantee and a contract for indemnity. Refer to a case which considers this difference.

Feedback on page 250

Revision question for study session 12

Describe the three tests applied by the courts when considering contract terms. Refer to case law in your answer.

Feedback on page 250

Revision question for study session 13

1 Describe TWO potential advantages of arbitration.
2 BR Builders have been contracted by Nursecare to build a new 20-bed nursing home. The contract contains a clause stating that any dispute arising out of the contract will be dealt with only by arbitration. Evaluate whether this is a valid clause.

Feedback on page 251

Revision question for study session 14

1 Explain TWO potential benefits to the buyer of e-sourcing.
2 As purchasing manager for your organisation explain why you would include the following *four clauses* in the contract for maintenance and servicing of the IT equipment which is critical for the business:
   • liquidated damages clause
   • time is of the essence clause
   • indemnity clause
   • dispute resolution clause.

Feedback on page 251

Revision question for study session 15

1 Zerum Ltd, a manufacturer of beds in the UK, agreed to sell them to Amber, a company in France. The contract was a cif contract and the goods were being transported by sea from Hull to Calais. Payment was agreed by way of a documentary credit through Banc Francais in France and the Bank of England in London. Zerum arranged for the loading of the goods and gave a clean bill of lading to the Bank of England. The beds were stored on the ship's deck and during a storm at sea the majority of the beds were damaged. The beds arrived at Calais before the bill of lading. Explain the obligation of Zerum under a cif contract and who carries the risk in the beds.

2   Draw a diagram explaining the documentary credit arrangement.

Feedback on page 252

Revision question for study session 16

1   Describe ONE Incoterm.
2   Explain the basic functions of Incoterms.

Feedback on page 252

Revision question for study session 17

1   Identify TWO of the five conditions for successful competitive
     tendering identified by the well-known American writers Dobler and
     Burt.
2   Describe the TWO major types of tendering process.
3   The tendering process has been carried out for two contracts, one
     for the purchase of stationery and the other for an innovative CRM
     package. You have received tenders for both contracts and now need to
     consider the tenders. Describe and contrast the evaluation criteria you
     would use to analyse the tenders for each of the contracts.

Feedback on page 253

Revision question for study session 18

1   Explain TWO remedies available to suppliers who can prove that the
     public sector buyer has breached the EU public procurement rules.
2   Analyse the truth or otherwise of the following statement:
     'Contracts which are subject to the EU directives can include
     specifications which refer to proprietary brands.'
3   Explain why compulsory competitive tendering (CCT) was introduced.

Feedback on page 254

Revision question for study session 19

1   As a purchasing professional, identify two ways of using electronics in
     the procurement process.
2   Explain why the issue of security is important to your organisation in
     the e-tendering process.

Feedback on page 254

Revision question for study session 20

1   Identify TWO categories of contract which will require extensive
     management.
2   Contract management only starts once the contract is awarded. Analyse
     the truth of this statement.

Feedback on page 254

Feedback on revision questions

Feedback on revision question for study session 1

1   Production materials used in manufacturing are usually raw materials, components and sub-assemblies or assemblies.

2   MRO means maintenance, repair and operating items. Your two examples could be from any of the following: fire and safety equipment, electrical supplies, caretaking requirements, repair parts or spares for plant and equipment.

3
    (a)   The grain/seed mixer machine falls within the category of capital equipment. Capital equipment is a tangible asset which provides utility or benefit to an organisation over a long period.
    (b)   The life cycle approach is the practice of obtaining, over the lifetime of the goods, the best use of the physical assets at the lowest cost to the entity. This approach can be considered under three headings: acquisition costs; operation costs; and disposal costs.
          Acquisition costs can include the initial costs of transportation, installation and commissioning and the cost of initial spares and training of the operator/supervisor. Operation costs include the costs of operators, supervisors and employment costs, as well as fuel and power expenditure, dealing with emissions or effluent, insurance, maintenance and downtime and cost of spares. Disposal costs include the costs of depreciation, estimated value on disposal if any and the costs of disposal including environmental costs.

4   MRO supplies are critical to an organisation and it is therefore important that the MRO purchasing professional takes a disciplined approach. The disruption to production by a shortage in an MRO item could be disastrous for an organisation. The MRO purchaser's role includes negotiation skills for the purchase and liaising with maintenance staff to ensure that information on cost, availability and delivery times is sufficient to avoid having a build up of unnecessary levels of stock. Their role also includes establishing a standardisation policy to avoid holding a variety of spares. They should suggest alternatives to purchasing such as outsourcing cleaning and catering for example, which will avoid the need to hold cleaning and catering items. They should aim to minimise administration and storage costs by using small order procedures and direct purchasing by users using call-off contracts. They should analyse proposed maintenance contracts and consider whether emergency or critical spares could be shared.

Feedback on revision question for study session 2

1   The classic definition of the purchasing task is considered by Lysons and Farrington (2006) in their book *Purchasing and Supply Chain Management.* The definition of the task is to obtain materials of the right quality in the right quantity from the right source delivering to the right place at the right time at the right price.

2   Difficulties arise because the corporate objectives differ from those of the purchasing department within an organisation. Corporate objectives tend to be strategic, long term and general, whereas the purchasing department's objectives are functional and are therefore tactical, short term and specific.

3   The procurement manager will need to take certain steps to ensure that the inputs an organisation acquires meet the requirements of the organisation. The steps include the use of specifications, performance measures and contract terms. The product or services should conform to their specifications. The specification is therefore an important part of the quality aspect of a product or service. The specification should give the supplier a clear picture of what is required by the organisation. Performance measurement measures how well a supplier is performing in supplying the required goods or services. The procurement function often needs to measure the quality of the products and services as well as supplier performance. Once agreement has been reached between the organisation and the supplier it should be set out formally in a contract. The contract should be clear as to the requirements of the organisation in terms of product or service to be provided by the supplier and it should make provision for what will happen in the event of difficulties arising.

4   Quality control is concerned with checking and inspecting a process or product during or after its production or online. Quality can be controlled this way, but it is generally a more expensive and less reliable method. Quality assurance on the other hand is concerned with prevention of errors in products and processes and therefore takes place in the preproduction stages. If total costs of quality are considered it is frequently established that this method is in fact a more resource efficient method of ensuring quality, particularly if failure costs are high. The disadvantages of separate inspection include additional stockholding costs, less flow in operations, more delays, less effort on the part of the supplier to ensure quality, and higher staff costs.

Feedback on revision question for study session 3

1   You have a choice of conformance or performance. A short answer is expected such as: Conformance specifications are strict and technical and usually describe the specific product or service. It limits a supplier's freedom.

2   Performance specifications state what the requirement is expected to do. It includes the typical performance expected and the minimum and maximum expectations. They encourage a supplier's freedom.

3   You should describe standards, brand or trade names, samples, drawings or blueprints, market grade, method of manufacture and physical or chemical properties. Provide a short sentence on each. For example,

standards could be A4 paper, manufacturer's standards, industry standards. Brand names could be BMW, but if using a brand then it is often more expensive and alternatives cannot be used. Sometimes the term 'or equivalent' is used. For samples, consideration has to be given to section 15 of the Sale of Goods Act 1979. In a construction project drawings are provided. And so on for the remaining methods.

4   The common agreement is a service level agreement (SLA). This allows purchasers to state their minimum service level needs clearly and unambiguously. SLAs enable providers to focus their resources on providing services at the required level. Table 21.1 shows what your table could look like.

Table 21.1

KPIs	Acceptable minimum level of service	Target level	How measured
Delivery time (include address of delivery)	85% same day	100% same day	Monthly customer survey
Pick-up time	85% collect within two hours	100% collect within two hours	Signature of receptionist
Damaged parcels	2%	0%	Monthly customer survey
Missing parcels	0%	0%	Data collation

5   Matters which are important differ between a purchaser and a supplier. Under the principles of English contract law the parties have freedom to contract. This means that the terms can vary from one contract to another as it is the parties' choice as to what they agree to include as express terms of their contract. Obviously each party will want the best terms for their organisation. Matters which have to be considered include delivery times; increase in production costs during the contract; when ownership of the goods passes, and so on. To cover each of these issues the terms to be included in the contract are: time is of the essence; price variation clause; retention of title clause and exclusion clauses.

Feedback on revision question for study session 4

1   When an offer is made, if an acceptance to the offer is made and it is clear and unqualified then the contract is concluded. If the acceptance is conditional or qualified it will be a counter-offer and it will destroy the original offer.

2   The acceptance in this case was acceptance by conduct. If conduct is silent it can still amount to acceptance as in the *Brogden* case where the plaintiff supplied coal to the defendant on a written annual contract. A new contract was sent to the plaintiff who amended it (this is a counter-offer), but the defendant filed it away and forgot to respond. However, the defendant accepted deliveries which conformed to the new contract. The court held that the defendants had accepted the new amended contract by their silent conduct, namely, accepting the deliveries.

3   This short case study is based on *Fisher* v *Bell* [1961] where a shopkeeper displayed a flick knife for sale in the shop window. The court held that by doing so it was an invitation to treat. This applies in

245

the case of the doll's house and the shop owner can refuse to sell it to Mrs S. The offer comes when Mrs S offers to buy and her offer of £20 is rejected so there can be no contract in this case.

4   An offer also comes to an end when an acceptance which is received is conditional as this is a counter-offer which terminates the original offer. An offer is terminated by revocation which is where the offeror, that is the person making the offer, changes their mind and no longer wishes their offer to be open. They take it back by revoking it. Of course revocation is only available until the offer is unconditionally accepted. Once unconditional acceptance takes place the offer cannot be revoked. An offer which is open only for a particular time will automatically end when that time expires. If no time is specified then an offer will expire after a 'reasonable' time.

Feedback on revision question for study session 5

1   Consideration is one of the essential elements of a contract. Consideration is something of value in the eyes of the law, which constitutes the price for which the promise of the other party is bought.

2   An agreement to meet a friend for dinner is classed as a social agreement and in the eyes of the law it is presumed that the parties had no intention of creating legal relations.

3   This case study is to do with privity of contract and the position of subcontractors. HS are subcontractors to CD. The doctrine of privity states that only a party to a contract can sue to enforce the contract or be sued. If this applied in this case study then there is no contract between HS and NTD so NTD would be unable to sue for damages for defective workmanship. However, this principle gave rise to many practical difficulties and so the law developed ways to deal with the problems caused by privity. One of the ways relates to subcontractors. A subcontractor, from a legal perspective, is someone that you do not have a direct contractual relationship with; in other words, they are a third party. This problem has been addressed in the area of English law in line with the law of other European systems with the Contracts (Rights of Third Parties) Act 1999. This provides rules by which third-party rights can be granted in the main contract. The Act can insert clauses into contracts to give rights to a third party who could then enforce them through the courts. So in these circumstances NTD could sue HS.

4   This case study is based on the case of *British Bank of the Middle East* v *Sun Life of Canada (UK) Ltd* [1983] where the plaintiff relied on the authority of one of the defendant's local managers to commit to a type of property transaction not usually undertaken by a life assurance company other than at head office level. The House of Lords held that as the written assurances given had come from senior local management not from general management then it was not binding. The practical steps you should take to avoid problems include having major contracts made by deed as the signature of either two directors or director and company secretary will be required. You could also request a certified copy of the board resolution that was passed when the contract was authorised. You could check the date when the company was incorporated. If the company is in liquidation then only the liquidator, administrator or receiver has the power to contract on its behalf.

Feedback on revision question for study session 6

1   You have a choice of describing the use of formal tendering; proper and careful management of all contract documentation; setting up of standard terms and conditions which are made clear to all suppliers before any contract is formally awarded; and e-contracts where the purchaser must click acceptance of the seller's terms and conditions before the contract can be made.

2   E-procurement means using the internet to operate the transactional aspects of requisitioning, authorising, ordering, receipting and payment processes for the required services or products.

3   The legal principles applicable to contract formation apply equally to e-contracts. E-contracts require the essential elements of offer, acceptance, consideration and intention to enter into legal relations. You must consider the information on the website carefully. You need to look at the general information as well as the terms and conditions on the website. If the website offers goods for sale which can be bought by purchasers by clicking acceptance on the website, then the website is making an offer and by clicking you are accepting that offer. Any subsequent emails are just confirmation of the contract which was already made at the time of clicking the acceptance button.
If the website merely advertises the supplier's goods then this is the same as displaying goods in a shop window. It will be treated as an invitation to treat just as the courts have held advertisements and displays to be invitations to treat in non e-contract cases. Case law that you can refer to includes *Partridge* v *Crittenden* [1968] and *Fisher* v *Bell* [1961].

4   This case study is based on the case of *BRS* v *Arthur B Crutchley Ltd* [1968] where the plaintiffs delivered whiskey to the defendants for storage. Their driver gave the defendants a delivery note which incorporated the plaintiff's terms. The defendants stamped the note that the goods were received under their terms and conditions. The court held that this was a counter-offer but the plaintiffs had accepted the counter-offer by their conduct when they handed over the whiskey. The contract was made on the defendant's terms and conditions. So in the present case study there is a valid contract and it is on BR's terms and conditions.

Feedback on revision question for study session 7

1   The effectiveness of a supply agreement depends on whether it does what it is supposed to do, whether it produces results and whether it produces the right results. The rights of purchasing include the right quality, right quantity, right source, delivered to the right place at the right time for the right price.

2   Once a supply agreement has been negotiated and the contract agreed it will then be performed. However, the effectiveness of the supply agreement can be affected by the commercial relationship between you and the supplier. You have to develop the appropriate relationship to ensure the effectiveness of the supply agreement. The style of commercial relationship depends on the type of items being procured. Bottleneck items are high risk but low spend. The seller is often in a powerful position and the buyer must behave accordingly. Strategic

items are high risk and high spend. These are critical to the purchasing organisation and it has a high spend. In this situation the purchaser should work closely with the seller to drive costs down and quality up. Non-critical items are everyday items which are low risk and low spend. Time and effort expended by the purchaser are unlikely to bring any benefit to the organisation. Leverage items are low risk and high spend. The main focus here is on price and there will often be many suppliers.

3   The effectiveness of a supply agreement will depend on various things such as specifications, what has been agreed during the negotiations and the contractual terms. You may need to evaluate its effectiveness by comparing it to other agreements. You may want to find out if it meets original expectations. You will need to look at whether it has achieved its objectives and you will need to measure its performance and whether it has complied with specifications and KPIs. You will need to carry out ongoing monitoring of performance, record measurements and score them in accordance with a scoring system. This is necessary to enable you to analyse and compare against other agreements.

Feedback on revision question for study session 8

1   You should explain that time of delivery is a warranty unless the buyer explicitly states that time is of the essence or similar in the contract documentation. The distinction is important as breach of condition allows an aggrieved party to terminate and claim damages.

2   This is an 'advertising puff', that is, an exaggerated statement found in an advertisement. Advertising puffs are not intended to be relied upon and have no legal effect. They can be ignored for contractual purposes.

3   This case study is to do with the difference between warranties, conditions and innominate terms and is based on the case of *Hong Kong Fir Shipping Co. Ltd* v *Kawasaki Kisen Kaisha Ltd* [1962] where the defendants had chartered a ship from the plaintiffs for two years. The charter stated that the ship was 'in every way fitted for ordinary cargo service'. However, the ship was in a poor state of repair and the engine crew were incompetent. The plaintiffs openly admitted this and consequently 20 weeks of the charter were lost. The statement 'in every way ...' was not stated to be a condition or a warranty in the contract. The defendants claimed that there was a breach of condition which entitled them to treat the contract as terminated. The plaintiffs claimed that the defendants were only entitled to damages. The court held that the term was an innominate term. The court then had to decide whether the defendants had been deprived of the whole of the benefit of the contract and if so then they were entitled to terminate and claim damages. In the *Hong Kong* case the court held that the defendants had not been deprived of a substantial benefit of the contract and could only claim damages. So in the short case study, if you follow the approach of *Hong Kong* and decide that the statement is an innominate term, you may decide that losing more than half of the contract period is substantial and that Robinson are therefore entitled to terminate and claim damages. You should explain that innominate terms are treated as such where there is no mention in the contract of whether the statement is a warranty or condition. However, you can also go on to explain that the courts are reluctant to follow the *Hong Kong* case and rather use

the traditional approach of declaring the term that had been breached as either a condition or warranty. If they decide it is a condition then it entitles the aggrieved party to terminate the contract and also claim damages, whereas if the term is a warranty then the aggrieved party is only entitled to claim damages.

Feedback on revision question for study session 9

1   An implied term is a term which has not been expressly agreed upon or included in the contract. It is implied into a contract by law irrespective of whether the parties agree to it or not.
2   Under SGA 1979, section 14 relates to quality and fitness of the goods, but only applies to goods sold in the course of business. Section 14(2) relates to satisfactory quality and section 14(3) relates to fitness for purpose.
3   Under SOGAS 1982, section 4(2) relates to satisfactory quality and section 4(3) relates to fitness for purpose.
4   Initially you may identify that this is a contract for sale of goods which turn out not to be of satisfactory quality. The appropriate section which applies would be section 14(2) Sale of Goods Act 1979. However, you should also identify that John will have no remedies under this Act as the contract for the sale of goods was not in the course of business.
5   The Unfair Contract Terms Act 1977 (UCTA 1977) and the Unfair Terms in Consumer Regulations 1999 control exclusion and limitation of liability in contracts. The 1977 Act established circumstances when a party to a contract can or cannot exclude or limit their liability by including an express term in the contract. Whether such a term is allowed depends on whether the contract is with a consumer and whether the term is reasonable. There can never be a term which excludes liability in respect of title under section 12 SGA 1979. When the term relates to sections 13–15 SGA 1979 then it will depend on the circumstances of each case. If a purchaser is a consumer then any express term in a contract excluding liability is deemed void under UCTA 1977. If the purchaser is not a consumer then the express term is subject to the reasonableness test.

Feedback on revision question for study session 10

1   Express terms are those which are stated within the contract and which have been agreed upon by both parties. Implied terms are those which are not stated within the contract but which may be implied by law depending on the circumstances of each case.
2   *Poussard* v *Spiers and Pond* [1876] related to the difference between conditions and warranties. An actress engaged to play the leading role in a play was unable to attend the opening night but attended one week after the season began. The producers had to hire a substitute and refused to allow the actress to play the role. The actress sued for breach of contract. The court held that the opening night was very important and by not turning up it amounted to breach of condition and therefore the contract could be terminated by the producers.
3   This short case study is similar to the case of *Bettini* v *Gye* [1876]. As you were able to attend a rehearsal and the actual event, it will be

held to be a breach of warranty and not a breach of condition as the rehearsals will be held to be ancillary to the contract. They had no right to terminate your contract and are only entitled to claim damages.

Feedback on revision question for study session 11

There is often confusion between what is meant by guarantee and indemnity. This is not surprising as many manufacturers use the word guarantee when referring to the quality of goods they are supplying whether the guarantee is contractual or not. If the contract is under a guarantee then the party compensating for the loss is liable to the party who suffered the loss. This is secondary to and depends on the liability of the principal contractor. It means that the party guaranteeing are standing in for the original party liable if the original party cannot pay.

However, in contracts for indemnity the party indemnifying the other party takes on the liability of the person being indemnified. This is separate to the original contract.

The case which considers the difference between guarantee and indemnity is the case of *Mountstephen* v *Lakeman* [1874]. In this case the courts decided that an indemnity had been provided when the defendant told the plaintiff builder to go ahead and undertake the work for the Local Board of Health. The defendant, who was the chairman of the local Board of Health, had told the builders, 'Do the work and I will see you paid'.

Feedback on revision question for study session 12

You should first of all state that the three tests are incorporation, interpretation and reasonableness. Go on to provide a paragraph explaining each of these.

Incorporation is where the courts will consider whether the clause has been included in the contract. This might seem obvious and simple, but it is not so. To be included in the contract it must be included validly and at the time the contract is made. The difficulty of whether this is so is illustrated in the case of *Olley* v *Marlborough Court Ltd* [1949]. A guest booked into a hotel. The contract was made at the reception desk. When the guest's belongings were stolen the hotel referred to their exclusion clause. The courts held that the exclusion clause had not been included in the contract as the contract was formed at the reception desk and the exclusion clause was only in the notice in the guest bedroom.

Interpretation of a term is considered by the courts when the term is incorporated or validly included in the contract. The courts can interpret all or any of the terms, but it is very important to exclusion clauses and a force majeure clause. When a party wants to rely on an exclusion clause then it must be drafted carefully. If there is any ambiguity then the clause will be interpreted *contra proferentum* which means that it will be interpreted against the person wanting to rely on it.

The reasonableness test is governed by the Unfair Contract Terms Act 1977 (UCTA 1977) and applies to exclusion or limitation clauses. These clauses will be void unless they pass the reasonableness test. The courts will consider the parties to the contract and whether the other party is dealing as a consumer.

Feedback on revision question for study session 13

1   Remember to describe only TWO!
    You have a choice of describing two of the following:
    - arbitration as being less formal both in relation to the hearings and the procedures; or
    - being more flexible as the arbitrators do not need to follow previous decisions (that is, there is no judicial precedent); or
    - the parties can choose who arbitrates, which means they can be an expert in a technical or specialist area and have greater knowledge of the subject in dispute; or
    - the fact that arbitration is held in private – there is no publicity; or
    - that it is less expensive as it usually takes less time and fees may even be reduced if legal representation is not encouraged; or
    - arbitration is quicker than litigation; or
    - the fact that the arbitrator's award can be enforced in the same way that a court judgment is enforced if the party at fault does not comply with the arbitrator's decision.

2   You should explain that the parties to a contract can decide to include a clause which will state what happens in the event of a dispute arising. However, you should also explain that a contract clause must not seek to prevent the parties having their rights determined by the courts. Such a clause would be void. So the word 'only' in this clause may cause difficulties if the parties have included this with a view to preventing parties having their right to go to court in the event of a dispute arising.

Feedback on revision question for study session 14

1   You have a variety of options for this question. You could start by stating that the basic requirements for formation of a contract still apply. Then go on to explain that information is available immediately via the internet; you will have less paperwork and administrative tasks; there will be lower transactional costs; you will have access to a wider range of suppliers and lower prices.

2   You would want to include liquidated damages clauses to provide for a genuine pre-estimate of anticipated loss on the occurrence of a given event. The clause should include a formula for calculating a fixed amount which will be paid by the defaulting party in the event of a delay in repair or late installation. The figure must be realistic. Where it is not, the courts may perceive it as a penalty and it will be struck out of the contract and you will have to sue for unliquidated damages.
    The time is of the essence clause is included in the contract so that you as buyer have the right to terminate the contract and sue for compensation should the supplier delay in delivery or performance of the contract.
    Including an indemnity clause ensures that you as buyer can pass liability to the machine supplier for claims arising from defective machinery.

The dispute resolution clause provides for the handling of any dispute by a specific process instead of going to court. The process can be arbitration or adjudication.

Feedback on revision question for study session 15

1   You should provide an explanation of a cif contract and explain that under such a contract there was an obligation on Zerum to arrange freight and insurance of the beds. According to the bill of lading the beds were dispatched in good condition. Once the beds crossed the rail of the ship in Hull the risk in the beds transferred to Amber. This means that the responsibility for the goods is with Amber and they should arrange for a remedy for the damage to the beds.
2   Your diagram should look like figure 21.1.

Figure 21.1

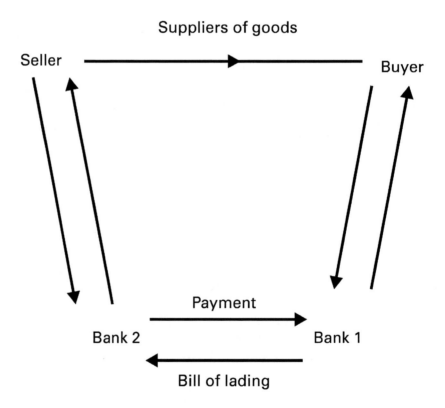

Feedback on revision question for study session 16

1   You have a choice of Incoterms: cif, fob, ddp, fas, exw to mention but a few. The usual ones to describe are cif or fob.
    *   CIF stands for 'cost insurance and freight', and responsibility is placed on the seller to arrange for the shipment of the goods and to insure them against loss or damage during the voyage.

- FOB stands for 'free on board' and places responsibility on the buyer to arrange for the shipment of the goods and to pay for insurance cover for the voyage. Responsibility of the seller stops when the goods are loaded on board the ship.
- DDP stands for 'duty paid' and the seller must deliver the goods to the buyer cleared for import and not unloaded at the named destination place. When the goods have been made available to the buyer at the named place in the import country then the seller has fulfilled his obligation. The seller bears the risk and costs including taxes, duties and delivery charges.
- FAS stands for 'free alongside ship'. In this contract the seller must place the goods, cleared for export, alongside the vessel at the named port of departure. The seller's obligations are fulfilled once the goods have been placed alongside the ship on the quay. The buyer then bears all costs and risks of loss or damage to the goods from then onwards.
- EXW means 'ex works'. There is minimum obligation for the seller. The seller must place the goods at the disposal of the buyer at the seller's premises or another named place which is not cleared for export and not loaded onto any vehicle. When the seller has made the goods available to the buyer at the seller's premises then the seller fulfils his obligation.

2 Incoterms are to make it clear how costs and risks are divided between the buyer and seller in relation to the delivery of the goods as required under the contract of sale. The main issues relate to delivery, risks and costs. There are different types of Incoterm and each of them clearly stipulates the responsibilities and obligations on the seller and buyer.

Feedback on revision question for study session 17

1 Your answer can be two of the following five:
- The value of the purchase must justify the time and effort spent on the tendering process.
- The specifications must be clear to everyone involved and the suppliers must know their costs of production.
- The sellers must actually want the contract and be technically competent.
- There must be sufficient time to carry out the tendering process.
- There must be an adequate number of sellers.

2 You should write a short paragraph about open procedure and restricted or selective procedure. In the open procedure the supplier is allowed to submit a bid for a contract. The downside to open procedure is the amount of work involved to identify which of the suppliers will actually be able to carry out the work. For the restricted or selective procedure you should explain that suppliers are invited to submit a tender. These suppliers are only the ones which are thought to be able to carry out the work. They may even have gone through a pre-qualifying procedure through an earlier supplier appraisal exercise.

3 Your answer should be in the form of an essay of 150 to 200 words. You should first of all identify that the stationery contract will fall into the low-spend/low-risk category whereas the innovative CRM is likely to fall into the high-risk/high-spend category of purchase. Then describe

each of the categories of high risk/high spend; high spend/low risk; high risk/low spend and low spend/low risk.

Feedback on revision question for study session 18

1   The suppliers have remedies through the High Court and these include having the contract declared void, having the contract varied and having an award of damages paid to the injured party.

2   Your answer should explain that where contracts are subject to EU directives then where possible they must refer to the British Standard that implements a European Standard. They should not refer to proprietary brands. However, if this is not possible then the brand can be included but the words 'or equal' should be inserted after the brand name.

3   CCT was introduced in the 1980s in the UK. The objective was to bring greater efficiency to local government and health services through the use of competition. The aim was to ensure that value for money was achieved for services directly used by the public sector organisations. The idea of best value authorities was introduced in the Local Government Act 1992.

Feedback on revision question for study session 19

1   There are a number of ways of using electronics and you can choose from any of the following:
*   e-sourcing – where you source suppliers and products and so on
*   e-transactions – where you carry out transactions via the internet or emails
*   e-contents – where you find out more about content for procurement
*   e-payments – where invoices and payments are made electronically
*   online contract management systems – where you manage your contracts via an online package such as one of the many software packages available.

2   Security is important because information is being made available outside your organisation. You should be aware of the difference between intranets (where information is passed within your organisation across departments) and the internet (where information is being passed to individuals and companies outside your organisation). It is good practice to have a privacy code which can be made available to suppliers and customers outside your organisation. You can set out details of your purchasing procedure and how you control information received and how it is safeguarded. You can explain that you must comply with the Data Protection Act 1998.

Feedback on revision question for study session 20

1   You should identify high risk/high spend with the emphasis on value or high spend/medium risk.

2   This is not true. To be truly effective contract management commences long before the contract is awarded. The contract should be managed

from the beginning of the process. In many organisations there will be a contract management team. Their job is to identify where problems might arise and these can be long before the contract is awarded. It is necessary to consider what roles each person involved in the contract will play and to know what the role is. It is important to manage how specifications are drafted, how suppliers are selected and how the contract is drafted. All this must be considered before the contract is awarded. Preparation is the key to building good commercial relationships. How you manage the contract process will also depend on the type of contract and category of purchase. You may wish to explain the Kraljic matrix and even draw it.

Appendix 1
The English legal system

If you are new to the study of law you will most likely be unfamiliar with the English legal system. Although in this course you will not be examined on how the English legal system works, you may find that this appendix provides useful background information to assist you with your understanding and application of contract law. You can find further information about the English legal system on the website of the Department of Constitutional Affairs at http://www.dca.gov.uk.

This course book refers to different types of law, namely case law, Acts of Parliament and statutory instruments as well as the laws applicable as a result of membership of the European Union and certain treaties in private international law.

Case law, or common law as it is sometimes referred to, has been developed in the English legal system since mediaeval times. Some cases decided as long ago as the sixteenth century are still valid law. The English courts have a hierarchy and when the higher courts in the system make decisions in cases, the courts which are lower in the hierarchy must apply the relevant legal principles and follow the higher courts' decisions when they deal with cases on the same legal point. This is known as binding precedent. Judges know what the decisions of previous cases are as they are published in law reports. Ever since cases were first reported several centuries ago, judges' decisions in cases have been recorded in writing. A vast body of information has developed in the law reports and these are available for study. If you wish to access information about the court system and read reports of decided cases you can look at the court service's website at http://www.hmcourts-service.gov.uk.

Parliament is now the major source of law in the UK. The Parliament at Westminster was established in the seventeenth century as a further source of law after the common law system had already been created and used for hundreds of years. Parliament creates Acts of Parliament, which are also referred to as statutes. You can find more information about how Parliament works, and how statutes are created, on the Parliament website at http://www.parliament.uk/works/newlaw.cfm. You can also read Acts of Parliament created since 1988, online at the website of the Office of Public Sector Information at http://www.opsi.gov.uk.

Sometimes, for various reasons, Parliament passes a very general statute simply setting out a framework of the new laws being created and giving authority to the relevant government department to create a Statutory Instrument which sets out the details of those laws. You can access Statutory Instruments at the website of the Office of Public Sector Information at http://www.opsi.gov.uk.

Not all of the laws made in the European Union have direct effect in the UK. Often these rules only become law in the individual Member States as a result of those states using their own legal systems to create the appropriate national laws to bring the state into line with the 'new European laws'. In the UK those laws are usually made by Parliament in the form of statutes and sometimes also by resulting Statutory Instruments.

The situation is the same with regard to private international law. When international treaties are signed, the rules agreed in those treaties do not automatically become directly applicable in the states which have been involved in the making of the treaty. Each state must take further action before the international rules set out in the treaty apply nationally. Sometimes this process can take several years. For example, following the international Hague Conference in 1964, two Uniform Laws known as the Hague Rules were adopted by various states including the UK but they did not become applicable to English law until several years later. Parliament passed the Uniform Laws on International Sales Act 1967 which brought the uniform laws into force in the UK in 1972.

Case law

This appendix contains summaries of the more significant legal cases mentioned in this course book.

Adams v *Lindsell* [1818]

In relation to the sale of some wool, the offeror was unaware that the offeree had validly accepted the offer by posting the offeror a letter. Before the letter was delivered to the offeror however, he sold the goods to another person. The court held that the offer had been validly accepted by the offeree and so a binding contract existed between the parties when the offeror sold the goods to someone else as acceptance was deemed to be communicated when the offeree put the letter of acceptance in the post.

Aluminium Industries Vassen BV v *Romalpa Aluminium Ltd*

The plaintiff, a Dutch company, sold aluminium foil to the defendant, an English company. The contract included a retention of title clause by which the plaintiff retained ownership of any unused foil in the defendant's possession until all payment was made. The clause also applied to any items made using the foil and such items or payment received for such items would be held by the defendant for the plaintiff. The defendant went into liquidation and the plaintiff sued to enforce the clause. The court held that the plaintiff could recover the unused foil still in the defendant's possession as well as the proceeds of sale of items made from the foil.

Atlas Express Ltd v *Kafco (Importers) Ltd* [1989]

A haulier insisted on increasing the price on a contract to transport the goods after a contract had already been made. The purchaser reluctantly agreed, but as the haulier was only providing the service that he had originally contracted to do, the court found that the haulier provided no additional consideration for the increased contract price and so the variation of the contract was not valid.

Bettini v *Gye* [1876]

A singer who was employed to perform for a whole season was required in the contract to attend rehearsals six days before the start of the season, but he only attended three days before the season started. The producers treated this as breach of condition and purported to terminate the contract so he sued for breach of contract. The court held that as the term relating to attending rehearsals was ancillary to the main part of the contract, it was a warranty, and on breach it gave rise to a claim for damages but not termination, so the producers only had the right to receive damages in the event of breach, they had no right to terminate the contract, so the singer's claim against them succeeded.

Blackpool & Fylde Aero Club Ltd v *Blackpool BC* [1990

The plaintiff invited tenders to run sightseeing trips from Blackpool Airport. The tenders were to be submitted to the council offices sealed in an envelope provided by 12 noon on a certain day. The plaintiff's tender complied with the requirements and was placed in the council's letter-box at 11 a.m. on the correct day but it was not collected by the council employees who should have emptied the letter-box and consequently it was treated as a late bid and not considered. The court held that there was a contract between the parties for the bid to be considered as it had been validly submitted and the defendant was in breach.

Borden (UK) Ltd v *Scottish Timber Products Ltd*

Resin was supplied under a contract which included a retention of title clause. After delivery a receiver was appointed for the purchasers, but the resin supplied had been mixed with other materials to produce chipboard and so it had lost its identity. Accordingly the court held that the retention of title clause did not preserve the seller's right of ownership.

Brogden v *Metropolitan Railway Company* [1877]

The plaintiff supplied coal to the defendant on a written annual contract. A new contract was sent to the plaintiff who amended it (counter-offer) and returned it to the defendant. The defendant filed it and forgot about it but continued to accept deliveries in keeping with the new amended contract until a dispute brought the matter before the court. The court held that the defendant had accepted the new amended contract by its silent conduct.

BRS v *Arthur B Crutchley Ltd* [1968]

The plaintiff delivered whiskey to the defendant for storage. The plaintiff's driver gave the defendant the delivery note, which said it incorporated the plaintiff's terms. The defendant stamped the note that the goods were received under its terms and conditions. The court held that this was a counter-offer, which the plaintiff accepted by conduct when it handed over the whiskey. The contract was made on the defendant's terms and conditions.

Butler Machine Tool Co v *Ex-Cell-O Corporation* [1979]

The plaintiff offered to sell machinery (on its own st&c) to the defendant. The st&c contained a price variation clause allowing the seller to charge the price applicable at the time of delivery. The defendant ordered the machinery on its own st&c which had no price variation clause but which had a 'tear off and return' acknowledgement slip. The plaintiff returned the slip indicating its acceptance of the defendant's st&c. Then there was a price increase and when the machinery was delivered, the plaintiffs tried to charge the higher price applicable at the time of delivery. The court held that as the plaintiff had accepted the defendant's st&c the price variation clause did not apply to the contract.

Carlill v Carbolic Smoke Ball Co [1893]

The defendants manufactured smoke balls which were supposed to prevent flu. Their advertisement stated they would pay £100 to anyone who contracted flu after buying and using the smoke ball correctly, and they also stated that they had deposited £1,000 in the bank to cover any such claims. The plaintiff bought and used the product correctly, caught flu and tried to claim her £100. The defendant refused to pay saying it was just an advert and was therefore an invitation to treat. The defendant also said that it was impossible to contract with the whole world and so it was impossible to make a unilateral offer. The court of appeal held that it was possible to make an offer to the world (a unilateral offer) and the defendant had done so in the very detailed advertisement which did constitute an offer and not an invitation to treat. The plaintiff had accepted that offer by her conduct. The court also held that there was presumption of intention on the part of the defendant to be bound.

Cehave NV v Bremer Handelsgesellschaft mbH, the Hansa Nord [1975]

Citrus pellets were sold subject to a term that they would be shipped 'in good condition'. On arrival some of the pellets were damaged and the buyers rejected the consignment but later bought the same cargo at a reduced price and then proceeded to use it for animal feed which had been the original purpose in their initial contract. The court of appeal held that it was an innominate term not a condition and as there had not been significant damage to the pellets the buyers had no right to reject them.

Collins v Godefroy [1831]

The plaintiff had promised to pay the defendant if he promised to attend court to give evidence, but the defendant was served with a subpoena and so was under a public duty to attend court. His claim for payment failed as the court held that as he was under an existing public duty to attend court, it could not be sufficient consideration for a contract.

Coward v Motor Insurance Bureau [1963]

The plaintiff's husband usually had a lift to work with a colleague and made a contribution towards the petrol. The men were killed in a road accident and when the widow sued the MIB, the court had to decide if the men had intended to create legal relations. The court held that it was a social arrangement and in the absence of evidence to the contrary there was no intention to create a legal relationship.

D&C Builders v Rees [1965]

The plaintiff did some building work for the defendant who, when it was finished, made only a part payment in cash of the sum due for the work. It was held by the court that this was insufficient to settle the debt. If you only pay part of a debt, it cannot usually be considered sufficient consideration to settle the debt in full.

Dunlop Ltd v *Selfridges Ltd* [1915]

The plaintiff sold tyres to a wholesaler (W) and inserted clauses into the contract to ensure the retail tyre price was fixed. W included the same clauses in its contract with the defendant, a retailer, but the defendant still sold the tyres below the price specified by the plaintiff. When the plaintiff sued the defendant the court held that the plaintiff had no contract with the defendant and so could not sue on it, the plaintiff's only contract was with W. W had correctly inserted the relevant clauses into its contract with the defendant and so it was not in breach of contract. There was a contract between W and the defendant but the loss was suffered by the plaintiff, not W, who would therefore not be able to claim damages for it.

Dunlop Pneumatic Tyre Co. v *New Garage & Motor Co. Ltd* [1915]

Dunlop supplied tyres to garages under an agreement for a minimum price on resale. In the event of the agreement being breached by sales below the minimum price, the agreement stated that liquidated damages of £5 were payable per tyre sold in breach. The court held that this was a genuine pre-estimate of loss and so it was a valid liquidated damages clause and not a penalty clause, which would have been void. The court established guidelines to identify when a clause is a penalty clause:

- when the sum payable in the event of breach is higher than the maximum loss;
- when the sum payable in the event of breach is higher than the sum due normally under the contract;
- where the contract specifies that the same sum is payable for different breaches both minor and major.

Edwards v *Skyways Ltd* [1964]

The plaintiff was made redundant by the defendant. In negotiations about his pension entitlement, instead of receiving a pension he agreed to receive a refund of his contributions and an ex gratia payment in respect of the employers' contributions from the defendant. The defendants then refused to make the ex gratia payment. The court held that the words 'ex gratia' did not negate the existence of a contract, it simply meant the defendants were not admitting to any prior liability. As a result of this they had not overturned the presumption and there was therefore an intention to be legally bound.

Felthouse v *Bindley* [1862]

The plaintiff was negotiating the purchase of a horse from his nephew and he wrote to his nephew saying that if he heard nothing further he would assume he could buy the horse. The nephew mentally accepted that his uncle would buy the horse but did nothing to communicate his acceptance. The animal was then sold to a third party by the auctioneers dealing on behalf of the nephew. The court held that the nephew's mental acceptance did not constitute contractual acceptance. Silence alone cannot amount to acceptance even if the offeror stipulates this.

Fisher v *Bell* [1961]

A shopkeeper displayed a flick knife for sale in his shop window. The court had to decide if the display amounted to an offer to sell it or an invitation to treat. The court held that it was an invitation to treat.

Grainger and Son v *Gough* [1896]

A wine merchant circulated a price list amongst potential customers and when a dispute arose about the sale of goods the circulation of the price list was held to be an invitation to treat and not an offer.

Hartley v *Ponsonby* [1857]

During a voyage a ship lost several crew members and the captain promised the remaining sailors additional wages to sail the ship back to port shorthanded. One of the sailors sued for the additional wages promised. The shortage of crew made the voyage extremely hazardous and so the judge took the view that the sailor was in fact doing a different, more hazardous job than he originally contracted for and held that he should receive the additional wages.

Harvey v *Facey* [1893]

The appellant sent a telegraph to the respondent asking, 'Will you sell us Bumper Hall Pen? Telegraph lowest cash price.' The respondent replied, 'Lowest price for Bumper Hall Pen £900.' The appellant's response was, 'We agree to buy Bumper Hall Pen for £900. Please send your title deeds in order that we may get early possession.' But no reply was received from the respondent. The court held that the respondent's reply was merely a statement of the minimum price he would accept if he decided to sell not an offer.

Hollier v *Rambler Motors (AMC) Ltd* [1972]

The plaintiff had left his car at the defendant garage three or four times in the previous five years, sometimes signing invoices containing an exclusion clause. The car was destroyed in a fire at the defendant's premises which was caused by the defendant's negligence. The court held that this was insufficient to constitute a previous course of dealings and the clause was not incorporated.

Hong Kong Fir Shipping Co. Ltd v *Kawasaki Kisen Kaisha Ltd*

The defendant chartered a ship from the plaintiffs for two years. The charter stated the ship was 'in every way fit for ordinary cargo service' but it was in a poor state of repair, the engine room crew were incompetent, the plaintiff openly admitted the ship was not seaworthy and consequently 20 weeks of the charter were lost. The term was not stated to be a condition or a warranty in the contract. The defendant treated the contract as terminated claiming it was breach of condition, but the plaintiff disagreed, claiming the defendant was only entitled to damages. The parties had not specified that the term was a condition or warranty. In deciding the case, the court considered whether the defendant had been substantially deprived of the whole of the benefit it was intended to have from the contract. The court found that they had not, and accordingly held that the termination was wrongful and the defendant only had the right to claim damages, so the plaintiff succeeded in its claim.

Hutton v Warren [1836]

A tenant was served with notice to quit his farm by his landlord, but as he was required to leave before harvest time he would not get the benefit of the crop that he had planted and tended. The agreement was silent on this point, but the court held that in accordance with local custom, the tenant was entitled to receive allowance for his expenditure on seeds and labour as the landlord would reap the benefit of the tenant's expense when the crop was harvested after the tenant's departure.

Hyde v Wrench [1840]

In this case the defendant offered to sell land to the plaintiff for £1,000. The plaintiff then made a counter-offer of £950 which was refused by the defendant. Afterwards the plaintiff said they would agree to the price of £1,000 but the plaintiff refused to sell the land to the defendant who then sued the plaintiff to try to force him to sell. The court held that the plaintiff's offer of £950 was a counter-offer which had destroyed the original offer of £1,000 and therefore the offer of £1,000 could not be accepted later in the negotiations as once destroyed the offer cannot be revived.

Interfoto Picture Library v Stiletto Visual Programmes Ltd [1988]

A standard form contract between the parties included a particularly onerous clause involving large penalty payments in the event of delay in returning the photographs to the plaintiff library. The court found that the plaintiff had not given appropriate notice of this clause and it was held that it was not therefore incorporated.

Kendall (Henry) & Sons (a firm) v William Lillico & Sons Ltd [1969]

An oral contract for the sale of animal feed was made and then the transaction was followed by a note of the sale containing an exclusion clause. The parties had been involved in over 100 such transactions in the previous three-year period and the court held that this was a previous course of dealings on those terms which meant the seller could rely on the exclusion clause when the goods sold were unfit.

Lampleigh v Braithwait [1615]

In this case the defendant requested the plaintiff to obtain a royal pardon on the plaintiff's behalf. Afterwards the defendant refused to pay the plaintiff, and the plaintiff sued. The court held that payment should be made.

Liverpool City Council v Irwin [1976]

The tenancies of some council tenants in a block of flats and maisonettes imposed obligations on the tenants but were silent as to obligations on the council to maintain the building. Lifts and rubbish chutes often broke down and when a tenant, in protest, refused to pay rent, the council sought possession of his maisonette. The court implied a term in all tenancy agreements that the landlord is obliged to take reasonable care to keep the common parts of the building in reasonable repair and usable.

Mountstephen v Lakeman [1874]

The defendant was Chairman of a Local Board of Health and in discussions with the plaintiff, a builder, he told the plaintiff to go ahead and carry out work for the Board saying, 'Do the work and I will see you paid.' The court held that the defendant had given an indemnity and that he was therefore personally liable to pay the plaintiff as there was no agreement with the board and so it could not be required to pay for the works carried out by the plaintiff.

Olley v Marlborough Court Ltd [1949]

The plaintiffs booked in to the defendant hotel. When they went up to their room there was a notice containing a clause excluding liability for theft. Some of their belongings were stolen and the hotel sought to rely on the exclusion clause to escape liability. However, the court held that as the contract had been made at the reception desk before having the opportunity to read the exclusion clause on the notice in the room, the clause was not incorporated into the contract and so the defendant could not rely upon it.

Partridge v Crittenden [1968]

An advertisement was placed in a newspaper for the sale of 'bramble finches, cocks and hens, 25 shillings each'. It was a criminal offence to offer to sell wild birds and the court had to decide whether the advertisement constituted an offer to sell or an invitation to treat. The court held that it was an invitation to treat.

Pharmaceutical Society of Great Britain v Boots Cash Chemists (Southern) Ltd [1953]

Purchasers were buying self-service goods from Boots the Chemist. The plaintiff alleged that Boots were breaking the law selling certain items in the absence of the pharmacist when goods were purchased 'self-service'. The court had to decide whether goods displayed on a shelf for self-service constitute an offer to sell or an invitation to treat. The court held that goods displayed on a shelf are an invitation to treat. The purchaser makes the offer when the goods are taken to a checkout.

Poussard v Spiers and Pond [1876]

An actress who was employed to play the leading role in an operetta for a season did not attend until a week after the season began. The producers engaged a substitute and refused her services when she eventually appeared. They purported to terminate the contract and consequently she sued for breach of contract. The court held that as the opening night was regarded as vital, the actress's absence amounted to a breach of a fundamental term of the contract. It was therefore breach of a condition of the contract, and as the producers were entitled to terminate the contract the actress's claim failed. The term breached was fundamental to the contract so it was a breach of condition permitting the other party to terminate the contract.

Re Casey's Patents, Stewart v Casey [1892]

The claimant managed the royalties from some patents on behalf of the respondents and he made a reasonable assumption that he would be paid. As a result of this the court held that he could sue to enforce the promise of payment even if it was made after the work was done.

Re McArdle [1951]

Several siblings inherited a property after the death of a parent. One of the brothers and his wife resided at the property. They carried out work which improved the property. The sister-in-law was told by the family that she would be reimbursed for what she had paid for the work but no payments were made to her. She sued and the court held that as the payment she was promised by the family related to past actions, and the promise to reimburse was made after the work was done, it could not be part of a contract and so she could not enforce the promise. The Court of Appeal held she could not enforce the promise.

Rose & Frank Co. v J R Compton & Bros Ltd [1925]

The defendants agreed to supply paper to the plaintiffs and a written marketing arrangement was made which included a clause providing that 'this … is not a … legal agreement … and shall not be subject to the law courts'. Before the end of the agreed period for the arrangement, the defendants refused to complete orders and terminated the arrangement without giving proper notice. The Court of Appeal found that each of the orders given and accepted constituted an individual contract and the defendant was obliged to fulfil the orders it had received but it was not obliged to fulfil future orders because the marketing arrangement specifically said that there was no intention for it to have legal consequences.

Routledge v McKay [1954]

The parties, who were private individuals, discussed the sale of a motorbike. The defendant said, in reliance on the vehicle registration document, that the bike was a 1942 model. A week later when the written contract was drawn up it did not mention the year of the bike and it was later discovered that it was a 1930 model. Due to the length of time between the discussion and the preparation of the written contract, and also as it was not later put into writing, the court held that the statement about the bike being a 1942 model was a representation not a term of the contract and the claim failed.

St Albans City and District Council v International Computers Ltd [1996]

In this case the defendant sold software to the plaintiff, a local authority. The software had an error which meant that the plaintiff miscalculated the Community Charge due. The contract included a clause by which the defendant sought to limit its liability to £100,000. The court held that the clause was unreasonable and so was invalid and the defendant could not therefore rely upon it.

Simpkins v *Pays* [1955]

The defendant owned a house where she lived with her granddaughter and the plaintiff, who was a paying lodger. They regularly entered a newspaper competition, the entry being submitted in the defendant's name. All three contributed to it although there was no regular arrangement about paying for it or posting it. When the parties won, the defendant refused to pay the lodger his share, claiming there was no intention to create a legal relationship. The court disagreed, finding that the presumption that it was a social arrangement and therefore there was no intention to create a legal relationship was rebutted. There was sufficient mutuality in the arrangements to establish a legally binding commitment to share any prize money.

Spencer v *Harding* [1870]

The defendant was instructed to offer the stock of a particular business for sale by tender and so issued a circular to that effect. The plaintiff submitted the highest bid which the defendant refused to accept. The plaintiff commenced proceedings arguing that the circular constituted an offer implying that the highest tender submitted would be accepted. The court held that the circular was in fact an invitation to treat which did not contain any implication that any tender would be accepted.

Stilk v *Myrick* [1809]

During a voyage a ship lost two crew members and the captain promised the remaining sailors additional wages to sail the ship back to port shorthanded. At the end of the voyage, however, the additional wages were not paid. When they were claimed through the court, it was held that as the sailors were already contractually bound to sail the ship home the claim failed as no additional consideration was given by the sailors; they were doing what they were contractually bound to do under their original contract.

The Moorcock [1889]

A ship that was moored on a jetty in the Thames was damaged by a rocky ridge on the bottom of the river when the tide went out. The court decided that as both parties envisaged the ship would rest on the river bed at low tide, there was an implied term that the bed around the jetty where the berths were available were reasonably safe.

Trentham Ltd v *Archital Luxfer* [1993]

The plaintiff, the main building contractor on a project, was negotiating a subcontract with the defendant, but work began before their negotiations were completed. Allegations were made that the defendant's work was defective, but when the defendant tried to argue that no contract existed (as there was no acceptance) in order to avoid the claims made against it, the court held that there had been acceptance by conduct and that a valid contract existed.

Tweddle v *Atkinson* [1861]

The fathers of a newly married couple agreed to pay a sum of money to the new husband. They agreed between themselves that if either of them failed to pay, the son/son-in-law could sue the defaulter. His father-in-law died before the money was paid and the deceased's executor refused to pay him, so the son-in-law sued his father-in-law's executor. The court held that the plaintiff's claim against the executors failed as he had given no consideration in the agreement. Consideration must move from the promisee (the person receiving the promise). Only someone who provides consideration for the contractual promise can enforce the contract. This rule of consideration follows the principle of privity of contract that only someone who is a party to the contract can enforce it, namely, can sue or be sued on it.

Legislation

This appendix contains relevant extracts from statutes referred to in this course book.

Unfair Contract Terms Act 1977

2 Negligence liability

(1) A person cannot by reference to any contract term or to a notice given to persons generally or to particular persons exclude or restrict his liability for death or personal injury resulting from negligence.

(2) In the case of other loss or damage, a person cannot so exclude or restrict his liability for negligence except in so far as the term or notice satisfies the requirement of reasonableness.

4 Unreasonable indemnity clauses

(1) A person dealing as consumer cannot by reference to any contract term be made to indemnify another person (whether a party to the contract or not) in respect of liability that may be incurred by the other for negligence or breach of contract, except in so far as the contract term satisfies the requirement of reasonableness.

6 Sale and hire-purchase

(1) Liability for breach of the obligations arising from—

(a) [section 12 of the Sale of Goods Act 1979] (seller's implied undertakings as to title, etc.);
cannot be excluded or restricted by reference to any contract term.

(2) As against a person dealing as consumer, liability for breach of the obligations arising from—

(a) [section 13, 14 or 15 of the 1979 Act] (seller's implied undertakings as to conformity of goods with description or sample, or as to their quality or fitness for a particular purpose);
cannot be excluded or restricted by reference to any contract term.

(3) As against a person dealing otherwise than as consumer, the liability specified in subsection (2) above can be excluded or restricted by

reference to a contract term, but only in so far as the term satisfies the requirement of reasonableness.

7 Miscellaneous contracts under which goods pass

(1) Where the possession or ownership of goods passes under or in pursuance of a contract not governed by the law of sale of goods or hire-purchase, subsections (2) to (4) below apply as regards the effect (if any) to be given to contract terms excluding or restricting liability for breach of obligation arising by implication of law from the nature of the contract.

(2) As against a person dealing as consumer, liability in respect of the goods' correspondence with description or sample, or their quality or fitness for any particular purpose, cannot be excluded or restricted by reference to any such term.

(3) As against a person dealing otherwise than as consumer, that liability can be excluded or restricted by reference to such a term, but only in so far as the term satisfies the requirement of reasonableness.

11 The 'reasonableness' test

(1) In relation to a contract term, the requirement of reasonableness for the purposes of this Part of this Act, section 3 of the Misrepresentation Act 1967 and section 3 of the Misrepresentation Act (Northern Ireland) 1967 is that the term shall have been a fair and reasonable one to be included having regard to the circumstances which were, or ought reasonably to have been, known to or in the contemplation of the parties when the contract was made.

(2) In determining for the purposes of section 6 or 7 above whether a contract term satisfies the requirement of reasonableness, regard shall be had in particular to the matters specified in Schedule 2 to this Act; but this subsection does not prevent the court or arbitrator from holding, in accordance with any rule of law, that a term which purports to exclude or restrict any relevant liability is not a term of the contract.

12 'Dealing as consumer'

(1) A party to a contract 'deals as consumer' in relation to another party if—

(a) he neither makes the contract in the course of a business nor holds himself out as doing so; and

(b) the other party does make the contract in the course of a business; and

(c) in the case of a contract governed by the law of sale of goods or hire-purchase, or by section 7 of this Act, the goods passing under or in pursuance of the contract are of a type ordinarily supplied for private use or consumption.

16 Liability for breach of duty

(1) where a term of a contract [or a provision of a notice given to persons generally or to particular persons,] purports to exclude or restrict liability for breach of duty arising in the course of any business or from the occupation of any premises used for business purposes of the occupier, that term [or provision]—

(a) shall be void in any case where such exclusion or restriction is in respect of death or personal injury;

(b) shall, in any other case, have no effect if it was not fair and reasonable to incorporate the term in the contract [or, as the case may be, if it is not fair and reasonable to allow reliance on the provision].

Schedule 2 'Guidelines' for Application of Reasonableness Test

Sections 11(2), 24(2)

The matters to which regard is to be had in particular for the purposes of sections 6(3), 7(3) and (4), 20 and 21 are any of the following which appear to be relevant—

(a) the strength of the bargaining positions of the parties relative to each other, taking into account (among other things) alternative means by which the customer's requirements could have been met;

(b) whether the customer received an inducement to agree to the term, or in accepting it had an opportunity of entering into a similar contract with other persons, but without having to accept a similar term;

(c) whether the customer knew or ought reasonably to have known of the existence and extent of the term (having regard, among other things, to any custom of the trade and any previous course of dealing between the parties);

(d) where the term excludes or restricts any relevant liability if some condition is not complied with, whether it was reasonable at the time of the contract to expect that compliance with that condition would be practicable;

(e) whether the goods were manufactured, processed or adapted to the special order of the customer.

Sale of Goods Act 1979

2 Contract of sale

(1) A contract of sale of goods is a contract by which the seller transfers or agrees to transfer the property in goods to the buyer for a money consideration, called the price.

12 Implied terms about title, etc.

(1) In a contract of sale, other than one to which subsection (3) below applies, there is an implied [term] on the part of the seller that in the case of a sale he has a right to sell the goods, and in the case of an agreement to sell he will have such a right at the time when the property is to pass.

(2) In a contract of sale, other than one to which subsection (3) below applies, there is also an implied [term] that—

(a) the goods are free, and will remain free until the time when the property is to pass, from any charge or encumbrance not disclosed or known to the buyer before the contract is made

13 Sale by description

(1) Where there is a contract for the sale of goods by description, there is an implied [term] that the goods will correspond with the description.

(3) A sale of goods is not prevented from being a sale by description by reason only that, being exposed for sale or hire, they are selected by the buyer.

14 Implied terms:i about quality or fitness

(2) Where the seller sells goods in the course of a business, there is an implied term that the goods supplied under the contract are of satisfactory quality.

(2A) For the purposes of this Act, goods are of satisfactory quality if they meet the standard that a reasonable person would regard as satisfactory, taking account of any description of the goods, the price (if relevant) and all the other relevant circumstances.

(2C) The term implied by subsection (2) above does not extend to any matter making the quality of goods unsatisfactory—

(a) which is specifically drawn to the buyer's attention before the contract is made,

(b) where the buyer examines the goods before the contract is made, which that examination ought to reveal, or

(c) in the case of a contract for sale by sample, which would have been apparent on a reasonable examination of the sample.

(3) Where the seller sells goods in the course of a business and the buyer, expressly or by implication, makes known—

(a) to the seller...

any particular purpose for which the goods are being bought, there is an implied [term] that the goods supplied under the contract are reasonably fit for that purpose, whether or not that is a purpose for which such goods are commonly supplied, except where the circumstances show that the buyer does not rely, or that it is unreasonable for him to rely, on the skill or judgment of the seller or credit-broker.

15 Sale by sample

(1) A contract of sale is a contract for sale by sample where there is an express or implied term to that effect in the contract

(2) In the case of a contract for sale by sample there is an implied [term]—

(a) that the bulk will correspond with the sample in quality;

(c) that the goods will be free from any defect, [making their quality unsatisfactory], which would not be apparent on reasonable examination of the sample.

61 Interpretation

(1) In this Act, unless the context or subject matter otherwise requires— 'goods' includes all personal chattels other than things in action and money, and in Scotland all corporeal moveables except money; and in particular 'goods' includes emblements, industrial growing crops, and things attached to or forming part of the land which are agreed to be severed before sale or under the contract of sale [and includes an undivided share in goods;]

Supply of Goods and Services Act 1982

2 Implied terms: about title, etc.

(1) In a contract for the transfer of goods, other than one to which subsection (3) below applies, there is an implied condition on the part of the transferor that in the case of a transfer of the property in the goods he has a right to transfer the property and in the case of an agreement to transfer the property in the goods he will have such a right at the time when the property is to be transferred.

3 Implied terms where transfer is by description

(1) This section applies where, under a contract for the transfer of goods, the transferor transfers or agrees to transfer the property in the goods by description.

(2) In such a case there is an implied condition that the goods will correspond with the description.

4 Implied terms about quality or fitness

(2A) For the purposes of this section and section 5 below, goods are of satisfactory quality if they meet the standard that a reasonable person would regard as satisfactory, taking account of any description of the goods, the price (if relevant) and all the other relevant circumstances.

(3) The condition implied by subsection (2) above does not extend to any matter making the quality of goods unsatisfactory—

(a) which is specifically drawn to the transferee's attention before the contract is made,

(b) where the transferee examines the goods before the contract is made, which that examination ought to reveal, or

(c) where the property in the goods is transferred by reference to a sample, which would have been apparent on a reasonable examination of the sample.

5 Implied terms where transfer is by sample

(1) This section applies where, under a contract for the transfer of goods, the transferor transfers or agrees to transfer the property in the goods by reference to a sample.

(2) In such a case there is an implied condition—

(a) that the bulk will correspond with the sample in quality; and

(b) that the transferee will have a reasonable opportunity of comparing the bulk with the sample; and

(c) that the goods will be free from any defect, [making their quality unsatisfactory], which would not be apparent on reasonable examination of the sample.

7 Implied terms about right to transfer possession, etc.

(1) In a contract for the hire of goods there is an implied condition on the part of the bailor that in the case of a bailment he has a right to transfer possession of the goods by way of hire for the period of the bailment and in the case of an agreement to bail he will have such a right at the time of the bailment.

8 Implied terms where hire is by description

(1) This section applies where, under a contract for the hire of goods, the bailor bails or agrees to bail the goods by description.

(2) In such a case there is an implied condition that the goods will correspond with the description.

9 Implied terms about quality or fitness

(2) Where, under such a contract, the bailor bails goods in the course of a business, there is an implied condition that the goods supplied under the contract are of satisfactory quality.

(2A) For the purposes of this section and section 10 below, goods are of satisfactory quality if they meet the standard that a reasonable person would regard as satisfactory, taking account of any description of the goods, the consideration for the bailment (if relevant) and all the other relevant circumstances.

(5) In that case there is (subject to subsection (6) below) an implied condition that the goods supplied under the contract are reasonably fit for that purpose, whether or not that is a purpose for which such goods are commonly supplied.

10 Implied terms where hire is by sample

(1) This section applies where, under a contract for the hire of goods, the bailor bails or agrees to bail the goods by reference to a sample.

(2) In such a case there is an implied condition—

(a) that the bulk will correspond with the sample in quality; and

(b) that the bailee will have a reasonable opportunity of comparing the bulk with the sample; and

(c) that the goods will be free from any defect, [making their quality unsatisfactory], which would not be apparent on reasonable examination of the sample.

13 Implied term about care and skill

In a contract for the supply of a service where the supplier is acting in the course of a business, there is an implied term that the supplier will carry out the service with reasonable care and skill.

14 Implied term about time for performance

(1) Where, under a contract for the supply of a service by a supplier acting in the course of a business, the time for the service to be carried out is not fixed by the contract, left to be fixed in a manner agreed by the contract or determined by the course of dealing between the parties, there is an implied term that the supplier will carry out the service within a reasonable time.

(2) What is a reasonable time is a question of fact.

15 Implied term about consideration

(1) Where, under a contract for the supply of a service, the consideration for the service is not determined by the contract, left to be determined

in a manner agreed by the contract or determined by the course of dealing between the parties, there is an implied term that the party contracting with the supplier will pay a reasonable charge.

(2) What is a reasonable charge is a question of fact.

Contracts (Rights of Third Parties) Act 1999

1 Right of third party to enforce contractual term

(1) Subject to the provisions of this Act, a person who is not a party to a contract (a 'third party') may in his own right enforce a term of the contract if—

(a) the contract expressly provides that he may, or

(b) subject to subsection (2), the term purports to confer a benefit on him.

(2) Subsection (1)(b) does not apply if on a proper construction of the contract it appears that the parties did not intend the term to be enforceable by the third party.

(3) The third party must be expressly identified in the contract by name, as a member of a class or as answering a particular description but need not be in existence when the contract is entered into.

(4) This section does not confer a right on a third party to enforce a term of a contract otherwise than subject to and in accordance with any other relevant terms of the contract.

(5) For the purpose of exercising his right to enforce a term of the contract, there shall be available to the third party any remedy that would have been available to him in an action for breach of contract if he had been a party to the contract (and the rules relating to damages, injunctions, specific performance and other relief shall apply accordingly).

(6) Where a term of a contract excludes or limits liability in relation to any matter references in this Act to the third party enforcing the term shall be construed as references to his availing himself of the exclusion or limitation.

Contract terms

This appendix contains examples of many of the types of draft terms studied in this course book.

Liquidated damages

If the supplier shall be unable to deliver goods by the contracted date then they shall pay, by way of liquidated damages, a sum representing 1 per cent of the contract price for every day of delay or part of a day beyond the contractual delivery date, up to a maximum of 20 per cent of the contract price.

Guarantees

The seller guarantees that if the goods fail due to defective workmanship or materials within 12 months of purchase, the seller will, in its absolute discretion, refund the purchase price, repair the goods or give new goods as a replacement. This guarantee is in addition to and does not affect the buyer's statutory rights.

Passing of risk and property

1   Risk in the goods shall pass to the purchaser when the goods have been delivered.
2   Notwithstanding delivery, property in the goods shall not have passed from the seller until the full contract price of such goods has been paid.

Retention of title

Goods delivered under this contract will remain the property of the supplier until such time as the buyer has paid for the goods in full. Notwithstanding the retention of title the goods shall be at the buyer's risk while on their premises and should be stored in such a way as to make them readily identifiable to the supplier.

Payment

Payment for goods supplied under this contract is due 30 days after delivery.

Confidentiality

The seller shall keep any confidential information, drawings, specifications or other materials which come into its possession in the course of design and manufacture, confidential, and shall return all such drawings and documents on completion of the contract.

Exclusion clause

The seller shall not be responsible for any defects in the goods under the contract beyond the cost of repair and/or replacement of the goods.

The seller will not accept any liability for shortages in delivery under this contract unless they are notified to the seller within two days of delivery.

Force majeure

If a delivery by the seller, or the acceptance by the buyer of a delivery, is delayed or prevented because the manufacture of the goods, their delivery to the buyer's works by usual route, or the consumption or use of the goods by the buyer in the ordinary course of his business has been or is being prevented or hindered by circumstances beyond the reasonable control of either party, including any form of government intervention, strikes and lockouts relevant to the contract, delays by subcontractors (but only where such delays were beyond the reasonable control of the subcontractor concerned), such delivery shall be suspended and if it cannot be made within a reasonable time after the due date, either party may serve the other with a written notice cancelling the delivery. Where more than one delivery is to be made under the contract, deliveries not cancelled will be resumed as soon as the circumstances causing the delay cease, but, except where both parties otherwise agree, the period during which deliveries are to be made will not be extended. The buyer shall pay the seller such sum as may be equitable in respect of work performed prior to cancellation.

Dispute resolution (including laws and venue)

The parties agree that the construction, validity and performance of this contract shall be governed by English law and all disputes which may arise under, or out of or in connection with or in relation to the contract shall be submitted to the arbitration of the London Court of Arbitration under and in accordance with its rules. The parties to this contract agree that service of any notice in the course of such arbitration at their address as given in the purchase order shall be valid and sufficient.

Variation

Any variation, amendment or addition to this contract shall not be valid unless agreed in writing between the parties and signed on their behalf by a duly authorised party.

Duration

This contract will last for two years from the commencement date unless ended sooner in accordance with its terms.

Default and termination

The buyer may terminate this agreement for any reason on giving 21 days' notice in writing thereof to the seller.

The buyer may terminate this contract with immediate effect on giving written notice to the seller if:

1   the seller fails to meet specified performance criteria on three consecutive occasions; or
2   the seller commits any material or persistent breaches of this agreement;
3   the seller becomes insolvent or has a receiver or manager appointed, commits an act of bankruptcy or commences to be wound up.

Indemnity

The seller shall indemnify the buyer against all claims, costs which the buyer may incur and which may arise, directly or indirectly from the seller's breach of any of its obligations under the contract.

Time

Delivery shall be made on the 15th of the month and time for delivery shall be of the essence of this contract.

Advice on answering examination questions

General tips for answering examination questions

Whilst studying this course you should not only be developing your knowledge and understanding of the subject, but also trying to improve your written communication skills. The skills you will be developing to improve your examination technique in writing essays and analysing case study/legal problem questions are also skills that are very useful professionally. They will enable you to select relevant information and organise that information in order to use it appropriately and communicate it clearly, effectively and efficiently.

As this course is assessed by examination it is important for you to develop appropriate skills in answering different types of questions. You will need to be able to write essays as well as answer questions based on a case study, which in this course will include questions about legal problems.

As a general tip, when you answer questions you should also consider whether you have any examples from your own professional experience which are relevant and to which you could refer in the examination. Relevant examples used well can enhance the quality of your answer and so improve your mark.

Essay questions

Some self-assessment tasks in this course book involve you writing your answer in essay form, and this will give you an opportunity to develop a good essay answering technique.

In order to achieve goods marks in an examination:

- It is important to read the question very carefully to establish exactly what is being asked. Do not just seize on certain words and then try to write everything you know on that topic! If you do that in an examination you are likely to receive poor marks for your essays.
- You might find it helpful to underline or highlight key words or phrases.
- Focus on the 'command' words such as *discuss, explain, evaluate* as these words will tell you what you should do in your answer. You must ensure that you know what typical command words expect you to do. You could check your knowledge with the list of common command words at the end of this appendix.
- You should note if there is more than one part to the question and if so ensure that you answer all parts.
- Ensure that you include examples in your answer.

- Always plan an essay as this will help you produce a well thought out answer instead of a written jumble of random thoughts. It will also help ensure that you do not miss out any important information.
- You should always write an essay using a definite structure.
- Firstly the essay should commence with an introduction, which should show that you understand what the question is asking you to do.
- Next the main body of the essay should follow, and it should be organised into sequenced paragraphs setting out the main points, arguments and examples. Remember that the reader must be able to follow your argument, so present it in a logical order.
- Finally, you should finish with a paragraph indicating what the conclusions of your argument are and any implications these may have.

When writing essays you should avoid bullet points but instead write in full sentences and set out your essay in paragraphs.

Answering questions based on the case study

Depending on what studies you have done before starting this course, you may already have experience of answering problem questions (or case studies as they are sometimes referred to in a business context). On the other hand, this may be the first time you have encountered this style of question. In order to achieve success in the examination it is very important that you know and understand the areas covered by the syllabus. However, it is also important that you are able to demonstrate your understanding in the examination questions as these will test your ability to apply that knowledge. Therefore, it is important that you have a good technique for answering case study/problem questions as this will help you maximise your marks in those questions.

When you are considering questions based on the procurement aspects of developing contracts you will be demonstrating your knowledge and understanding of the syllabus as well as using your experience as a procurement professional in commenting on the situations in the case study in order to apply relevant procurement principles methods and procedures. You will be able to draw upon your experience as a procurement professional to illustrate your answers with examples from your own experience as well as from your studies.

When answering case study questions/problem questions based on the legal parts of this course you may not have as much practical experience as you have on the procurement aspects, but you will have the knowledge and understanding gained from your studies in this course and you have examples of laws to illustrate your answers in the form of the cases and statutes that you study.

When judges hear civil cases they listen to the case presented by the claimant and defendant which includes oral evidence from witnesses, they read any reports or documents that are used in evidence and hear legal argument from the barristers or solicitors instructed by the parties. At the end of the case they must come to a decision as to whether the claimant has proved their claim, and what, if any, remedies they will grant. In arriving at this decision, the judges consider the legal principles and rules which they know apply to the situation presented in the case. They may find these principles in case law or there may be statutes or statutory instruments (regulations) which may apply.

The judges must also carefully consider the facts presented in evidence and identify which of them are relevant.

The judges then apply the legal principles to the relevant facts. They do this in the 'judgment' which is their explanation for their decision in finding that the claimant has either proved their claim or not, as the case may be.

When you answer legal problem questions, you should approach the questions in the same way that a judge would come to a decision in a case. The examiner is very interested in how you arrive at your decision that, for example, Co. X will succeed in its claim. The examiner wants to see that you can identify the relevant principles and apply them to given situations. The ability to apply rules appropriately in problem questions illustrates your understanding of that topic.

Remember that you will be faced with problem questions in different programmes of study with CIPS. If you develop a good technique in this course answering problem questions on legal matters you will be able to apply that technique in other courses too. You should aim to develop an analytical and methodical approach to problem-solving questions which will produce a considered and well-organised answer.

Once you understand the principles in contract law you will also be able to put them to practical use in applying them to real-life situations as a purchasing professional to enhance your practice.

Problem questions require you not only to know the topics on your course but also to understand them, as in these questions you will be applying your knowledge to given situations. Planning is important in problem questions just as it is in essay questions, and especially so if you are answering a large problem question or if you are under pressure in an examination situation, as, if you do not plan your answer, you could miss out some important information and it is unlikely to present a logical well-structured argument.

In this study guide appendix 3, Legislation and appendix 2, Case law set out some important cases and relevant statutes for this course. When you refer to legal principles in your answers you should try to remember to state where the principle is found. It may be in a section of a statute or it may be in a decided case. When you refer to cases in the examination, the examiner will not be looking for you to repeat the facts of the case in great detail. Whilst it is useful to know the facts of a case, as this will help you understand it, the importance of a case is the legal principle involved and how it is applied by the court hearing the case. Therefore, when you are studying cases, try to briefly summarise the relevant facts but ensure that you understand fully the legal principle involved.

Remember, when you are analysing a legal case study/problem question, you are using the same skills that judges use when deciding cases.

- You identify the relevant legal principles involved.
- You identify the relevant facts.

- You apply the relevant principle to the relevant facts.
- You reach your conclusion.

Improving your examination technique

Sample essay question

Define life cycle costing and explain how it can assist in making capital expenditure purchasing decisions.

In considering the question you should follow the guidelines set out in this appendix.

Firstly you should read the question carefully to establish what the command words are and what you are expected to do. You should also decide how many parts there are to the question.

The command words are 'define' and 'explain' and there are two parts to this question. If you do not know how to deal with the command words you should consult the list at the end of the appendix.

As to the structure of your essay, you should plan it with an introduction, followed by the main part of the essay and then the conclusion.

As to the content your essay should include:

- A definition of life cycle costing and an explanation that as some costs must be estimated when budgeting for the whole life of the item, life cycle costing is not an exact science.
- An explanation that life cycle costing could be considered under the headings of acquisition, operation and disposal costs. Each of these should be explained in detail and examples given to illustrate what is involved and how they affect the life cycle costs. For example, with acquisition costs the price may be low, but if transportation costs from overseas were involved the total costs would be higher but would reflect the true cost of the item. With disposal costs, environmental issues may be relevant and disposal costs may be significant. It is also possible that there would be some benefit in some circumstances where there was a residual value on disposal as the organisation could receive payment on sale.

Sample case study/problem question

(This case study is not exam specific)

You are a senior procurement officer at Branch Ltd. Tailor Ltd offer to supply your organisation with a consignment of goods at a price of £50,000. One of the directors of BL, who often tries to get involved in procurement, is in your department when the offer is received. He immediately contacts Tailor Ltd and tells them that Branch Ltd will buy the consignment for £48,000 not £50,000. You then discover that none of your other suppliers can supply you with the goods in time and therefore you will have to purchase them from Tailor Ltd. Tailor Ltd

offer to supply Branch Ltd with the same consignment but the price has now risen to £52,000.

Explain Branch Ltd's legal position to your director.

After reading the question carefully and underlining any key words or phrases, you should have recognised that the relevant legal principles which apply relate to contract formation and more particularly to the elements of agreement. In considering the problem you should examine the principles relating to offer, acceptance and counter offer, and you should refer to relevant cases from those sections of your course book.

Once you have identified the relevant legal principles, you should identify the relevant facts and then apply the legal principles to the facts to arrive at your conclusions.

The introduction to your answer could state that legal principles relating to contract formation and more particularly agreement apply to this question.

You should then proceed to the main part of your answer where you identify the relevant facts and apply the legal principles to them. Your answer should explain that Tailor Ltd made an offer to sell at £50,000. There is no unconditional acceptance of this offer by Branch Ltd, but there is a counter offer of £48,000 from Branch Ltd which extinguishes the original offer. You could refer to the case of *Hyde* v *Wrench* [1840] here. It does appear that the director had rejected the original offer in any event. The only offer capable of being accepted therefore is the offer to buy by Branch Ltd at £48,000, but Tailor Ltd is not interested in accepting it indicating perhaps that they are not prepared to negotiate a lower price.

Then a further counter offer is made by Tailor Ltd for £52,000 which extinguishes the previous counter offer. This further counter offer by Tailor Ltd to sell to Branch Ltd is then the only offer capable of acceptance.

Your advice to your director about Branch Ltd's legal position would be that if Branch Ltd wants to purchase the goods from Tailor Ltd (remember that now they are your only source of those goods), it seems Branch Ltd will have to accept the counter offer and agree to pay £52,000. (The original offer of £50,000 made by Tailor Ltd was extinguished and cannot now be revived by Branch Ltd.) If Branch Ltd unconditionally accepted the latest counter offer the contract would be made at a price of £52,000.

Command words

Here are some of the more common command words with explanations as to how you should approach questions using them.

- Criticise – make a judgement of the merits of the opinions or theories based on your discussion of the evidence or reasons given.
- Define – give the exact meaning of a word or phrase.
- Describe – give a detailed account.
- Discuss – explain, then give two or more sides of the issue and any implications.

- Evaluate – determine the worth or validity or value of something; weigh something up.
- Explain – give reasons for; interpret and account for something.
- Outline – give the main features or general principles of a subject, do not include minor details but concentrate on the structure and argument.

Useful websites on study skills

If you want to improve your study skills and general skills in answering questions or preparing for examinations there are several websites which you may find helpful.

- http://www.hope.ac.uk/gnu – go to Student Help where you can access information on matters such as note taking, essay writing, effective revision and exam techniques.
- http://www.jcu.edu.au/studying/services/studyskills/online.html – in the Online Learning Skills Resources you will find guidance on matters such as studying for exams (in Organisation), note taking (in Lectures and Tutorials) and essay writing (in Academic Writing) as well as other aspects of studying and learning.
- http://www.mmu.ac.uk/academic/studserv/learningsupport/studyskills/practical.html.
- You will find general links to many study skills sites at http://www.support4learning.org.uk/education/revision_and_study_skills_.cfm – you should look in the general study skills section.

References and bibliography

This section contains a complete A–Z listing of all publications, materials or websites referred to in this course book. Books, articles and research are listed under the first author's (or in some cases the editor's) surname. Where no author name has been given, the publication is listed under the name of the organisation that published it. Websites are listed under the name of the organisation providing the website.

Cannon, S (2005) *Procurement Policy, Strategy and Procedures*, 1st edition. London: Spiro Press.

Carter, R and S Kirby (2006) *Practical Procurement*, 1st edition. Cambridge Media.

Chartered Institute of Purchasing & Supply (CIPS): http://www.cips.org

Department for Constitutional Affairs: http://www.dca.gov.uk.

Cambridge Dictionaries Online: http://www.dictionary.cambridge.org.

Dobler, D and D Burt (1996) *Purchasing & Supply Management*, 6th edition. Europe: McGraw-Hill.

Europa: http://europa.eu.int.

Fuller, G (2002) *Purchasing Contracts: A Practical Guide*, 1st edition. London: Spiro Press.

Griffiths, M and I Griffiths (2002) *Law for Purchasing and Supply*, 3rd edition. Harlow: Pearson Education.

Hong Kong International Arbitration Centre: http://www.hkiac.org.

HM Courts Service: http://www.hmcourts-service.gov.uk.

GNU: http://www.hope.ac.uk/gnu.

International Chamber of Commerce: http://www.iccwbo.org.

JCU Study Skills Online: http://www.jcu.edu.au/studying/services/studyskills/essay.

Juran, JM (1988) *Quality Control Handbook*. McGraw-Hill.

University of Oslo, Status of UNCITRAL Conventions and Model Laws: http://www.jus.uio.no/lm/un.conventions.membership.status.

Kraljic, P (1983) 'Purchasing must become supply management', *Harvard Business Review*, September/October.

London Court of International Arbitration: http://www.lcia-arbitration.com.

Longman Dictionary of Contemporary English Online: http://www.ldoceonline.com.

Lysons, K and B Farrington (2006) *Purchasing and Supply Chain Management*, 7th edition. Harlow: Pearson Education.

Marrian, J (1965) 'Marketing Characteristics of Industrial Goods and Buyers'. In *The Marketing of Industrial Products*, ed. A Wilson. London: Hutchinson.

Manchester Metropolitan University: http://www.mmu.ac.uk/academic/studserv/learningsupport/studyskills/practical.html.

BBC News: http://news.bbc.co.uk/1/hi/world/default.stm.

Office of Government Commerce: http://www.ogc.gov.uk.

Office of Public Sector Information: http://www.opsi.gov.uk.

The United Kingdom Parliament: http://www.parliament.uk/works/newlaw.cfm.

Risley G (1972) *Modern Industrial Marketing*. New York: McGraw-Hill

Singleton, S and R Lawson (2002) *Commercial Contracts: A Practical Guide to Standard Terms*, 1st edition. Croydon: Butterworths Tolley.

SITPRO: http://www.sitpro.org.uk.

Support 4 Learning: http://www.support4learning.org.uk/education/revision_and_study_skills_.cfm.

[http://www.telegraph.co.uk, *Telegraph* newspaper online].

Times Online: http://www.timesonline.co.uk.

UNCITRAL, United Nations Convention on Contracts for the International Sale of Goods (1980): http://www.uncitral.org/pdf/english/texts/sales/cisg/CISG.pdf.

UNCITRAL, International Sale of Goods (CISG) and Related Transactions: http://www.uncitral.org/uncitral/en/uncitral_texts/sale_goods.html.

Wyborn, J (2000) *One Stop Contracts*, 2nd edition. London: ICSA Publishing Ltd.

Index